Also published by *The Woodfield Press*

The Wicklow World of Elizabeth Smith (1840-1850)
edited by DERMOT JAMES and SÉAMAS Ó MAITIÚ

The Sligo-Leitrim World of Kate Cullen (1832-1913)
revealed by HILARY PYLE

Ballyknockan: A Wicklow Stonecutters' Village
SÉAMAS Ó MAITIÚ and BARRY O'REILLY

*The Tellicherry Five: The Transportation of Michael Dwyer
and the Wicklow Rebels*
KIERAN SHEEDY

John Hamilton of Donegal 1800-1884: This Recklessly Generous Landlord
DERMOT JAMES

Red-Headed Rebel: A Biography of Susan Mitchell
HILARY PYLE

CHARLES DICKENS'S IRELAND
AN ANTHOLOGY

including an account of his visits to Ireland

JIM COOKE

THE WOODFIELD PRESS
in association with
RTE COMMERCIAL ENTERPRISES

This book was typeset by
Gilbert Gough Typesetting for
THE WOODFIELD PRESS
17 Jamestown Square, Dublin 8

A catalogue record for this title
is available from the British Library.

ISBN 0-9528453-8-5

Printed in Ireland
by Genprint Ltd

For Sophie, Alison, Aoife and Aengus

Contents

Foreword

Charles Dickens is perhaps a little out of fashion now, despite our cinematic taste for caricature and the grotesque, but the creatures of his irrepressible imagination still have a universal appeal, and there was never greater need for the profound humanity of his vision or the ordinary decent values he celebrated in his novels. This book is a curious and remarkable compendium of material, attempting to create a sense of the age of Dickens as it was experienced in Ireland. It contains original material by Dickens, on Irish and related subjects and accounts of his three tours of Ireland in 1858, 1867 and 1869 as well as miscellaneous material with an Irish relevance garnered from the various magazines he edited.

A specific invitation to Dickens came from Cork in 1852, the year of the great Cork Exhibition, when it was suggested he might perform in aid of the Dickens Guild of Literature – a kind of primitive Aosdána, intended to recognise and help struggling writers. He didn't finally come to Dublin until 1858 arriving on the 21st August. His first reading in the Rotunda was the splendidly unseasonable "A Christmas Carol". Dickens's description of the loud mouthed tardiness of Dublin audiences will be familiar to contemporary theatre goers in the city.

In letters during this visit he remarks on the comparative scarcity of "spirit shops" (how much things have changed) and the loquacity of jarveys – the equivalent of modern day taxi men – who have "something to say about everything" (how little things have changed!) although his attempts to capture the Dublin accent of his driver show surprisingly that like the rest of his countrymen, as far as the Irish accent is concerned, Dickens had a tin ear. Curiously this can be contrasted with a later contribution to one of the miscellanies in the book.

The venue for successive Dublin readings was the round room of the Rotunda, and it must surely make today's Dubliners ache to read of the splendour and sense of occasion involved, when one thinks of the present equivocal state of the building, with half the seats torn out and only the balcony open for the sporadic showing of films.

Dickens at first thought that Irish audiences were less sympathetic to his sense of pathos and comedy, which may actually have demonstrated a greater sophistication on the part of his Dublin listeners, but he was gratified at the tears indulged in subsequently by a large part of the audience at the death of little Paul Dombey. The notices for the daily papers which are reprinted here are fascinating. Whether in Dublin, Belfast or Limerick they commence with a review of the audience generally described as "immense in number and brilliant in appearance" (shades of Oscar Wilde and his remarks at the opening night of "The Importance of Being Earnest"). To a modern ear or eye there is much in the review material that would seem affected and even to invite satire "Who is there who has not read with delighted interest the exquisite delineation – so graceful, so tender, so poetical, of the dreamy, imaginative, thoughtful child, which Mr Dickens has given to the world in little Dombey?" But *autre temps – autre moeurs*. The final Dublin reading included a narrative of the ventures of the unfortunately named Richard Double Dick, which apparently left the audience unmoved, although no doubt nowadays audiences would respond with ribald laughter.

David Norris
10 September 1999

Preface

When I gave a lecture on Charles Dickens's visits to Dublin to the Old Dublin Society in 1989, Dickens's connections with Ireland had been largely forgotten. I then decided to prepare this anthology of Irish articles from the journals edited by him and to include an account of his visits to Ireland.

The articles included here are only a fraction of the total number of Irish articles published in his journals. Perhaps a revitalised Dublin branch of the Dickens Fellowship might take on the joyful task of providing a second anthology.

I wish to thank the librarians of Trinity College Dublin, the National Library of Ireland and the staff of the Dickens House Museum, London for unstinting assistance in my research. I also wish to thank Séamas Ó Maitiú for reading the typescript and especially my publisher Terri McDonnell of The Woodfield Press for her constant support and guidance in bringing the text to book form. My thanks are also due to Odile Hendricks and Paul Candon.

Laurence Foster, drama producer at Radio Telefís Éireann, has been popularising Dickens for some time with his one-man shows after the manner of Dickens's own readings and he has kindly applied his talents to this book.

The inimitable Joycean scholar and literary raconteur, Senator David Norris, has written a lively and colourful foreword.

Jim Cooke
10 September 1999

CHAPTER ONE

Dickens in Ireland: 1858

C harles Dickens first visited Ireland in 1858 as part of his first professional readings tour, at the age of 46 years. He had been invited over on an earlier occasion but had regretfully declined.

As early as 1839 Dickens intended to go "in the midsummer or autumn either to Ireland or to America and to write from thence [for his weekly *Master Humphrey's Clock*, then about to be started] a series of papers descriptive of the places and people I see, introducing local tales, traditions and legends, something after the plan of Washington Irving's Alhambra".

But by March 1841 he was writing "I am disposed to make Scotland my destination in June rather than Ireland". He did tour Scotland in June and

The Old Curiosity Shop

July and was granted the Freedom of the City of Edinburgh. He also travelled
to the United States (in 1842) and Italy (in 1844) for his purpose "to enlarge
my stock of description and observation".

Writing to a friend, John Cay of Edinburgh, in July 1841 Charles Dickens said:

> I am delighted to hear that you got home again undamaged. I was half
> afraid to look into the print shop at Glasgow as I rode through the town,
> lest I should see a lithographic representation (on the model of the
> picture of Captain Cook's death) – the Zoffany painting of the clubbing
> to death of Captain James Cook by the Sandwich Islands natives in
> 1797 – of certain Irish excavators beating you to death with clubs. I
> bless my stars – and the Military – for your preservation.

A violent quarrel had broken out between the Highlanders and Irish labourers working on the Edinburgh and Glasgow Railway. On 27 June several
Highlanders were severely injured by bludgeons; and the next day the
Linlithgow authorities called in military aid from Edinburgh to prevent a battle between 1500 Irish and a larger number of Scots. As sheriff of
Linlithgowshire, Cay would have been closely involved.

Following the Great Exhibition in Hyde Park in 1851 a similar great
exhibition was organised for Cork in 1852, and one of the organisers, Mr
J.W. Bourke, wrote in May of that year to Charles Dickens inviting him to visit
and perform at the exhibition on behalf of Dickens's Guild of Literature and
Art. This was founded in 1850 to help writers in difficulties with a system of
annuities and pensions. Dickens's small theatre company, which was performing short plays in London at this time, would perform plays and he would
also give lectures to raise funds for the guild's purposes.

Bourke in his letter suggested that if the founders of the guild meant "to
extend its benefits to the fugitive genius of Ireland", sympathies could be best
enlisted by a series of such performances during the exhibition which would
also be "a delightful feature" in its "brilliancy and attractiveness of our coming season".

Charles Dickens replied:

> after considering the subject well, that the distance it would be necessary for the large body concerned, to traverse; and the very great
> difficulties in the way of an absence from London prolonged beyond
> four or five days consecutively; combine to impose upon me the disagreeable task of declining the visit you suggest. I discharge the duty, I
> assure you, with great reluctance.

Since Dickens's "only objection" was "on the score of time", a special committee of "leading citizens" was formed to make such arrangements as might overcome this.

Bourke wrote again with detailed proposals for the visit but Dickens replied on 11 June:

> I am very anxious indeed to visit Ireland in connexion with the Guild, because your assurances only confirm my confidence in the warm-hearted reception we should have; and because it seems but right that Ireland, which sends so many young men into the struggles of literary aspiration here – to say nothing of the Fine Arts – should be especially addressed in such a cause. For this reason I would have made a great exertion to have effected a trip to Cork with the whole Amateur Company, and to have proceeded thence to Dublin. By going to the two places we might have made the expedition sufficiently remunerative, if the receipts at Cork could have been raised to a larger amount. But, as it is, and on the scale of returns you set before me, I do not feel justified in proposing the hazard to the gentlemen associated. The result in figures, on the creditor side of the account, would scarcely warrant the trouble, wear and tear, and inconvenience.

In 1858, the first announcement of Dickens's forthcoming visit to Ireland was made in an advertisement which appeared in the Dublin daily papers for a week previously, and ran as follows:

MR. CHARLES DICKENS
will read in the Round room,
ROTUNDA, DUBLIN,
On Monday evening, August 23, 1858, at Eight o'clock, his
CHRISTMAS CAROL;
On Tuesday evening, August 24, at Eight o'clock, his
CHIMES;

On Wednesday, August 25, at Three o'clock,
THE STORY OF LITTLE DOMBEY;

On Thursday evening, August 26, at Eight o'clock,
THE POOR TRAVELLER, BOOTS AT THE HOLLY-TREE INN,
and MRS. GAMP

Dickens arrived in Dublin with his manager, Mr Arthur Smith, on Saturday,

21 August 1858, and made Morrisson's,[1] then the fashionable hotel, his headquarters.

His son Charley had visited him at his home, Gad's Hill at Rochester, Kent, earlier in the month and "talked of passing his fortnight's holiday in Ireland with me. I encouraged him in the idea, as I thought it would do him more good than any other Holiday he is likely to take." But Charley did not travel to Ireland.

Soon before coming to Ireland Dickens had a bad cold but by 17 August he wrote: "After dinner yesterday, I began to recover my voice, and I think I sang half the Irish Melodies to myself as I walked about, to test it."

On his first day in Dublin, Monday 23 August 1858, he had formed his first impressions of Dublin:

> The Dublin audience are accustomed to do nothing in the way of taking places, until the last moment, or until they actually "take them" by walking in at the Doors. We are therefore quite in the Dark. I read the Carol here tonight – the Chimes tomorrow – Little Dombey on Wednesday morning – and the Poor Traveller &c on Thursday evening. We had a five hours passage from Holyhead in the night of Saturday, and it was very, very, nasty. . . . Arthur was quite insensible when we got to Dublin, and stared at our luggage without in the least offering to claim it.
>
> I am greatly surprised by this place. It is very much larger than I had supposed, and very much more populous and busy. Upon the whole it is no shabbier than London is, and the people seem to enjoy themselves more than the London people do. The old town of Edinburgh is a thousand times more squalid than the bye places I have seen in Dublin; and I have wandered about it for 6 or 8 hours in all directions. It may be presumed that it has greatly improved of late years. There are far fewer spirit shops than I have been used to see in great cities. And even Donnybrook Fair (which is on now, though sought to be abolished) is less disagreeable than Chalk Farm; and I have seen numbers of common people buying the most innocent and unlife-like of Dolls there, for their little children.

In a letter to his daughter Mary, he further expanded on his impressions:

> The man who drove our jaunting-car yesterday hadn't a piece in his

---

1. This hotel, situated at the corner of Nassau Street and Dawson Street, was pulled down some years ago, and was replaced by the splendid offices of the North British and Mercantile Insurance Co. The buildings are now occupied by the Ulster Bank.

coat as big as a penny roll, and had had his hat on (apparently without brushing it) ever since he was grown up. But he was remarkably intelligent and agreeable, with something to say about everything. For instance, when I asked him what a certain building was, he didn't say "courts of law" and nothing else, but "Av you plase, sir, it's the foor coorts o'looyers, where Misther O'Connell stood his trial wunst, ye'll remimber, sir, afore I tell ye of it." When we got into the Phoenix Park, he looked round him as it if were his own, and said: "THAT's a park, sir, av yer plase." I complimented it, and he said: "Gintlemen tills me as they'r bin, sir, over Europe, and never see a park aqualling ov it. 'Tis eight mile roond, sir, ten mile and a half long, and in the month of May the hawthorn trees are as beautiful as brides with their white jewels on. Yonder's the vice-regal lodge, sir; in them two corners lives the two sicretirries, wishin I was them, sir. There's air here, sir, av yer plase! There's scenery here, sir! There's mountains – thim, sir! Yer coonsider it a park, sir? It is that, sir!"

The Irish Times wrote:

The Round Room of the Rotunda where the Readings took place was admirably adapted to the purpose, and capable of accommodating about three thousand persons comfortably. It was then, the principal hall for concerts and indoor entertainments of all kinds. On the occasion of the first Reading, on Monday, August 23rd, 1858, the building was completely filled, with the exception of a few seats in the reserved portion, by a most brilliant audience. The piece chosen by Dickens for the occasion was A Christmas Carol. The fittings of the platform upon which he stood were simple in the extreme. A small table, covered with green cloth and having a stand for his book, stood in the centre of the platform. At the back was erected a chocolate-coloured screen, which was to assist in throwing the reader's voice forward into the apartment. Overhead a smaller screen was hung longwise, from behind which a row of gas jets threw a flood of light on the figure below. These comprised all the "scenic effects."

The *Freeman's Journal* reported:

Dickens made his appearance on the platform and was greeted by a burst of applause than which we have never heard anything more spontaneous, general, or enthusiastic. He was evidently much pleased with the cordiality of his reception, and acknowledged it by bowing repeatedly. His appearance is eminently prepossessing. His figure is tall, slight and graceful – his features regular and sharply chizelled, and his shaven cheeks, moustache, and pointed beard, after the American fashion, render still more striking and peculiar a face remarkable for character, energy and expression. He has a broad and high forehead, underneath which flash eyes so deep and lustrous that lighted up by them even the plainest countenance would seem beautiful. When the applause with which he was received had subsided, Mr. Dickens, in a clear and sonorous voice, thus addressed the audience: – Ladies and Gentlemen – Let the first public words I have spoken on Irish ground be words of thankfulness to you for your cordial and generous welcome. You cannot, believe me, be more glad to see me than I am to see you (applause). This little book which I am to have the honour and pleasure of presenting to you tonight is divided into four parts. I shall pause with your permission for about five minutes at the end of the second part. I am quite sure beforehand that you will be as easy and natural with me as I shall try with all my heart to be with you; and I therefore earnestly hope that you will (. . .) to any emotions which the story may be calculated to call forth the freest expression. You need be under no apprehension of disturbing me thereby, as nothing can be more delightful to me than to receive any assurance that you are interested. Mr. Dickens then proceeded to read the Carol. . . .

All the points were brought out in the most vivid manner, and the interest of the audience never flagged from the beginning to the end of the reading, which lasted exactly two hours. Peals of laughter at the comic passages, which were given with exquisite drollery – bursts of applause at the enunciation of generous and noble sentiments – and the tears which were drawn from many of the audience at the deep pathos displayed in the delineation of the child cripple, Tiny Tim, testified to the extraordinary dramatic talent of the reader.

They followed him throughout with marks of the deepest interest, and caught up with quick and ready appreciation of his points, whether comic or sentimental. At the conclusion of the reading he was again enthusiastically applauded. The "Chimes," another Christmas story, will be read this evening.

Earlier, on the tour in England, Dickens had found his feet as a dramatic artist. The people were amazed and delighted and every reading was booked to capacity. "They don't quite understand beforehand what it is, I think", Dickens wrote from Worchester to Wilkie Collins, "and expect a man to be sitting down in some corner, droning away like a mild bagpipe". What they were given was a brilliant series of carefully rehearsed impersonations, in which Dickens recreated the characters of his tales before their eyes. There was no precedent for such a thing, and Dickens was equally delighted with his success. "It is very curious", he wrote to Miss Coutts, afterwards the Baroness Burdett Coutts, who did some philanthropic work in Ireland, "to see how many people in black come to Little Dombey. And when it is over they almost uniformly go away as if the child were really Dead – with a hush upon them".

On Wednesday, 25 August the *Freeman's Journal* reported on the last night's performance of "The Chimes".

THE CHIMES – a goblin story of some bells that rang an old year out and a new year in – was the subject in which Mr. Dickens displayed last evening his remarkable powers as a dramatic reader. Less varied in its character and incidents than the Christmas Carol – more solemn in its general purport, and less exuberant in the play of humour than that charming production, it did not afford Mr. Dickens so good an opportunity as he had on the previous evening of evincing that nice perception of the humorous and those versatile powers of comic expression which he possesses in so high a degree. But whatever the Chimes may have lost in animation, variety, or drollery – and it is only as compared with the Carol that it can be said to have been at all deficient in these points – it gained in depth, in earnestness, in solemnity, and in pathos. The work, as its author informed his audience, was written some twelve years ago, when certain events, occurring within the compass of a single week, appeared to him to render a few earnest words necessary, advocating compassionate and merciful remembrance of the poor. And surely no nobler sermon could be preached to those who bask in worldly prosperity than this – in which, pictured by the hand of genius, the sorrows, the sufferings, the hard trials, and the bitter privations of our poorer brethren, accompanied often, thank Heaven! by the noblest virtues and the most heroic fortitude, are displayed in vivid colours before us. No man can read unmoved the series of affecting scenes in which Mr. Dickens inculcates so strongly the duties of charity, of kindness, and of consideration towards the poorer and humbler classes of our bellow-beings. But how much deeper must be the impression, when the person is personally enforced with earnest voice and glowing features by the great teacher himself. We have no doubt that many left the Rotunda last night with softened hearts, and minds more disposed perhaps than before to look earnest sympathy upon the joys and sorrows of those beneath them. The man who can teach such lessons and produce such effects as these deserves to be ranked amongst the benefactors of his kind – and such a man is Mr. Charles Dickens.

In another little snippet the same day elsewhere in the paper, reporting a London bankruptcy case, it said:

> THE ROAD TO RUIN. – Charles Dickens calls pawnbrokers duplicates "turnpike tickets, obtained by travellers on the road to ruin." Mr. John Townsend, M.P. for Greenwich, appears to have gone a few stages on the aforesaid road, and to have possession of an adequate number of the turnpike tickets.

Writing to his sister-in-law, Georgina Hogarth, the same day, Dickens wrote:

> Morrison's Hotel, Dublin
> Wednesday, Aug. 25th, 1858.

I begin my letter to you to-day, though I don't know when I may send it off. We had a very good house last night, after all, that is to say, a great rush of shillings and good half-crowns, though the stalls were comparatively few. For 'Little Dombey', this morning, we have an immense stall let – already more than two hundred – and people are now fighting in the agent's shop to take more. Through some mistake of our printer's the evening reading for this present Wednesday was dropped, in a great part of the announcements, and the agent opened no plan for it. I have therefore resolved not to have it at all. Arthur Smith has waylaid me in all manner of ways, but I remain obdurate. I am frightfully tired, and really relieved by the prospect of an evening – overjoyed.

They were a highly excitable audience last night, but they certainly did not comprehend – internally and intellectually comprehend – 'The Chimes' as a London audience do. I am quite sure of it. I very much doubt the Irish capacity of receiving the pathetic; but of their quickness as to the humorous there can be no doubt. I shall see how they go along with Little Paul, in his death, presently. . . .

We meant, as I said in a letter to Katie, to go to Queenstown [meaning Kingstown or Dun Laoghaire] yesterday and bask on the seashore. But there is always so much to do and we couldn't manage it after all. We expect a tremendous house to-morrow night as well as to-day; and Arthur is at the present instant up to his eyes in business (and seats), and, between his regret at losing to-night, and his desire to make the room hold twice as many as it will hold, is half distracted. I have become a wonderful Irishman – must play an Irish part some day – and his only relaxation is when I enact 'John and the Boots', which I consequently do enact all day long. The papers are full of remarks upon my white tie, and describe it as being of enormous size, which is a wonderful delusion, because, as you very well know, it is a small tie. Generally, I am happy to report, the Emerald press is in favour of my appearance, and likes my eyes. But one gentleman comes out with a letter at Cork, wherein he says that although only forty-six I look like an old man. He is a rum customer, I think.

All manner of people have called, but I have seen only two. John has given it up altogether as to rivalry with the Boots, and did not come into my room this morning at all. Boots appeared triumphant and alone. He was waiting for me at the hotel-door last night. 'Whaa't sart of a hoose, sur?' he asked me. 'Capital'. 'The Lard be praised fur the 'onor o' Dooblin!'

Arthur buys bad apples in the streets and brings them home and doesn't eat them, and then I am obliged to put them in the balcony because they make the room smell faint. Also he meets countrymen with honeycomb on their heads, and leads them (by the buttonhole when they have one) to this gorgeous establishment and requests the bar to buy honeycomb for his breakfast; then it stands upon the sideboard uncovered and the flies fall into it. He buys owls, too, and castles, and other horrible objects, made in bog-oak (that material which is not appreciated at Gad's Hill); and he is perpetually snipping pieces out of newspapers and sending them all over the world. While I am reading he conducts the correspondence, and his great delight is to show me seventeen or eighteen letters when I come, exhausted, into the retiring-place. Berry has not got into any particular trouble for forty-eight hours, except that he is all over boils. I have prescribed the yeast, but ineffectually. It is indeed a sight to see him and John sitting in pay-boxes, and surveying Ireland out of pigeon-holes.

Same Evening before Bed-time.

Everybody was at 'Little Dombey' to-day, and although I had some little difficulty to work them up in consequence of the excessive crowding of the place, and the difficulty of shaking the people into their seats, the effect was unmistakable and profound. The crying was universal, and they were extraordinarily affected. There is no doubt we could stay here a week with that one reading, and fill the place every night. Hundreds of people have been there to-night, under the impression that it would come off again. It was a most decided and complete success.

Arthur has been imploring me to stop here on the Friday after Limerick, and read 'Little Dombey' again. But I have positively said 'No'. The work is too hard. It is not like doing it in one easy room and always the same room. With a different place every night, and a different audience with its own peculiarity every night, it is a tremendous strain. I was sick of it to-day before I began, then got myself into wonderful train. . . .

We walked out last night, with the intention of going to the theatre; but the Piccolomini establishment[2] (they were doing the "Lucia")[3] looked so horribly like a very bad jail, and the Queen's[4] looked so blackguardly, that we came back again, and went to bed. I seem to be always either in a railway carriage, or reading, or going to bed. I get so knocked up, whenever I have a minute to remember it that then I go to bed as a matter of course.

Dickens was invited to call on the Rutherfords, whom he knew, who lived in Dublin, but he declined.

Morrison's Hotel, Dublin
Wednesday Twenty Fifth August | 1858

My Dear Mrs. Rutherford

I owe you many thanks for your kind note, and I much regret that the constant occupation of my time during my hurried visit here disables me from making any engagements or calls whatever. I am a perfect galley-slave at this time. Nor have I any of my family with me; for, though it would have been delightful to me to bring my girls, my movements are so rapid and comfortless, that I denied myself that pleasure too.

I am sorry to receive so Nelsonic an account of Major Rutherford's right hand. But I am sure he knows that he cannot have a better one than he finds in you.

With kind regard to him and all your house, I am ever

Dear Mrs. Rutherford | Faithfully Yours
CHARLES DICKENS

The Wednesday 25th night's reading of 'Little Dombey' was reported in the *Freeman's Journal* as follows:

---

2. The Italian Opera were performing at the Theatre Royal, with Mlle Marietta Piccolomini (1834-99) as the leading soprano. The performances were enthusiastically reviewed in the *Dublin Evening Post*.
3.   They performed Donizetti's *Lucia di Lammermoor* on 21 and 26 August.
4.   The Queen's Theatre, Great Brunswick Street, South: a small theatre, "well adapted for the production of melodramas, farces &." (*Dublin: What's to be Seen*, 1872). [Source: *The Letters of Charles Dickens*, pilgrim edition, editors Madeline House, Graham Storey, Kathleen Tillotson (Clarendon Press, Oxford, 1995), Vol. 8, 1856–58, p. 639.]

MR. CHARLES DICKENS

The reading of 'Little Dombey', yesterday afternoon, attracted an audience, immense in point of numbers, and most brilliant in appearance, including as it did a very large proportion of ladies. There was not a single vacancy in the reserved stalls, and the other compartments of the Round Room were crowded to excess, whilst not a few were unable to obtain accommodation, and had to turn away disappointed from the doors. The hour at which the reading took place, as well as the interest involved in the subject of it, combined, as might have been anticipated, to bring this vast assemblage together. Who is there that has not read with delighted interest the exquisite delineation – so graceful, so tender, so poetical, of the dreamy, imaginative, thoughtful child which Mr. Dickens has given to the world in 'Little Dombey'? Who has not felt pained, as if he had suffered some personal, affliction when as the story progresses it becomes apparent that death has marked that fragile form for his own – and who has not felt the tears start unbidden to his eyes at the inexpressably affecting description of the death bed of the gentle child? Let us admit that the character of Little Dombey is overdrawn, and somewhat unnatural. How much stronger then is the testimony to the genius of the author, who has invested this delicate creature of his imagination with such an aspect of reality and truth, that we all seem to have known and loved him. The reading of yesterday afternoon was a selection from the novel of 'Dombey and Son', and consisted solely of those passages in which the brief life of little Paul is told. We must confess that upon the whole we were not as much pleased on this occasion as by the two previous readings of the Christmas Carol, and The Chimes. Very many passages, it is true, were read with great feeling, and the most perfect expression; the dramatic talent of Mr. Dickens was as varied and striking as ever; but when the author spoke in his own person his utterance was generally too rapid and occasionally too indistinct to allow his meaning to be perfectly caught by many of the audience. Of course those who were provided with a book could follow him with ease; but much of the effect was lost by the effort necessary to catch many of his sentences. These observations do not apply to the dialogues, which were read with the utmost distinctness, point and expression. The conversations of Little Paul with his sister Florence, and the death scene with which the reading concluded, were faultlessly rendered; and in the humorous parts, the comic talents of Mr. Dickens shone conspicuously. The pompous Dr. Blimber; the erudite Cornelia; Toots – the gruff-voiced, stupid headed, good-hearted Toots; the airy Mrs. Chick, and her obsequiously polite satellite Miss

Tox, were all presented most vividly to the minds of the audience by
that wonderful flexibility of voice and feature, and those appropriate
and expressive gestures which Mr. Dickens can command with such
rapidity and ease. Indeed, in all the humorous portions of the reading
Mr. Dickens achieved the most genuine and complete success. This
evening the reading, the fourth and last of the series, will be composed
of three distinct pieces – 'The Poor Traveller', 'Boots at the Holly Tree
Inn', and 'Mrs. Gamp'.

Dickens at this time had not learned to read with the ease and precision for
which he eventually became famous, and at the start of his career as a reciter
he occasionally suffered from hoarseness due to the unaccustomed strain the
readings involved. This probably accounts for the indistinctness complained
of. Nevertheless, in the "Dombey" reading he achieved the most genuine and
complete success, and was awarded tumultuous applause when the reading
ended.

Dickens, writing to his daughter Mary from Belfast a few days later, described his reception in Dublin which his manager Arthur Smith tried to cope
with:

When I went down to the Rotunda at Dublin on Thursday night, I said
to Arthur, who came rushing at me: "You needn't tell me. I know all
about it." The moment I had come out of the door of the hotel (a mile
off), I had come against the stream of people turned away. I had strug-
gled against it to the room. There, the crowd in all the lobbies and
passages was so great, that I had a difficulty in getting in. They had
broken all the glass in the pay-boxes. They had offered frantic prices
for stalls.

Eleven bank-notes were thrust into that pay-box (Arthur saw them)
at one time, for eleven stalls. Our men were flattened against walls, and
squeezed against beams. Ladies stood all night with their chins against
my platform. Other ladies sat all night upon my steps. You never saw
such a sight. And the reading went tremendously! It is much to be
regretted that we troubled ourselves to go anywhere else in Ireland.
We turned away people enough to make immense houses for a week.

The Thursday night and final Dublin reading was reported in the *Freeman's
Journal* again as follows:

MR. CHARLES DICKENS

Mr. Dickens's reading, yesterday evening, was composed of three distinct pieces, and possessed, therefore, the powerful attraction of variety, though wanting in that continuous interest which attaches to a single story. The charm of variety, most probably, but still more the fact that this was known to be the last appearance of Mr. Dickens in Dublin (for the present, at least), as a reader of his own works, had the effect of bringing together an overflowing audience. The crush at the entrance doors was immense, and long before the reading commenced there was scarcely a seat unoccupied. The reception which the distinguished author met with was even more marked and enthusiastic than the cordial welcome which greeted his first appearance on last Monday evening before an Irish audience. The applause which hailed him, when he stepped upon the platform, and which was repeated at frequent intervals during the evening, was so hearty and vigorous that it may be said without exaggeration to have assumed the form of a popular ovation. The first piece which he read was a tale, entitled 'The Poor Traveller', published in one of the Christmas numbers of 'Household Words'. Amusing and interesting to a certain extent it could hardly fail to be: but it must be admitted that it is not a production calculated either to exhibit his genius as a writer, or his talents as a dramatic reader to the best advantage. It is highly melodramatic and unrelieved by that quaint and genial humour in the expression of which Mr. Dickens has achieved his greatest successes. The 'Poor Traveller' is a narrative of the adventures of a dissipated youngster, Richard Doubledick, who, enlisting in the army, is reclaimed by an officer, with 'deep dark bright eyes' and rises through the various grades of Sergeant Richard Doubledick, Sergeant Major Richard Doubledick, Ensign Richard Doubledick, &c. The manner in which Mr. Dickens repeats and dwells upon the name and titles of his hero, and constantly introduces the 'dark bright eyes' of the officer is rather theatrical and affected. Very different and most charming throughout is 'Boots at the Holly Tree Inn' – one of those graceful trifles which no one can write so well as Mr. Dickens – and evidently thrown off by him in one of his happiest moments of inspiration. The story is that of a little couple – the boy eight, the girl seven years old – who fell in love and eloped together with a view to marriage at Gretna-green, and having arrived at the Holly Tree Inn were kept there for two or three days until the father of the young gentleman came and took him home, during which time they were the objects of wondering and delighted interest to the host and hostess, the chambermaids, and the boots, by the latter of whom the narrative is told. The utter impossibility of the circumstances, which removes the story at once out of the region of fact, only increases the charm of the exquisite humour, the graceful fancy, the happy and natural touches, the acute observation, and most graphic word painting which imparts so much reality and truth to the writings of Mr. Dickens. Conceived in a happy moment the story is worked out in his best style. The Boots is a younger brother of Sam Weller – graver and less exuberant in his wit than our old friend – but nevertheless a distinguished specimen of his order, and most characteristically portrayed. The way in which Mr. Dickens read this piece was inimitable, and kept his audience convulsed with merriment, which would have been more demonstrative but for their fear of interrupting him. The chuckling tone and merry twinkle of the eye with which he gave expression to the salient points of the story were wonderfully effective, and impossible to be described. It was evident that Mr. Dickens entered thoroughly into the spirit of the thing and enjoyed the fun quite as heartily as his hearers. There was, of course, great curiosity to hear 'Mrs. Gamp'; and Mr. Dickens introduced that remarkable female and her invisible friend, Mrs. Harris, to his audience with the most complete success. Mrs. Gamp is one of the best conceived and most artistically finished characters in the whole range of the humorous creations which we owe to the fertile fancy of Mr. Dickens – and her peculiarities, so pointedly brought out by the admirable reading of the author, were productive of the greatest amusement. At the conclusion of his reading Mr. Dickens was enthusiastically applauded, and the cheers having been renewed after he had left the platform, he returned and bowed his acknowledgments. We believe he will commence his series of readings this evening at Belfast.

Dickens and his party travelled by train to Belfast next day and his first impressions of that city were expressed in a letter to Forster that he liked Belfast quite as much as Dublin but in a different way:

> A fine place with a rough people; everything looking prosperous; the railway ride from Dublin quite amazing in the order, neatness, and cleanness of all you see; every cottage looking as if it had been whitewashed the day before; and many with charming gardens, prettily kept with bright flowers.

Belfast heralded his arrival with a notice in the *Northern Whig* that the steamer pilot would sail for Bangor on Saturday 28th at 5.30 pm (instead of 5.00 pm) "to accommodate parties attending Mr. Dickens's 3.00 pm reading that day". Those people living in Bangor and in the bathing places adjacent would be afforded the opportunity to hear Dickens in the Victoria Hall, Belfast.

Dickens's first Belfast reading was at 8 o'clock on Friday 27 August to a crowded audience "to whom he has so long and so intimately been known through his words. . . . In him the Christmas Carol assumes new features of beauty, of humour, and of pathos".

The *Northern Whig*, reporting the Friday night event, said that the audience had been brought back to classic times when writers found their audiences in the Forum. "Some make a polite protest against public appearances of authors on the grounds that it makes undue concession to the vulgar curiosity which craves an acquaintance with the personality of great men." This the writer dismissed and said Charles Dickens's performance was less reading than dramatic monologues – a finished little play in which scenes of dialogue are given with a variety of intonation and a command of mimicry "which surpasses Mrs Fanny Kemble's readings".

Every set was taken and hundreds were turned back at the doors. It had been a most pleasing and enjoyable entertainment.

The Saturday afternoon performance of 'Little Dombey' was also moving. "There were tears on many fair cheeks throughout the hall and grave old men, whose youthful sympathies had long been closed, found a strange dimness in their eyes."

The evening performance of Richard Doubledick, Boots at the Holly Tree Inn and Mrs Gamp was another success. Dickens, writing to his daughter Mary that day from Belfast, described his reception in Belfast where again his manager, Arthur Smith, was at his wits' end to cope with the confusion and two near accidents during the performances:

> We arrived here yesterday at two. The room will not hold more than from eighty to ninety pounds. The same scene was repeated with the additional feature, that the people are much rougher here than in Dublin, and that there was a very great uproar at the opening of the doors, which, the police in attendance being quite inefficient and only looking on, it was impossible to check. Arthur was in the deepest misery because shillings got into stalls, and half-crowns got into shillings, and stalls got nowhere, and there was immense confusion. It ceased, however, the moment I show myself; and all went most brilliantly, in spite of a great piece of the cornice of the ceiling falling with a great crash within four or five inches of the head of a young lady on my platform (I was obliged to have people there), and in spite of my gas suddenly going out at the time of the game of forfeits at Scrooge's nephew's, through some Belfastian gentleman accidentally treading on the flexible pipe, and needing to be relighted.
>
> We shall not get to Cork before mid-day on Monday; it being difficult to get from here on a Sunday. We hope to be able to start away to-morrow morning to see the Giant's Causeway (some sixteen miles off), and in that case we shall sleep at Dublin to-morrow night, leaving

here by the train at half-past three in the afternoon. Dublin, you must understand, is on the way to Cork. This is a fine place, surrounded by lofty hills. The streets are very wide, and the place is very prosperous. The whole ride from Dublin here is through a very picturesque and various country; and the amazing thing is, that it is all particularly neat and orderly, and that the houses (outside at all events) are all brightly whitewashed and remarkably clean. I want to climb one of the neighbouring hills before this morning's 'Dombey'. I am now waiting for Arthur, who has gone to the bank to remit his last accumulation of treasure to London.

Our men are rather indignant with the Irish crowds, because in the struggle they don't sell books, and because, in the pressure, they can't force a way into the room afterwards to sell them. They are deeply interested in the success, however, and are as zealous and ardent as possible.

Dickens could not have visited the Giant's Causeway which is 60 miles away. He probably visited the Giant's Cradle, a rocking stone in Browne's Bay, near Larne, c. 20 miles away.

According to Percy Fitzgerald, who met him in Dublin three days later, Charles Dickens thus described Belfast: "Tremendous houses, curious people, they seem all Scotch, but quite in a state of transition." Dickens also told him that he "walked a long way by sea to Carrickfergus" (in Co. Antrim, 9 ½ miles north of Belfast).[5]

Dickens left Belfast on Sunday 29 August from the Ulster Railway on the 3.30 train to Dublin en route to Cork.

Dickens had a shrewd business sense and kept track of his financial takings. Writing to his sister-in-law, Georgina Hogart, that night from Morrison's Hotel, Dublin, he wrote:

For novelty's sake, I will give you some statistics. To understand which, you must be informed that Arthur charges every place with its proportion of the next prospective expenses. For instance, before my profit is declared here, it is debited with the journey to Belfast; and before my profit is declared at Belfast, it is debited in its turn with its share of our expenses home to London. After all these deductions, and after paying Arthur's share, I made here £210, and at Belfast (in two days) £130. With a good return at Cork, and nothing very great at Limerick from which we don't expect much (except pretty women, for which it is famous), I shall have made a handsome Thousand Pounds since I left

---

5. *Memories of Charles Dickens*, pp. 7-8.

Gad's Hill on our country Tour! That is, no doubt, immense; our expenses being necessarily large, and the travelling party being always five.

The success at Belfast has been equal to the success here. Enormous! I think them a better audience on the whole than Dublin; and the personal affection there, was something overwhelming. I wish you and the dear girls could have seen the people look at me in the street – or heard them ask me, as I hurried to the hotel after reading last night to 'do me the honor to shake hands Misther Dickens and God bless you Sir; not ounly for the light you have been to me this night; but for the light you's been in mee house Sir (and God love your face!) this many a year.' Every night, by the bye, since I have been in Ireland, the ladies have beguiled John out of the bouquet from my coat. And yesterday morning, as I had showered the leaves from my geranium in reading Little Dombey, they mounted the platform after I was gone, and picked them all up, as keepsakes.

I have never seen men go in to cry so undisguisedly as they did at that reading yesterday afternoon. They made no attempt whatever to hide it, and certainly cried more than the women. As to the Boots at night – and Mrs. Gamp too – it was just one roar with me and them. For they made me laugh so, that sometimes I could not compose my face to go on...

Tell the girls that Arthur and I have each ordered at Belfast a trim, sparkling, slap-up Irish jaunting car!!! I flatter myself we shall astonish the Kentish people. it is the oddest carriage in the world, and you are always falling off. But it is gay and bright in the highest degree. Wonderfully Neapolitan.

What with a sixteen mile ride before we left Belfast, and a sea Beach walk, and a two o'Clock dinner, and a seven hours' railway ride since, I am – as we say here – "a thrifle weary". But I really am in wonderful force, considering the work. For which I am, as I ought to be, very thankful.

Arthur was exceedingly unwell last night – could not cheer up at all. He was so very unwell that he left the Hall (!) and became invisible after my five minutes' rest. I found him at the Hotel in a jacket and slippers, and with a hot bath just ready. He was in the last stage of prostration. The local agent was with me, and proposed that he (the wretched Arthur) should go to his office and balance the accounts then and there. He went, in the jacket and slippers, and came back, in 20 minutes, perfectly well, in consequence of the admirable balance. (He is now sitting opposite to me ON THE BAG OF SILVER (£40; it must be dreadfully hard), writing to Boulogne.

I suppose it is clear that the next letter I write, is Katie's. Either from Cork, or from Limerick, it shall report further. At Limerick I read in the Theatre: there being no other place.

Fancy FREDERICK presenting himself here, in this house, to me, last Thursday a few minutes before Dinner. I was dreadfully hard with him at first; but relented.

Dickens's brother Frederick was, like his father, always in debt and on this occasion had followed Charles to Ireland to get money from him. Charles Dickens's success created this occupational hazard of being a target for relieving others' financial distress. Though irritated by such approaches Dickens was generous with the supplicants.

Dickens travelled to Cork on Monday 30 August 1858, and stayed in the Imperial Hotel. The reading was in the Athenaeum. The following account details his visit to Cork. That he kissed the Blarney Stone was no doubt claimed by Corkonians to have ensured his future success:

CHARLES DICKENS IN CORK

On Monday evening CHARLES DICKENS, both personally and in his writings the most popular of living novelists, made his first appearance before a Cork audience. The house was well filled all through, though the cram in the galleries showed intellectual entertainment to be most favoured amongst the democracy. Almost precisely at the time appointed, the distinguished visitor made his appearance, and was greeted by a hearty cheer, which he cordially acknowledged. The platform on which he took his place had been carefully adapted to throw out into the strongest possible relief the figure of the reader, and to enable the audience to see in the most distinct manner the movements of his form, and the workings of his marked and expressive lineaments. The peculiarities of his appearance, the extreme elegance of his toilette, his handsome, yet care-worn features, his American moustache and beard, and those large, wonderful eyes which seem to fascinate everyone's attention, have been already fully described. Audiences must be favourably impressed with the quiet, gentlemanly manner in which he invites, the natural expression of any emotion to which the little book he is about to read 'may be fortunate enough' to give rise, and listeners and declaimer commence their intercourse with an easy feeling on both sides. The 'little book' was the Christmas Carol, one of the most exquisite prose idylls in any language. Full of strange character-sketching, of queer conversations, of genial loveable humour, of quaint, pathetic tenderness, and withal founded upon a violent improbability – the sudden conversion of a miser by a dream – those who read it rush through its pages with a fascination which works of graver import and perhaps higher merit cannot command. But those who have so perused it know comparatively little of its power, until they have heard its strange fancies, its odd whimsical conceits, its bits of thrilling pathos, its flashes of brilliant fun, proceeding from the lips of its author. Mr. DICKENS is a consummate actor. His voice is full and mellow – strong without being noisy, and of most versatile quality. Then he can speak with every muscle and line of his face, and then he does startle with somewhat vehement or fantastical action. All these aids are combined to make Scrooge more miserly, hard and exciting; his nephew more good-humoured and forebearant [sic]; the ghost of Marley more transparent; the buttons of his coat behind more visible through him; the once questionable fact of his having no bowels more self-evident; the chain he had forged for himself of cash boxes, ledgers, steel purses etc. more firmly binding about him. The rich, flexible voice and the speaking glances make more droll that picture of Christmas at Bob Cratchit's, 'Tiny Tim and all', which is one of the drollest, pleasantest sketches that has ever been drawn. Who that looks at and listens to the author, as he details all the events of that astounding festivity, cannot see almost with his own eyes the two juvenile Cratchits thrusting their spoons into their mouths lest they could not restrain themselves until their time came to be helped, and should actually shriek for goose? Who does not sympathise in the hopes and fears regarding the well-being of the pudding, and follow almost in person its triumphant procession when it is found to be miraculously successful? It needs all the powers of the actors, as well as the author, to help us to realize the agility of old Fezziwig, whose legs shone so that at the last cut they seemed to wink. Without his reading, imagination cannot picture the full absurdity of believing that Topper in reality was blind during that game of blind man's buff, which took place at Scrooge's nephew's, or had any other design than that of catching the plump sister – 'her in the lace tucker.' In fact, all that touched or amused in the written work had its merit heightened and made more vivid by thus proceeding, living as it were, out of the mouth of him who conceived it. Nor could it be forgotten that it was no mere actor was before you; no adaptable instrument that entered the music made by another; but the man who, out of his own rich imagination, had drawn all those shapes of beauty which dwell so fondly in our memories, whose exuberant wealth of humour had left us the legacy of fun which has been made the property of high and low, and whose generous, warm heart had conceived all the benevolent homilies of love and charity, of which this Christmas Carol is one of the most touching.

It is almost needless to say that the two hours' reading held the attention of the audience rivetted, except when some passage elicited a spontaneous burst of laughter, or some generous sentiment evoked a cheer; and that at the end the gratified listeners saluted the departure of their illustrious entertainer with a hearty and cordial farewell...

Our illustrious visitor availed himself of the leisure moments in the intervals of his entertainments to visit the scenery in the vicinity of Cork, having gone yesterday to Queenstown, and this day to Blarney. He spent a quarter of an hour on the top of the Castle, surveying the pleasant prospect, and before departing kissed the famous stone. Whether Mr. DICKENS thought this ceremonial necessary to increase the magic with which his tongue is tipped, we do not know; but surely it was not the opinion of the visitors to the Athenaeum on Monday and Tuesday evenings. We understand that Mr. DICKENS expressed the most intense delight at the natural aspect of the neighbourhood, and most agreeable disappointment at the outer condition of our people. We believe in a pecuniary point of view his visit has been very successful.

The Cork Examiner, Wednesday, 1 September 1858.

Writing from Cork on Tuesday, 31 August to Mrs Richard Madden in Dublin, he regretfully declined her request to read again in Dublin. It would have given him the greatest pleasure to do so had such a thing been possible, he said. He had also been urged by his manager to return to Dublin, after Limerick, to read "Little Dombey" again, but notwithstanding that he knew that he "could easily fill the Rotunda every night for a week", he refused. "I have positively said 'No'. The work is too hard." Dickens was of course right to refuse, to prevent exhaustion, and as it was this latter condition which is credited with causing his premature death at the age of 58 years, he would have been advised to refuse more often, notwithstanding the large amounts of money he could so readily earn.

Writing to Frank Finlay of Belfast from Limerick, he said:

Cork was an immense success. We found upwards of a thousand Stalls let, for the three readings. A great many people were turned away too, on the last night. I did not think them, when I read the Carol, nearly as good an audience as Dublin or Belfast, in respect of demonstrative satisfaction. But they were excellent as to Dombey and the Boots too. Perhaps, on the occasion of the first reading, the fault was in myself. For I was not in very good spirits that evening.

Dickens arrived in Limerick on Wednesday 1 September and read for two nights in the Theatre Royal. The *Limerick Chronicle* of 4 September 1858 recounts his performances with one little reservation:

MR. CHARLES DICKENS

A practice which was necessary in olden times, when printing was unknown, for literary men to bring their works under notice by reading them before the public has been revived in modern times by Mr. Russell, the historian of the Crimean war, and by Mr. Charles Dickens, the great novelist, the immortal 'Boz', and the inimitable delineator of Pickwickian characters. Mr. Dickens has been reading his works in Limerick on Wednesday and Thursday evenings before crowded and fashionable audiences. His merits as a writer – clothing the common incidents of every day life with a touching interest – and ever leaning to the side of the weak and injured – are universally known and appreciated by the reading public. As a general reader we cannot give him unqualified praise, for though he undoubtedly possesses dramatic talents of a first rate order for personifying characters, yet he recited several passages of a descriptive nature in a sing-song, schoolboy style that was below par. On Wednesday evening Mr. Dickens read his Christmas Carroll [*sic*], and this production of his genius is, we trust, too well known to need any recapitulation.

On Thursday evening Mr. Dickens read 'The Poor Traveller' 'Boots at the Hollytree Inn,' and 'Mrs. Gamp.' 'The Poor Traveller' is a story of a reckless man, who for his ill conduct had been discarded by the woman whose affections he had won, and who therefore enlisted in the line in the year 1799. Private Richard Doubledick, as he called himself, became the worst character in the regiment, and was on a fair way to the triangles when his captain, who alone possessed influence over him, brought about a change. Doubledick became the best and bravest soldier in the army, rose from the ranks, and so the tale ends happily for him; and not without a lesson for those who heard it. 'Boots at the Hollytree Inn' is a capital contrast to the story of Richard Doubledick. Boots is his own historian, and the accent of Mr. Dickens as he personated that individual was a fruitful source of laughter. 'Sairy Gamp' was however, the strong point of the evening. It was a little comedy in two chapters, in which all the characters were performed by the reader. The oily hypocrite, Picksniff; the piping imbecile, Chuffey; the voluble undertaker, Molds; and the inimitable Gamp herself, were distinct personations, and as far as voice and accent were concerned, became distinct realities.

In Limerick he stayed in the Royal Hotel and in a letter, commented to Frank Finlay of Belfast: "There is not much to be done here, but it is a charming little Theatre for seeing and hearing (I read in the Theatre), and they were a highly sensitive, quick, and agreeable audience last night."

And in another letter from Limerick to his friend W.H. Wills, assistant editor of *Household Words* and later *All the Year Round*:

> This is the oddest place – of which nobody in any other part of Ireland seems to know anything. Nobody could answer a single question we asked about it. There is no large room, and I read in the Theatre – a charming Theatre. The best I ever saw, to see and hear in. Arthur says that when he opened the doors last night, there was a rush of – three Ducks! We expect a Pig to-night. We had only £40; but they seemed to think that, amazing! If the two nights bring £100, it will be as much as we expected. I am bound to say that they are an admirable audience. As hearty and demonstrative as it is possible to be. It is a very odd place in its lower-order aspects, and I am very glad we came – though we could have made heaps of money by going to Dublin instead. . . .
>
> Arthur sends you his kindest regard. He has been nearly torn to pieces in the shilling rushes, and has been so flattened against walls that he is only now beginning to "come round" again. My kindest remembrance to Mrs. Wills.

He arrived home to Gad's Hill Place, Higham by Rochester, Kent, on 4 September and wrote to friends:

> I am only just now at home for eight and forty hours, direct from Ireland. My success has been something wonderful.
>
> The work is very hard – sometimes, almost overpowering. But I am none the worse for it, and arrived here quite fresh.

CHAPTER TWO

Dickens and Daniel O'Connell

Charles Dickens (1812–1870) was born in Portsmouth on 7 February 1812. His father was John Dickens who was employed in the Navy Pay Office there. His mother was Elizabeth Barrow whose family came from Bristol. Her sister Mary, Charles Dickens's "Aunt Fanny" died in Ireland in 1822 when Charles was 10 years old, having come to Cork with her second husband Mathew Lamert, an army surgeon. Lamert later became Deputy Inspector-General of Military Hospitals and he too died in Cork.

Though John Dickens had quite reasonable means from his salary in the Navy he was continually falling into debt, and now living in Chatham with a London posting he moved house a number of times until he was arrested for debt in 1824 and imprisoned in the Marshalsea. Charles was taken out of school and went to work in Warren's Blacking Warehouse through the agency of his cousin James Lamert. After a few months John Dickens was released from debtors' prison and Charles returned to school.

John Dickens continued to be troubled by debt. In 1827 Charles, at the age of 15 years, began as a solicitor's clerk in Gray's Inn. John Dickens had retired from the Navy Office in 1825 on a small pension. By 1828 he had learnt shorthand and was working as a reporter for the *Morning Herald*. By the following year Charles too had learnt shorthand and became a freelance reporter at the Doctors' Commons, a law court which dealt with ecclesiastical (including divorce) probate and admiralty cases. In 1830 Charles Dickens was admitted as a reader at the British Museum and in the following year, at the age of 19, began working for his uncle, John Henry Barrow, reporting for the *Mirror of Parliament*. It was here that he came into contact with Daniel O'Connell, the Liberator and architect of Catholic Emancipation.

Daniel O'Connell (1775–1847) was educated in Ireland and France which he fled a few days after the execution of Louis XVI during the French Revolution. He spent the next three years as a law student in London, then came to Dublin and was called to the bar in 1798. He built up a large practice at the Irish bar, having entered politics in 1800 to organise a meeting of Dublin Catholics to oppose the Act of Union that year. By 1805 he was active in the Catholic Committee to achieve full freedom and equality for Catholics so that they could enter parliament and government service. In 1823 he formed the Catholic Association which proved to be the first great popular democratic

Mr Weller attacks the Executive of Ipswich (*Pickwick Papers*)

organisation in politics. By 1828 O'Connell was emboldened to contest a by-election for Co. Clare, the first Catholic to stand for Parliament since the 17th century. O'Connell won the seat but was debarred as a Catholic from taking his seat at Westminster. The Duke of Wellington as Prime Minister and Sir Robert Peel as Home Secretary (the minister in charge of Ireland) decided that Catholic emancipation must be enacted. Accordingly, in the spring of 1829 Peel introduced the Bill which was passed by both houses of Parliament without difficulty and received the royal assent in April.

Once elected to Parliament, O'Connell applied his energies to a large number of causes. These included the extension of the parliamentary and local government suffrages; the Tolpuddle Martyrs; the Poles persecuted by czarist Russia; Jewish emancipation; separation of church and state in Catholic as well as in Protestant countries, and even in the Papal States; free trade and especially the repeal of the Corn Laws; and the abolition of black slavery. In pursuing these aims, he was the leading Radical in the British Parliament in the 1830s.

The Reform Bill of 1832 set out to correct the defects of the old system of parliamentary representation whereby seats were not distributed according to population which had greatly relocated since the industrial revolution. The franchise was limited and based on no uniform system, and many seats were held as hereditary right by the landed aristocracy. By the 1820s, the middle classes were determined to secure reform.

On 1 March 1831, Lord John Russell in a Whig-led government introduced the first Reform Bill and the debate on the first reading continued until 9 March. There is indirect evidence in one of his letters that Charles Dickens reported this debate in which 70 to 80 members spoke and the *Mirror of Parliament* had full verbatim accounts. O'Connell spoke on 8 March and strongly supported the Bill as "an effectual measure of Reform", although he ideally wished for universal suffrage "as a matter of right". He requested more seats for Ireland while continuing to support the Bill. He also deplored the exclusion of the 40 shilling freeholders from the franchise in Ireland under the terms of the 1829 Catholic Emancipation Act raising the qualification to vote to £10.00. In a long speech (28 columns in *Hansard*) he railed against the "rotten boroughs" and called on the Government to do justice to Ireland as to England by passing this Bill. As it happened, the Bill was defeated in Committee and King William IV, who was personally in favour of reform, dissolved Parliament. It was not until June 1832 that the third Reform Bill passed the House of Lords when the king threatened to create a majority of Whig peers.

With the passing of the Catholic Emancipation Act in 1829 O'Connell hoped for great things for Irish Catholics, but the Tories and more conservative Whigs were determined to exclude Catholics from public office. O'Connell therefore proceeded with his "agitation" for further reform. The year 1832 was one of great disturbance in Ireland with many agrarian outrages committed in the country. The government decided to bring in a harsh Coercion Act.

Charles Dickens had moved to the *True Sun* as a reporter in 1832 and was well recognised now as a supreme shorthand writer. When Lord Edward Stanley, Chief Secretary for Ireland, spoke in the House of Commons on 27 February 1833 to the Coercion Bill, concerning the condition of Ireland, he was unhappy with newspaper reports of his speech and sent for Charles Dickens whom he knew of by reputation as a parliamentary reporter. He dictated his speech to Dickens who recorded it, in a private session, in shorthand and reproduced a faithful account of it which Lord Stanley had issued as a pamphlet.

O'Connell brought his campaign for "Justice for Ireland" all over England and Charles Dickens, now with the *Morning Chronicle* (since August 1834) reported the famous Ipswich speech of O'Connell on 28 May 1836.

O'Connell's main attack was against the Tory-dominated House of Lords for blocking the Municipal Corporations (Ireland) Bill.

In a letter to his wife Kate on 27 May 1836, Dickens wrote: "It is now half past one and huge mobs are assembled to greet O'Connell who is every moment expected. From the appearance of the crowd, and the height of party feeling here, I rather expect a Row." Scuffles did take place, and "the gold-banded cap, which decorated the Liberator's brow, was wrested from it by some ruffianly hand". O'Connell obtained a hearing with the greatest difficulty, "and the conduct of the Tories was most outrageous and disgraceful". O'Connell himself was told to "get back to Ireland", but his supporters greeted him with great applause.

An interesting article, "Dickens reports O'Connell: a legend examined" by William J. Carlton, appeared in the *Dickensian* in 1969:[1]

> So many passages in Dickens's writings bear witness to his acute sensitivity whenever an unusually flagrant case of man's inhumanity to man, woman or child came to his attention that some of his critics have not found it difficult to base on one or more of them a charge of excessive sentimentality. Professor George H. Ford, who devotes a chapter of Dickens and his Readers to this aspect of the novelist's work, reminds us, however, that his fondness for sentimental scenes was shared with his contemporaries, many of whom wept unashamedly over the death of Little Nell. Long ago I quoted an anecdote which, if its authenticity could be established, might have some relevance to this question.
>
> During the passage of the Irish Coercion Bill through the House of Commons (so the story ran), a speech by Daniel O'Connell had such an effect on young Dickens, who was reporting the debate for the *Morning Chronicle*, that he was constrained to lay down his pencil, so moved was he by the orator's vivid picture of a widow seeking her only son among the peasants killed by soldiers in a tithe riot, and on another occasion of a young girl shot down whilst leading her blind grandfather along a country lane.[2]

Throughout his letters Charles Dickens wrote on a number of occasions: "I

---

1.   Volume 65.
2.   W.J. Carlton, *Charles Dickens: Shorthand Writer*, 1926, p. 88.

have 'registered a vow' (in imitation of Mr. O'Connell)" in relation to various decisions he had made to important everyday matters. This referred to O'Connell's statement in the House of Commons in 1830. On killing J.N. D'Esterre in a duel in 1815 O'Connell had made a vow never to fight again. After refusing a challenge from Sir Henry Hardinge in 1830, he was taunted in Parliament, and replied: "There is blood upon this hand", raising his right hand, which was covered with a black glove. "I regret it deeply; and the honourable and learned gentleman, the Solicitor-General for Ireland, knows it. He knows that I have made a vow to Heaven, else he would never venture to use those taunts which in this House he has safely resorted to."

Dickens could sometimes be critical of O'Connell's speeches, however. Writing to Forster from Italy in June 1844 he told him that they were "the old thing: fretty, boastful, frothy, waspish at the voices in the crowd, and all that; but with no true greatness".[3]

Dickens had completed *The Old Curiosity Shop* by January 1841 and its serialization was completed in *Master Humphrey's Clock* in February of that year. It was at this time that Daniel O'Connell was reading the final instalment of *The Old Curiosity Shop* on a train journey and, on meeting with the death of Little Nell, "burst into tears, groaned, 'He should not have killed her' and despairingly threw the volume out of the train window". An account of a similar reaction was preserved "for its comicality" by Dickens's friend and biographer Forster in a letter from a Mrs Jane Greene, of Dublin, written after publication of his first volume of *The Life of Charles Dickens* (1872). Her uncle, she says, "like Mr Landor, was so enchanted with *Little Nell* that any-one might have supposed she was a real living child in whose sad fate he was deeply interested. One evening while silently reading . . . he suddenly sprung from his chair, flung the book violently on the ground, and exclaimed 'The Villain! The Rascal!! The bloodthirsty scoundrel!!!' His astonished brother thought he had gone mad, and enquired aghast of whom he was speaking? 'Dickens,' he roared, he would commit murder! He killed my little Nell – He killed my sweet little child!'"

A more sober account of O'Connell's reaction to the death of Little Nell is that given by the editor of his correspondence, W.J. Fitzpatrick, who comments:

> O'Connell's interest in the writings of Dickens reached its climax in the "Old Curiosity Shop". He followed quite excitedly the adventures and vicissitudes of little Nell; but when Dickens prematurely killed her he flung away the book, declaring that never again would he read a line

---

3.   *Forster's Life*, ed. J.W.T. Ley, 1928, p. 341.

that "Boz" wrote. It was obvious, he said, that the author had not sufficient talent to maintain Nell's adventures with interest to the end and
bring them to a happy issue, so he killed her to get rid of the difficulty.
O'Connell's resolve never again to read Dickens must be taken cum
grano. It was one of the impulsive speeches of a naturally good-hearted
man which, once uttered, he thought no more of.

Fitzpatrick also quotes a letter from O'Connell to Richard Barrett which indicates his true view of Dickens, one of admiration.

To Richard Barrett.

Merrion Square: 23rd March, 1843.

My dear Barrett, – I saw with great surprise in the last Pilot a paragraph which you certainly took from some other newspaper, headed
"O'Connell and Dickens", and purporting to be a quotation from an
alleged letter of mine to the editor of a Maryland newspaper, published
at Baltimore, and called the Hibernian Advocate. The thing is from
beginning to end a gross lie. I never wrote a letter to that newspaper,
nor am I in the habit of corresponding with the editors of American
papers.

I am surprised that you did not take notice that this forgery was
published in a slave-holding state – a state in which there is that moral
contamination about the press which, I think you ought to know, would
preclude me from having any communication with it.

Hibernian Advocate! Oh, miserable wretch, you are, indeed, fit to
circulate fictitious documents, for even your very name must be a forgery.

Few people admire more the writings of Dickens, or read them with
deeper interest, than I do. I am greatly pleased with his "American
Notes". They give me, I think, a clearer idea of every-day life in America
than I ever entertained before. And his chapter containing the advertisement respecting negro slavery is more calculated to augment the
fixed detestation of slavery than the most brilliant declamation or the
most splendid eloquence. That chapter shews out the hideous features
of the system far better than any dissertation on its evil could possibly
produce them, odious and disgusting to the public eye.

Forster also noted O'Connell's indignant disclaimer ". . . of a forged letter
with his signature that had 'gone the round of the American press' and as
quoted in the *New York Herald*, included the remark 'Thank God Dickens is
not an Irishman'."

Charles Dickens's views on slavery were incorporated into the American chapters of his new novel *Martin Chuzzlewit* which he began writing in December of 1842. In July of 1843 he was staying in Yorkshire for a rest from writing the novel.

> While here he read the newspapers, too, and in *The Times* he saw reports of American support for Daniel O'Connell and his campaign for Home Rule (Repeal of the Union) in Ireland, support which was hastily withdrawn in some quarters when O'Connell attacked slavery in one of his more fiery speeches. Dickens kept the material, and on his return to London from Yorkshire included it in one of the novel's American chapters which he was now writing.[4]

---

4. *Dickens*, Peter Ackroyd (Sinclair–Stevenson, London, 1990), p. 402.

CHAPTER THREE

The Irish in America

Emigration from Ireland was a permanent feature of Irish history from the 18th century. Emigration increased as a result of famine, espe cially the Great Famine 1845–47. Between 1841 and 1925 gross overseas emigration included 4¾ million to the United States of America, 70,000 to Canada, and over 370,000 to Australia, while countless thousands crossed the Irish Sea to Britain.

On 4 January 1842 Dickens and his wife Catherine set sail on their first visit to America, arriving back in England on 1 July. Within a month he had begun writing *American Notes* which were published in October.

In New York, Dickens describes the passing street parade of its inhabitants and lights on two characters near him on the sidewalk:

> . . . and let us see what kind of men those are behind ye: those two labourers in holiday clothes, of whom one carries in his hand a crumpled scrap of paper from which he tries to spell out a hard name, while the other looks about for it on all the doors and windows.
>
> Irishmen both! You might know them, if they were masked, by their long-tailed blue coats and bright buttons, and their drab trousers, which they wear like men well used to working dresses, who are easy in no others. It would be hard to keep your model republics going, without the countrymen and countrywomen of those two labourers. For who else would dig, and delve, and drudge, and do domestic work, and make canals and roads, and execute great lines of Internal Improvement! Irishmen both, and sorely puzzled too, to find out what they seek. Let us go down, and help them, for the love of home, and that spirit of liberty which admits of honest service to honest men, and honest work for honest bread, no matter what it be.

En route from Pittsburgh to Cincinnati on board a steamboat on the Ohio River (which enters the Mississippi) he again describes the other passengers:

> Further down still, sits a man who is going some miles beyond their

Paul and Florence (*Dombey and Son*)

place of destination, to 'improve' a newly-discovered copper mine. He carries the village – that is to be – with him: a few frame-cottages, and an apparatus for smelting the copper. He carries its people too. They are partly American and partly Irish, and herd together on the lower deck; where they amused themselves last evening till the night was pretty far advanced, by alternately firing off pistols and singing hymns.

Ensconced in his hotel in Cincinnati he, by chance, witnessed a temperance parade in which the Irish were particularly noticeable.

There happened to be a great Temperance Convention held here on the day after our arrival; and as the order of march brought the proces-

sion under the windows of the hotel in which we lodged, when they
started in the morning, I had a good opportunity of seeing it. It comprised several thousand men; the members of various 'Washington
Auxiliary Temperance Societies'; and was marshalled by officers on
horseback, who cantered briskly up and down the line, with scarves
and ribbons of bright colours fluttering out behind them gaily. There
were bands of music too, and banners out of number: and it was a
fresh, holiday-looking concourse altogether.

I was particularly pleased to see the Irishmen, who formed a distinct society among themselves, and mustered very strong with their
green scarves; carrying their national Harp and their Portrait of Father
Mathew,[1] high above the people's heads. They looked as jolly and
good-humoured as ever; and, working (here) the hardest for their living
and doing any kind of sturdy labour that came in their way, were the
most independent fellows there, I thought.

His chapter on slavery made a great impact in favour of the abolitionists, by
reproducing literally pages of newspaper advertisements of slave owners seeking to recover their slaves. The following is only a small part of these pages:

- Ran away, Negress Caroline. Had on a collar with one prong turned
  down.
- Ran away, a black woman, Betsy. Had an iron bar on her right leg.
- Ran away, the negro Manuel. Much marked with irons.
- Ran away, the negress Fanny. Had on an iron band about her neck.
- Ran away, a negro boy about twelve years old. Had round his neck
  a chain dog-collar with 'De Lampert' engraved on it.
- Ran away, the negro Hown. Has a ring of iron on his left foot. Also,
  Grise, his wife, having a ring and chain on the left leg.
- Detained at the police jail, the negro wench, Myra. Has several marks
  of LASHING, and has irons on her feet.
- Ran away, a negro woman and two children. A few days before she
  went off, I burnt her with a hot iron, on the left side of her face. I
  tried to make the letter M.

I could enlarge this catalogue with broken arms, and broken legs, and
gashed flesh, and missing teeth, and lacerated backs, and bites of dogs,
and brands of red-hot irons innumerable.

---

1. Fr Theobald Mathew (1790–1856), the much loved and honoured Irish Catholic friar and
temperance preacher. After signing the pledge in 1838, he preached temperance with remarkable
success throughout Ireland, in London in 1843, and in the principal American cities from
1849–51. Numerous American temperance societies were named after him.

He then turns to a comparison of the Whiteboy agrarian disturbances in Ireland; and the native American Indian:

> What! shall we declaim against the ignorant peasantry of Ireland, and mince the matter when these American task-masters are in question? Shall we cry shame on the brutality of those who ham-string cattle: and spare the lights of Freedom upon earth who notch the ears of men and women, cut pleasant posies in the shrinking flesh, learn to write with pens of red-hot iron on the human face, rack their poetic fancies for liveries of mutilation which their slaves shall wear for life and carry to the grave, breaking living limbs as did the soldiery who mocked and slew the Saviour of the world, and set defenceless creatures up for targets! Shall we whimper over legends of the tortures practised on each other by the Pagan Indians, and smile upon the cruelties of Christian men! Shall we, so long as these things last, exult above the scattered remnants of that race, and triumph in the white enjoyment of their possessions? Rather, for me, restore the forest and the Indian village; in lieu of stars and stripes, let some poor feather flutter in the breeze; replace the streets and squares by wigwams; and though the death-song of a hundred haughty warriors fill the air, it will be music to the shriek of one unhappy slave.

*   *   *

Later, near the end of his life, Dickens published an article by another author in his magazine journal (for which he commissioned and edited articles) on the Irish in America:

THE IRISH IN AMERICA[2]

"There are few more suggestive sights to a thoughtful mind than that which may be witnessed, several days in each week, at Queenstown, the harbour of Cork. It is there that the hundreds of poor Irish emigrants who every week flock on board the westward-bound Atlantic steamers, walk for the last time on their native soil, and gaze for the last time upon their dear home-friends. No one can see the embarcation of these multitudes of forlorn creatures, the long painful parting from country and from friends, the crowding of the steerage deck as the steamer slowly swings out of the harbour into the open sea, the tearful eyes, covering the rude visages with honest moisture, straining to catch a last glimpse of the dear people who stand on the shore, the exclama-

---

2. *All the Year Round*, 1 May 1869, London, pp. 510-514.

tions and growing out of arms as the beloved slopes of the Irish coast gradually recede from the view, no one with a heart can see this sight unmoved, or
without feeling a keen sympathy for the motley, even ludicrous-looking, crowd
which is huddled together in the 'forward' part of the ship.

Why have they left their native land, and what will they do when they
reach America? Poverty and hardship, the impossibility of existing in their
own crowded country, the accounts which have come from friends in America,
and the wonderful narratives of lucky neighbours, who have returned to tell
how the poor man thrives on the Western Continent, these are the causes
which have determined the bold venture. What they will do when they reach
the other shore, few of them have the remotest conception. They are haunted
by visions of broad acres and vast meadows which await the first comer; by
prospects of great fortunes easily acquired; by hopes of penetrating to the
mines, and drawing thence endless nuggets of gold and silver. Some go in
response to the urgent entreaty of relatives who have already tried the experiment. This old man is going to join his daughter Biddy, a prosperous
maid-of-all-work in New York; or to see his lusty son, Pat, who has subdued a
government-given tract of forest and prairie land in the Far West, so that it
now yields him goodly crops of wheat, and enables him to live in ease and
contentment. These brawny fellows have had a message from a townsman,
who is happy as a prosperous builder of railroads, and has told them that they
have only to get over, to prosper likewise.

With what self-denial have the poor souls hoarded up their pennies and
sixpences, until they grew to the six sovereigns requisite to buy a steerage
passage! And how crowded and huddled together are they over there in the
forward part of the steamer, living scantily on the limited allowance of bread,
water, and occasional saloon leavings! They manage, nevertheless, to make a
right merry voyage of it, after the home-sickness and sea-sickness are somewhat worn off, and a general acquaintance has been scraped; and on many a
night, at sea, you and I, ensconced in the saloon, may hear their merry laughter, their rollicking songs, and the measure of their Irish jigs. And when the
last morning comes, ushered in by cries of 'Land!' 'There's Long Island!'
'There's Staten Island!' 'There are the masts of the vessels anchored at New
York!' perhaps there is no one aboard the steamer who strains eyes shore-
ward with such anxious gaze, as do these poor Irish emigrants, come to a
strange land and among a strange people to seek the means of bare existence.

Of the Irish emigrants who thus land at the American ports, a very large
majority remain where they first set foot on American soil. It is characteristic
that, while French, German, Italian, and Scandinavian emigrants are prone
to scatter themselves, to penetrate to the Western States, to become settlers
on the vast fertile lands which the American Government parcels out and
divides among those who will take and till them, to find out new and growing

towns, and there establish themselves, the Irish almost invariably confine themselves to the vicinity, or the district of country round about the place where they reach the new continent. Thus it is that in nearly, if not all, of the Eastern cities there is, in the suburbs, a distinct Irish colony huddled together, living in little shanties, or in big houses which accommodate twenty or thirty families, and which is usually nicknamed by the native population 'Dublin'. According to the census, a large preponderance of the foreign population of the Atlantic cities is Irish; in the Western cities they are exceeded by the Dutch and Germans. Even the Frenchman, belonging to that nation which, of all civilised nations, travels least, is found in America to take more kindly to the life of a backwoodsman than the native of Erin. The Irishman is essentially a social animal; he sticks close to civilisation, hanging about its skirts; he huddles with groups of his own race near to populous cities and towns. The foreigner who visits New York for the first time is called upon to visit a certain notorious district in that metropolis, known, the land over, by the name of the 'Five Points'. It is in the heart of the lower town, and its name is derived from the junction of five narrow and filthy streets, which meet in a kind of open space in its centre. Here the Irish herd in squalid masses, living in houses where several families occupy a single room, issuing thence in the daytime to earn, or to pilfer, the pittance which is to keep them from starving for the next twenty-four hours. Here one sees the Irish in their state of lowest degradation. Here they are, thieves, vagabonds, murderers, garotters, burglars, here it is unsafe for the well-dressed citizen to pass, even in broad daylight, without an escort: so frightfully desperate is the misery of its low Irish denizens. Still, this 'Five Points' district is, in a manner, a political power. Universal suffrage gives the people of the Five Points control over the elections. There exists a coterie of wretched native American 'roughs', bar-room-keepers, gamblers, prize-fighters, who, by acts corrupt, yet shrewd, have managed to get this Irish population under their leadership. The result is seen in the election of corrupt mayors, of more corrupt judges, and of pugilists and gamblers to seats in the national congress. Electoral corruption, intimidation, and bribery, are here carried on openly, unblushingly, and unmolested. it is unsafe for any man to approach the polls in the 'Five Points' for the purpose of giving a vote against the favourite candidate. The polls are guarded by troops of ruffians; the population of this quarter is a perpetual mob, ever ready for action; even if the police were not kept away by the corrupt authorities which the 'Five Points' have put into power, they would hardly dare to engage with so formidable a mass of desperate vagabonds. The riots which now and then break out in the American metropolis have their rise in the 'Five Points', without exception.

It may be here remarked that the criminal statistics of New York, indeed those of all the large Eastern cities, prove that a great majority of the murders, thefts, and arsons committed, are the work of the foreign population, and especially of the Irish. The 'Five Points' and the 'Dublins' of the Atlantic cities are very pandemoniums of strife and quarrelling; and it is hard to conceive a more abandoned ruffian than the downright bad Irishman. The same spirit which commits agrarian crime on the soil of Erin, survives the Atlantic voyage, crops out on the other side, and fills the American courts and prisons with criminals of a most desperate and incorrigible class. All the virtue and patriotism in New York has hitherto been unavailing to destroy the political power which has its seat in the 'Five Points'.

But this is the darker side of the picture; it is a necessary penalty for the hospitality which America extends to the vagrants of all nations. While, however, the lower, desperate, poverty-stricken stratum of the Irish do certainly constitute a great sore on the face of all the large American cities, the better and more honest class of Irish are a highly important element in American society. The vast majority of the Irish who emigrate to the Western continent, not only succeed in getting a good living, and comfortable situations, but they give in return an ample equivalent in their industry, and capacity for hard rough work. Probably every railroad in America was built by Irish hands; nearly all the heavy, disagreeable drudgery to be performed in the country is done by them. It is the Irish, and the Irish alone, who clean the streets, dig the gutters, build the roads, make the sewers; the farms teem with Irish labourers; they are the best fellers of wood and diggers of potatoes. They are, in America, emphatically toilers by the sweat of their brow. . . . The Irishman works heartily and sturdily. He is impudent, he is obstinate, he is inclined to get into hot discussion with his comrades – but he works with a will. I have often seen Irishmen working on new England farms; I never saw one with an inclination to indolence. This indefatigable capacity for hard toil enables the Irishman to outbid every competitor. And his lot is not to be despised. Let him once find work on a New England farm, and he has capital wages, comfortable lodging, healthy meals, good land to work on, plenty to drink, and people to bicker with. He was never born to manage a farm; he is not thrifty; as good a piece of ground as there is in the peerless Shenandoah valley of Virginia would go to ruin under his control; but set him his farm work – leave him no option but to dig this acre of potatoes, or reap that field of wheat – and he stands unrivalled. The rule is, of course, not an universal one; there are exceptional Irishmen who, from obeying, do learn to command; from inhabiting a farm, and plodding on it, these get to be thrifty and able to manage. Such an Irishman sometimes takes his place among the independent farmers; one of the richest farmers in Massachusetts – a man who gets from his land some three or four thousand dollars a year – is an Irishman who emigrated to America twenty years ago without twenty shillings in the pockets of his patched trousers, who plodded and plodded, bought a little plot, added to it, and now sends his daughters to fashionable boarding schools, his sons to the university, and his wife to town in a two-horse carriage. Among the farmers in the rural districts of New England – and especially in New Hampshire – it is the custom to treat the labourers and servants much as if they were members of the family. The Irish 'helps', male and female, take their places at the table with the farmer, his wife, sons, and daughters; they are helped from the same dishes; they join in the conversation, they enjoy their post prandial pipes with the 'boss', on the little lawn in front of the farmhouse. They are provided with bedrooms in no respect inferior to those occupied by the master and mistress; they join in many of their amusements – go a-fishing or picnicing with them; they sit in the parlour and hear the papers or books read in the evening; and, in short, partake of all the comforts and enjoyments of home. And the constant companionship of the average New England farmer's family is no mean advantage to the poor, ignorant Irish emigrants.

The New England farmer who so democratically admits his poorest and most ignorant 'hand' to his table and his family circle, is almost without exception a man of some education, and of vigorous and independent habit of thought. He is not only capable of reading and writing, but he has a keen love of papers and books; is admirably posted in the politics and events of the day; is himself a most enthusiastic politician, and fairly revels in argumentation with a rustic opponent. He has been educated at one of those free schools of which New England people are justly proud: working on the farm, when a boy, during the summer months, and availing himself of the bleak winters to attend the little rustic school which a wise legislation has provided for him. Thus the Irish labourer, separated from the association of other ignorant Patlanders like himself, having in the association of the farmer's family and in the comforts of the farmer's house an efficacious substitute for the public-house, becomes more intelligent and more industrious, and is gradually moulded into an useful member of democratic American society. Treated as an equal, ambition of a worthy kind is begotten in him; if he be as good as the 'boss', and worthy to break bread with him, why not aspire to be a 'boss' himself? And so it comes about that now and then examples appear, of Irishmen becoming landed proprietors. But the larger part of the emigrants who penetrate beyond the cities, are of a nomadic, restless, roving disposition. They wander about the country in the summer time, picking up a farming job here and there, indisposed to remain long in one place, working with a will, but thriftlessly spending their earnings as fast as they make them. Labour is so much in demand, that they never have to go far without employment, and in return for whatever work they do, they receive what must seem to them, coming from over-crowded Ireland, a very handsome wage. Notwithstanding all its advantages, the Irishman in America does not appear to take so kindly to farm work as to the irksome drudgery which is his lot in the cities. After all, he prefers to live in 'Dublin', if it be only the imitation Dublin which hangs on the outskirts of every American city. Here he has his mates and his wife, and here he cheerfully digs gutters, and clears streets, for the privilege of living in an over-crowded and dirty nest of children of Erin like himself. And here, in the cities, he is a godsend to the corporations, who get their more humble jobs done better and cheaper by the Paddies than by any other workmen.

The mass of Irish remain in the Northern and Eastern States. To the South the Irishman is loath to go, for he finds in the negro a competitor who contests the market with him at great advantage. No white race can compete with the negro on a cotton, rice, or sugar plantation. The Irishman cannot exist on so little as the black man. The Irishman is the more vigorous labourer in the North; but the Southern sun melts him, gives him sunstroke, paralyses him, while the hotter the day, the livelier the negro. It is amusing to note what an instinctive antipathy exists between these two rival races for securing the work of the American employer. Each seems to be conscious of this rivalry – each seems to feel that the other is in his way. Each affects a profound contempt for the other; and as both are gifted with a facile use of the tongue, and a perfect arsenal of epithets, a hostile dialogue between the white and the black is one of the most unique and amusing imaginable. Sometimes, in the more northerly of the States where slavery formerly existed, Irish and negroes are found huddled together in the same quarter or suburb; then there is constant quarrelling and strife.

It is odd that, much as the Irish like to huddle together and live in crowds, such a thing is scarcely ever heard of as an Irish colony in the vast plains of the West. Natural farmers as they are, you never hear of their associating together, taking a westward course, and settling on the rich domains which the American government offers free to all who will 'squat' and till. In Michigan there is a famous Dutch colony, where nothing but Dutch is spoken, nothing but Dutch dishes are eaten, nothing but Dutch pipes are smoked, and none but Dutchmen hold office; a colony imported from Amsterdam. Further South – in those States which formerly composed part of the French colony of Louisiane – French colonies may be found, where you would starve before you found a man who could understand your order for dinner in English. In Missouri, Nebraska, and Kansas, German settlements may be found quite as characteristic and exclusively foreign. There is so large a leaven of the Teutonic element in Missouri, that a German refugee has just now been elected United States senator to represent that great and growing state. But the Irish have not, as a mass, a capacity of self-reliance. They must cling as dependents upon another civilisation; so they remain in the East, and leave the emigrants of other nations to patiently build up communities stamped with their own national traits in the boundless West.

What becomes of the Irish girls who constitute a large majority of the emigrants? The great mass of them become cooks, maids-of-all-work, chambermaids, household servants of some sort. Probably the chambermaids and scullerymaids of every hotel in New York, Philadelphia, Chicago – all the cities – are buxom Irish girls. At least nine-tenths of the servants in the private houses in the North and East are of the same nation. The healthy Irish girl who leaves her own country to seek her fortune beyond the ocean, has in her excellent stuff for the fulfilling of household duties. She is strong, she is quick to learn, she is willing to work, and wherever she is wanting in taste, tutelage by the mistress goes far to mend it. Many family matrons prefer to take a raw emigrant rather than a girl who has been long in America. She is more honest, she is not troubled with too many beaux and acquaintances, she blunders yet is willing to learn, she does her best, and she has not yet acquired those grand notions of dress and independence which the Irish girl long resident is apt to have picked up. She is capable of making a really good plain cook, and if she be taken straight from shipboard, may be educated to her mistress's peculiar style of cookery – every mistress, be it said, having a style and dishes of her own. The main trouble with the Irish servant is, that she is prone to be too social in character, readily makes acquaintances, and holds high carnival in the kitchen with the family provisions. Still, with all her shortcomings, she is nothing less than invaluable to American households. It is only in the far West, and back in the rural districts of New England, that native American girls are found in service. The negro 'Mammies', now free, are probably destined to become rivals of the Irish 'Biddies'; still, the former usually prefer their native South to the bleak and unfruitful North.

During the war of the Rebellion, the Irish naturalised citizens of the United States did sterling service for the Federal cause. Throughout the land, volunteer regiments were formed composed exclusively of Irishmen; and more than one illustrious name among the Union generals betrays the Celtic origin of its bearer. Sheridan, now second in command of the American army, was the son of Irish parents; the gallant Colonel Corcoran, of the New York Irish Regiment, was one of the most brilliant soldiers and best loved commanders of the epoch. The revival of Fenianism since the war, is often attributed to the martial spirit engendered among the Irish soldiers during that great struggle; and this is no doubt partially true. But the spirit of hostility to England among the emigrant Irish of America was universally prevalent long before the war; and while that event gave greater force to the movement in favour of Irish independence, it by no means developed any greater rancour than that previously felt towards the mother country. Fenianism owes much encouragement to native American demagogues who have hounded it on for their own political purposes; but it chiefly owes its popularity among the American Irish to the energy, boldness, and eloquence of a few Irish leaders, most of whom were Federal officers in the war. If anything were wanting to prove the incapacity of the Irish character for self-government, the course of Fenianism in America proves it. They are too bellicose among themselves; they never have been cordially united; they are credulous, and allow swindlers to rob them; they are quarrelsome, and dissipate their energy and resources in internal dissension. The poor Irish servant, ardently attached to 'darling Erin', and excited by the harangues against England, saved her little weekly pittance, and cheerfully gave it up to Fenian 'circles' to be devoured by the leaders of the cause, and to be embezzled by the swindlers to whom they confided it.

The Irish in America, although, as has been said, they are clannish, do yet gradually merge themselves into the general community, and become part and parcel of the American population. The second generation of the emigrant Irish are educated at the free public schools, rise to a higher sphere of labour than their parents, in many instances become Protestants, and then freely mingle with the rest of the community as thoroughly Americanised citizens. Many of the most eminent American statesmen, scholars, and merchants have been the children of emigrants, or have come from the generation next succeeding the native Irish generation. Presidents Jackson and Buchanan were sons of Irish parents; so was Vice-President Calhoun, one of the greatest of American orators. A.T. Stewart, the merchant prince of New York, was a native of Belfast. James T. Brady, foremost of criminal advocates in New York; Meagher, the general and writer; were Irish. This proves that the boast of Americans, that their country offers its prizes to all who will compete for them, is not unfounded; it also proves that there are characteristics, even among the poor classes of Irish who are driven to emigration for existence, while are capable of development into the power of leading men, and into a high influence upon the age."

CHAPTER FOUR

Bentley's Miscellany

C harles Dickens left the staff of *The Morning Chronicle* in November 1836. His ambition was to produce his own journal and this was facilitated by Mr Richard Bentley asking him to edit a new magazine, *Bentley's Miscellany*, having George Cruikshank as illustrator. This he did from 1 January 1837 until 31 January 1839, and many Irish articles and poems appeared in it.

By December 1836 Charles Dickens had organised copy for *Bentley's Miscellany* which was launched on 1 January 1837 and he indicated in a letter to Bentley on 5 December that, among others, he was pleased with Samuel Lover's contribution. This was a serialised story, *The Adventures of Handy Andy*, which was later published as a novel. Samuel Lover (1797–1868)

The Meeting (*Oliver Twist*)

was a miniature-painter, song-writer, novelist and dramatist. Born in Dublin, his "Rory O'More" was published by Bentley in 1837. In 1833 he had been one of the founders of the *Dublin University Magazine*. He moved to London in 1835, becoming a notable man of popular fiction and drama, and a member of Lady Blessington's salon circle. His "Handy Andy" is the great, amiable, awkward, moronic lout of Irish literature. In more recent times the novel was edited and reprinted by Sean O'Faolain who introduced it as follows:

'Handy Andy' is a classic of Irish humour: indeed, of its kind, one of the classics of the English language. It is also a memorable picture of Irish life in the 19th century. For that alone it is well worth reading.

The novel is full of high spirits. It has done more than any other book – barring the novels of Charles Lever, and the stories of Somerville and Ross – to establish the picture of the light-hearted, devil-may-care, hot-tempered, amiable Irishman. In a large degree Lover defined this lighter side of the Irishman's character. That alone was an achievement.

The novel as Lover wrote it has not really a great deal to do with the central character of 'Handy Andy', the blundering, good-natured servant. Indeed, he plays a quite minor part. The main adventures are provided by the local squires, O'Grady and Egan, the bucks, solicitors, and ladies of Ballysloughguttery, and the visiting Civil Servants from Dublin. The central incident is a rousing Election, given, as it was fought in the fine, slashing old-time style. Andy comes in only as a sort of minor *deus ex machina* to upset an occasional apple-cart. Indeed, once that main adventure is disposed of, Lover lets the tale straggle off a little, and the sub-plots of his love-stories become rather confusing. Besides, in the fashion of the day, Lover never hesitated to interrupt his flow with a good yarn, no matter how irrelevant, just as he was very fond of putting in some of his songs and verses.

The essence of the character of Handy Andy will, however, appear clearly in the major incidents of this modern condensation – the election and his absurd 'abduction'. So will other things, such as the merits and peculiarities of Lover's work; the loose style and manner of Irish fiction at this stage in its career: and the reader may well see through the exaggerations of Lover's extravaganza, a vivid picture of the rough and tumble of Irish life in the hard days of the 19th century when only the highest spirits and an unquenchable humour saved the people from despair. Of the book as a whole one's only regret is that Lover telescoped the conclusion of it so that Andy's absurd adventures in London are barely touched on.

Lover was interested in all the vagaries of human character, and could not desist from illustrating human folly so long as he could, like his own bucks, enjoy the spectacle in high spirits to the sound of rollicking laughter. Books so amiable and so free-and-easy are rare to-day. If they spill over into farce that is their only weakness. Times have changed, and the Handy Andys of Ireland have disappeared with the social revolution of our times. But though the modern Handy Andy has not, like the Handy Andy of this story, become a peer, and in position and wealth found that there can be as much unhappiness upstairs as downstairs, one may hope that his chief richness remains – his natural humour, his kindness, and his easy content with all the whirligigs of life.

In the March edition Samuel Lover contributed Song of the Month:

OUR SONG OF THE MONTH
No. III March, 1837

March, March! why the de'il don't you march
Faster than other months out of your order?
You're a horrible beast, with the wind from the East,
And high-hopping hail and slight sleet on your border:
Now, our umbrellas spread, flutter above our head,
And will not stand to our arms in good order;
While, flapping and tearing, they set a man swearing
Round the corner, where blasts blow away half the border!

II

March, March! I am ready to faint
That St. Patrick had not his nativity's casting;
I am sure, if he had, such a peaceable lad
Would have never been born amid blowing and blasting:
But as it was his fate, Irishmen emulate
Doing what doom, or St. Paddy may order;
And if they're forced to fight through their wrongs for their right,
They'll stick to their flag while a thread's in its border.

III

March, March! have you no feeling,
E'en for the fair sex who make us knock under?
You cold-blooded divil, you're far more uncivil

Than Summer himself, with his terrible thunder!
Every day we meed ladies down Regent-street,
Holding their handkerchiefs up in good order;
But, do all that we can, the most merciful man
Must see the blue noses peep over the border.

Charles Dickens's own *Oliver Twist* began serialization in the February 1837 edition of *Bentley's Miscellany*. It was an instant success and in September of that year we find Daniel O'Connell writing from his home, Derrynane Abbey, Co. Kerry, to P.V. Fitzpatrick, in London: "Send me 'Tait's Magazine' and 'Bentley's Miscellany' for this month. The story of 'Oliver Twist' is continued in the latter, and I am most impatient to see it."

Legends form a significant part of the writings in *Bentley's Miscellany* and later in *Household Words* (1850–58) and *All the Year Round* (1859–88), which Dickens edited up to his death in 1870.

THE LEGEND OF BOHIS HEAD[1]

"One of the most south-western points of Ireland is the promontory of Bohis, which forms the northern shore of the bay of Balinskeligs. A singular conformation of rock is observable upon the extremity of the wild cape, it being worn by the incessant beating of the billows into a grotesque resemblance of the human profile. The waves, however, are not suffered to claim undisputed this rude sculpture as their own; a far different origin being attributed to it by the legends of the country around.

In times long, very long ago . . . Bohis Head, instead of the abrupt, broken cliffs that now terminate it, presented a lofty and uniform wall of rock to the assaults of the Atlantic. Upon the topmost summit . . . there stood, at the period of our tale, the castle of a very celebrated personage, generally known in those parts as the Baon Ri Dhuv – in Plain English, 'The Black Lady', – a title partly bestowed on her, on account of her dark hair and face, and partly on account of the cruelty and tyranny which she exercised upon all those who were subject to her dominion. She must have been redoubtable in no small degree, as, besides the possession of a large army, which she could at any time connect from her numerous array of vassals, she was a deep proficient in the art of magic, and was even said to have once, by the potency of her spells, prevented a drop of rain from falling upon her territories (which included the whole of Munster) for a week together. But as the south of Ireland at least has never since been known to be so long without showers, this

---

1. *Bentley's Miscellany*, Vol. I, 1837, pp. 519-524.

feat is not so implicitly believed as other of the traditions about her. However that may be, this at least is certain, that she wanted for nothing that force or fraud, fair means or means the most unholy, could give her; and she was deemed the happiest as well as the most powerful being in the world.

Those who said this, did not judge truly. In the midst of all her splendour and state, caressed, feared, flattered, obeyed as she was by all, she was not happy: and it is strange that her tenants and servants did not find this out, as her usual method of easing her feelings was by ill-treating and abusing them. She was not happy; and simply because, among her myriad of vassals, flatterers, and slaves, she had not one friend. There was the whole secret. In her inmost soul she – that proud, tyrannical, haughty, hard-hearted woman – felt that, all feared and all potent as she was, she still was no more than mortal; and that within her own breast there was that which tyrannized over herself – the innate longings of our nature for sympathy, for companionship, for affection. The humblest hind that served her, had a comrade – a friend; while she, the queen and mistress of all, was the object of detestation as universal as the slavish obedience that met her at every step. At first she scoffed and spurned at the dull internal aching; it was a weakness, she thought, that needed but to be fought against, to be for ever quelled. She sought wars and conflicts; she dived deeper than ever before into the unholy mysteries of the 'Black Art'; she revelled, she feasted, and she succeeded in quelling the rebel feeling for a time – but only for a time. There came a reaction to her excitement; and, while her spirits and all else seemed exhausted and worn out, this dull yearning was stronger and more aching than ever. At length, one day, after a long and painful reverie, she started up, striking her forehead violently, and vowed that she would have a friend – a companion – nay, even (as her sentimentality increased with indulgence) a husband – or perish in the attempt! As the oath passed her lips, a tremendous peal of thunder rolled over the castle towers and passed off to seaward, dying away in the distance with a sound not unlike a wild and prolonged shout of laughter.

She had not much time to lose, if she intended to marry. The little servant-boy, who had been allowed to get drunk on the night of rejoicings for her birth, was now a grave and sedate major-domo of most venerable age. She herself, but some fifteen or sixteen years his junior, was long past the time when the grossest flattery could make her believe that she was young; and her years had not passed over her head without leaving their traces behind. She had been in her best days what is called by friends 'rather plain', which generally means 'very ugly'. Her forehead bowed out and overhung her nose, which endeavoured to stretch out to some decent length, but was unfortunately foiled by the want of a bridge. The mouth, as if it perceived this failure on the part of the feature immediately above it, modestly declined the contest, and retreated far inward. The chin, however, amply made up for all intermediate deficiencies, and even surpassed the forehead in the hugeness of its proportions, or disproportions. Her hair was black, as has been said, and hung in long, lanky clusters about her face. Time seldom improves the human countenance, and certainly made no exception in favour of the Baon Ri Dhuv. At the time of her vow many wrinkles had made their appearance, and unequivocal grey hairs chequered the once uniform sable that covered her head. Magic had not then arrived at the pitch of perfection to which it afterwards attained in the times of Virgilius and Apollonius Rhodius; and, among the inventions yet in the womb of time, were the charms for restoring youth and imparting beauty.

The lady of the castle set off, one fine morning, on the back of a cloud which she had hailed as it was drifting over her chimney-tops, driven inland by the fresh breeze from the ocean. As she was borne along, she looked anxiously right and left down upon the earth, to spy out, if possible, the desired companion. But she found she had grown very fastidious, now that the means of ridding herself of her troublesome desires appeared open to her. She looked at no women; she felt instinctively that none of her own sex could be the friend that would satisfy her heart: but all the young men that she passed over, she scrutinized, as if her life depended upon it. They in their turn stared a good deal at her, as well they might; for it was no common thing, even in those days, to see a woman perched up on a cloud, sailing over your head before a rattling breeze of wind. Perhaps it was their staring at her, so different from the downcast eyes and humble mien of her slaves at home – perhaps it was their rude remarks that displeased her; whatever it was, on she went without making her choice, until towards the close of the day she found she had nearly crossed Ireland in a diagonal line from south-west to north-east, the wind blowing in that direction. As it still blew merrily, and it was full-moon night, she determined to go on to Scotland, and try whether Sawnie could please her, better than Paddy. With this resolve she had not proceeded more than half a league from the shore of Ireland, when she perceived she was going over a mountain-islet some five or six miles in girth, and apparently very fertile in its soil, for large herds of cattle were grazing upon its sides. It is a trite and true saying, that those who possess much, are often covetous of more; and in her case it was especially true. With a word she stayed the cloud over the island; the wind falling all at once, in obedience to her will. . . Over the island she hung, gazing down upon it, and gloating on its richness and fertility, while she inwardly resolved to strain her magical powers to the utmost, to transfer it from its present position to the neighbourhood of her own coast. Her attention, however, was soon withdrawn from all other objects, and concentrated on one that had just caught her eye: it was a young man, the only one she had as yet seen who did not stare up at her, rudely and impertinently. Indeed he did not look up at all. He seemed to have no eyes, no soul, for any one but a young girl who was by his side. The lady on the cloud could see by the moonlight that the girl's face was exceedingly beautiful; that is to say, as much as could be perceived of it when she occasionally, and but for a moment, raised her eyes from the ground, on which they were riveted.

'Speak! will you not speak to me?' were the words of the young man: 'but one word, Eva – dearest Eva – to tell me have I offended by my boldness?'

The girl blushed ten times deeper than before, and her lips quivered as at length she slowly murmured out, 'No, Conla!'

'Thanks! thanks!' was his rapturous exclamation; 'a thousand times thanks, my own, my... Hallo! what is this? Whence came you?' These latter words were addressed to the Black Lady, as, to his utter astonishment, she alighted from the cloud right in his path. Eva shrieked, and hid her face in his bosom.

'I am the Baon Ri Dhuv,' said the enchantress, trying to look dignified, and to smooth away the scowl that had darkened her visage since she perceived his companion – 'the Queen of the South!'

'And what can the Baon Ri Dhuv, the Queen of the South, want with Conla, a shepherd of the north?'

'Young man, mock me not,' replied she, frowning most awfully: 'you know not, but you may be made to feel, my power. Listen to me,' continued she in a milder tone, and putting on what she intended to be a most amiable and engaging look; but which gave her coarse lineaments a still more grotesque hideousness, that almost made the young shepherd laugh in her face, despite the secret dread he felt creeping on his heart. 'I am the ruler of a vast tract of country; I have a vast army to do my will; nay, more, I have dominion over the elements in their fiercest rage, and spirits obey my bidding. I am rich beyond counting. You smile, and believe not. Look here!'

As she spoke, she struck the ground three times with her foot, muttering rapidly to herself, when up sprang close to her, a tall tree of the purest gold, the glittering branches laden with jewels beyond all price. Seizing one of these, a magnificent emerald, and pulling it off the branch, again she stamped her foot, and the tree disappeared, leaving the jewel in her hands.

'Here,' continued she, putting it into Conla's passive hand, 'here is the earnest of my wealth; leave that weak girl, and come with me to wealth and happiness!'

Conla had hitherto been kept dumb by the strange scene before him; but now, rousing himself, he looked at his Eva, and meeting her gaze of deep, whole-hearted, confiding affection, he dashed the glittering jewel on the ground, and cried,

Away, sorceress! I spurn your gifts, your accursed power, yourself! With Eva will I live or die!

The face of the Black Lady showed horrible in the pale moonlight, as, with a withering scowl of hatred and vengeance, she again spoke:

> You shall not die, insolent wretch! You shall live in agonies to which death were mercy; ay, and she, too – that worthless thing you prefer to me – she, too, shall suffer!

As she spoke, she described a circle in the air with her hand round the island. At once the moon became obscured, and a terrible darkness fell upon all, while a sudden storm swept over the island. Conla and his Eva tried to fly to some cave for refuge, but were arrested by the sight that met their eyes when the transitory darkness cleared away. The moon again shone out brilliantly, and by its light the lovers perceived, to their great horror, that the island itself was in motion! A little ahead of its southernmost point their persecutor was scudding over the waters in a bark, the traditional accounts of which, represent it as a good deal resembling the steam-boats of modern days, for there was smoke issuing out of it; and two or three respectable individuals, with black faces, fiery eyes, horns on their heads, and tails twirled in graceful folds, might be seen through an open hatchway, employed in much the same manner as the hard-working, hard-drinking steam-packet engineers of our own times, while a clacking and clanging of iron was continually heard, similar to the sounds that annoy sea-sick passengers at present. From the taffrail of this inviting-looking vessel, three or four strong cables stretched to the island, and were rove through an immense hole in a huge projecting rock, that seemed as if it had been bored for this especial purpose. The steamer tugged gallantly, and the island plashed and splashed heavily along, at the rate of twenty or thirty knots an hour; the cows and sheep upon the latter, not having their sea-legs aboard, tumbled and rolled about in fine style. Eva got exceedingly sea-sick, and Conla exceedingly indignant: but there was no use in his anger. On the island went.

On and on – past Belfast, Drogheda, Dublin – rattling and splashing along, greatly to the astonishment of the fishes, who, besides being then quite unaccustomed to public steaming, had never before seen an island on the move. Between Dublin and Holyhead there was a little difficulty; for the island, which was exceedingly unmanageable, fetched away to starboard, and took the ground a little outside of Howth. This was a cause of great delight to the lovers, who thought their voyage was now at an end; but they were much mistaken: two of the amiable gentry who manned the tug-boat jumped lightly on the island, and cut away with a couple of strokes of an axe the part that was aground, it breaking into two pieces, which remain to this day, proofs of the truth of this tale, under the names of Lambay and Ireland's Eye. On went the steamer again, and on went the island merrily and clumsily as ever, and the

Black Lady looked back and laughed at the disappointed lovers.

Wicklow went by – Wexford – and now the shores of the county Waterford hove in sight; and the vessel and island, rounding Point Carnsore in gallant style, issued out from the Irish Channel into the waters of the Atlantic.

Morning had broken by this time, and a bright and beautiful morning it was. Eva, overpowered by fatigue, had sunk to sleep; Conla sate beside her, deep anxiety lowering on his brow, and his soul rent with the most agonizing emotions. Meantime his body was just as much disturbed, for the island was now heaving and pitching worse than before, upon the longer billows of the ocean; and he occasionally had to hold on with both his hands to the stones and shrubs near him, to prevent himself from being what sailors would call "hove overboard" by the violent motion of the strange craft in, or rather on, which he was embarked. Disliking his situation exceedingly, and greatly fearing that he would have still more reason to do so, he saw that there was no chance of his delivery from it, if he could not succeed in mollifying the enraged enchantress. Espying her again seated upon the steamer's taffrail, he therefore hailed her, and sought by humble prayers and entreaties to induce her to release him and his Eva; or, if one should suffer, to set her free, and vent the heaviest vengeance upon his head. But the Black Lady let him talk on. He had a very sweet voice, and she liked to hear that; and, when he had done, she contented herself with simply shaking her head in token of refusal: then, as he again stooped his proud spirit to still more vehement entreaties and supplications, and raved in the intensity of his anguish, she mocked at him, and laughed loud and long in scorn, till at length, wearied out and despairing, he sunk his head upon his bosom, and was silent. Slowly the day wore on, but quickly the headlands and bays of the southern shore of Ireland glided by; and great was the wonder and amaze of those who looked to seaward from that shore. . . .

The sun was sinking gloriously into the bosom of the slow-heaving main as the steamer, with the island in tow, rounded Dursey Head, and hove in sight of their destination, the promontory of Bohis. With exultation in her eyes, the Baon Ri Dhuv pointed out her lofty castle, shining in the distance with the last rays of the departing orb of day. Eva was now awake, and her and Conla's supplications were poured out for mercy and for pity; but they might as well have been uttered to Bohis Head itself. The leagues between the latter place and Dursey Head were rapidly traversed, and now the island had been towed within a mile of its final destination, which was the promontory on which the castle stood. At this moment another sudden storm, such as that of the preceding night, passed athwart the scene; and, when it cleared away, the steamer had disappeared, and the Black Lady was to be seen, upon the headland tugging at the island to bring it closer.

"Is there no help in Heaven!' cried Conla, as, after another appeal in vain to their persecutor, he threw his eyes up with a reproachful glance.

"Hush, Conla! reproach not the powers above; they are most merciful, and will protect us. Hark! they answer!'

At this moment a heavy peal of thunder crashed over head, and, rolling towards the castle, seemed to expend itself over its summit.

"Dread lady,' cried Eva, animated to unusual courage by the omen, "hearken to that, and yield to the powers of Heaven! – they declare against thy tyranny!'

"Never!' roared the tyrant, her eyes flashing baleful fire. "Sooner will I become part of his mountain on which I stand mistress, than ye shall escape me!'

As she spoke, she gave a pull with her utmost strength to the chains. At the moment a vivid flash of lightning darted from the clouds, and the chains snapped right asunder. With the force of the shock the Black Lady was precipitated into the sea, the island at the same time rebounding back and becoming fixed for ever about half-way between Dursey and Bohis Head.

The Baon Ri Dhuv's tenants and servants spent the night in vainly searching for her. The morning revealed to them a terrible sight. Upon the extremity of the cape her well-known visage appeared, but transformed to stone, and doomed for ages to remain there, lashed by the raging billows of the ocean. Thus was her fatal wish accomplished!

The island so strangely brought round, remains where it recoiled to, and is now known by the name of Scariff. It is still rich land, and feeds many herds. . . . Conla and Eva lived happily for the rest of their days where they were, and left a numerous progeny. . . .'

* * *

THE LEGENDS OF THE TORRY ISLANDERS[2]

The famous legends of Torry Island were recounted in *Bentley's Miscellany.*

"Torry Island, situated on the north-west coast of Ireland, is probably the least known of any of her majesty's European possessions. Although so near the main, the communication is difficult and infrequent. The island has but one landing-place, and that can only be entered with leading winds, while, during the prevalence of the others, it is totally unapproachable.

Within the memory of people still alive, the natives of Torry were idola-

---

2.   *Bentley's Miscellany*, Vol. II, 1837, pp. 530-531.

ters. They were ushered into life, and quitted it for the grave, without either rite or ceremony. Marriage was la Martineau, nothing but "a civil contract', and their notions of the Deity, rude and untutored as Kamschatdales or New Zealanders. Latterly, priests from the main have occasionally landed on the island, and there introduced the formulae of religion; but visits dependent on winds and waves are "few and far between', and the state of Torry may still be termed more than demi-savage. When some adventurous beadsman ventures on a clerical descent, during his brief sojourn he finds that his office is no sinecure: children are to be christened by the score; and couples, who took each other's words, to be married by the dozen. During the long interregnum, a large arrear of omitted ceremonies has accrued, and the daring clerk returns from this "ultima Thule' a weary, if not a wiser man.

Nothing can be more wretched than the appearance of the island and its inhabitants: the one, cold, barren, and uncultivated; the other, ugly, dwarfish, and ill-shapen. The hovels are filthy to a degree; and all within and about Torry is so sterile and inhospitable, that a dread of being wind-bound deters even the hardiest mariner from approaching its rock-bound shores.

That "holy men' should venture among the Heathen, is, as it ought to be; and that savans will go desperate lengths to obtain bones, oyster-shells, and other valuable commodities, is equally true. For spiritual and scientific Quixotes, Torry opens an untried field; and any philosopher who can digest dog-fish, and possesses a skin impervious to entomological assaults, may here discover unknown treasures: none having yet been found – for none have sought them.

It was, probably, expectations such as these that induced the late Sir Charles Geisecke to visit this unfrequented island. Whether his geological discoveries compensated his bodily sufferings, the gentleman who perpetrated his biography leaves a scientific mystery. Certain it is, that in after-life the worthy knight never touched upon this portion of his wanderings without shuddering at the recollection.

Three days he sojourned among the aborigines and three nights he sheltered in the chief man's hovel. He left Ards House[3] in good spirits, and fat as a philosopher should be; and when he returned, his own dog, had he possessed one, would not have recognised his luckless owner. He came out a walking skeleton, and the ablutions he underwent would have tried the patience of a Mussulman. He had lost sleep; well, that could be made up for. He lost condition; that too might be restored. But to lose hair, to be clipped like a recruit, and have his garments burned at the point of a pitch-fork – these indeed would daunt the courage of the most daring entomologist.

---

3.   Ards is situated on the main, near the wild promontory of Horn Head, and is the seat of the Stewart family.

Pat Hegarty, the knight's guide, used to recount the sufferings they underwent. Their afflictions by day were bad enough; but these were nothing, compared to their nocturnal visitations. "My! what a place for fleas!' said an English femme de chambre who happened to be an accidental listener. "How numerous they must have been!'

"Numerous!' exclaimed the guide, "mona mon diaul, if they had only pulled together, they would have dragged me out of bed!'

Since the knight's excursion, Torry has been more frequently visited. In executing the Ordnance survey, a party of Sappers and Miners were encamped upon the island, and the engineer officer in command amused many of his solitary hours by collecting traditionary tales from the narration of an old man, who was far more intelligent than the rest of the inhabitants. The two [following] legends were taken from the patriarch's lips, and they afford an additional proof of that fondness which man, in his savage state, ever evinces for traditions that are wonderful and wild."

*   *   *

THE LEGEND OF BALLAR[4]

"The most ancient of the kings of Torry was Ballar the Dane. . . . His manners were anything but amiable; his temper violent; his disposition sanguinary and revengeful; while, in his notions regarding the doctrines of 'meum and tuum', there was not a looser gentleman of his day.

In personal appearance Ballar was dark, stern, and gigantic; and, in an excess of her bounty, Nature had been graciously pleased to gift him with a third eye. This extra optic was placed in the back of his head; and such was the malignity of its influence that one glance extinguished animal life, a forest was withered by a look, and all those bare and herbless hills upon the mainland which lie in scattered groups beneath the scathed pinnacles of Argyle, may – if tradition can be trusted – date their barrenness to an optical visitation they underwent from their dangerous neighbour the king of Torry. As, even in the darkest character some lighter shading may be found, Ballar – to give the devil his due – perfectly aware of the destructive properties of his third eye, kept it carefully concealed by a curtain.

Ballar had 'one fair daughter, and no more', and an oracle had foretold that, unless killed by his grandson, he should exist for ever. Determined to outlive Methuselah, Ballar resolved on leaving his native country, and seeking out some abiding place where the celibacy of the young lady might be secured. Accordingly he set out upon his travels, and, after an extensive tour,

---

4.   *Bentley's Miscellany*, Vol. II, 1837, pp. 527-530.

visited Donegal, and chose Torry for his residence; and, faith! a nater spot for a gentleman who wished retirement could not have been selected. There he built a castle for himself, and a prison for his daughter. To 'make it all right,' the young lady was placed under the surveillance of twelve virgins; whence the latter were obtained, history doth not say.

Ballar's nearest neighbours on the main were called Gabshegonal, and Kien Mac Caunthca. The latter was possessed of two brave boys, while the former was owner of a white heifer: Glassdhablecana, or 'the grey-flanked cow' was the envy of the country. Nothing from Dingle to Donegal could match her; she was a dairy in herself; and Ballar, regardless of justice, and not having the fear of the going judge of assize before him, determined to abstract her if he could. Like other autocrats, he found no difficulty in trumping up a title, for he asserted that those resident on the mainland were his vassals, and claimed and exacted certain seignorial rights, which, much to the satisfaction of persons entering into matrimony, have been allowed to sink into desuetude.

Like those of all bad monarchs, his ministers were no better than himself; and the chiefs of his household, Mool and Mullock, were worthy agents of their three-eyed master. As his demand upon Gab's cow had been peremptorily rejected, the tyrant of Torry determined to obtain by fraud, what force could not effect; and Mool and Mullock received instructions accordingly.

Ballar's intentions having transpired, Gabshegonal assumed the defensive, and called to his assistance the sons of Kien Mac Caunthca. Gab, it appears, was the most celebrated sword-cutler of his day, and he promised to forge a weapon for each of the young men; they undertaking, in return, to watch the grey-flanked cow for a given time.

The elder of the Mac Caunthcas performed his part of the contract with the smith, and obtained the promised sword; and the younger commenced watch and ward in turn. For some time his vigilance secured the white cow; but, unhappily, it occurred to the youth that it would be desirable to have his name engraved on the sword-blade which Gab was then polishing. He ran to the forge to make his wishes known; and, short as his absence was, alas! upon his return the cow was gone! The spoilers were discovered from the top of Argyle; the younger Mac Caunthca observed Mool and Mullock driving Glassdhablecana along the beach; and, without his being able to overtake them, they embarked for Torry with their prey. Enraged at the occurrence, the smith retained the elder brother as a hostage, and swore that, if the cow were not recovered, he would behead him, to avenge her loss.

The unhappy watchman, overwhelmed with grief and shame, fled from his home, and wandered recklessly along the rock-bound coast. To reach Torry was impossible, and he abandoned himself to sorrow and despair.

Suddenly, a little red-haired man appeared unexpectedly at his elbow, and with sympathetic civility inquired the cause of his lamentations. Mac Caunthca informed him of the misfortune, and the red dwarf offered his condolence, and volunteered to assist him to reach the island. Mac embraced the little gentleman and his offer; and, having ascended the summit of Cruicknaneabth, he placed his foot upon the dwarf's hand, who rose with him into the air, and, passing over the small islands between Torry and the main, fast as the wind itself, landed in safety beneath the castle walls of Ballar. Both the youth and his conductor were 'the nonce' rendered invisible. With little difficulty the cow was found; and the dwarf engaged that, ere morning, she should be safely returned to her lawful owner, the honest sword-cutler, Gabshegonal.

Whether the little gentleman with the red beard preferred daylight for his aerial trips, does not appear; but, certain it is, that his protegé remained that night upon the island, and was introduced by the obliging dwarf to the prison of the princess, where he remained until dawn broke. Safely was he then conducted to the place he had left on the preceding evening. The red man took an affectionate leave. The grey-flanked cow was before him at the owner's. His brother was released; the promised sword honestly delivered by the maker; and the whole adventure ended prosperously.

Time rolled on. Nine months had elapsed since his visit to the island, when the young Mac Caunthca was honoured by a call from the little red gentleman, who requested his company to make a morning call upon the imprisoned princess. They crossed the arm of the sea with the same rapidity that marked their former flight; and, on entering the well-remembered tower, what was MacCaunthca's delight and surprise on finding that he was the father of a large and healthy family! The princess had just given birth to a son; and the twelve young ladies, following, as in duty bound, the example of their mistress, had each produced 'a chopping boy'.

But, alas! the pleasures of paternity were speedily ended. Ballar detested children. Twins would drive a Malthusian distracted; and what apology could be offered for thirteen? Nothing remained but to remove the young Mac Caunthcas in double quick; and the dwarf, with his usual good nature, proposed the means. A curragh[5] was procured; the tender pledges of the maids of honour were placed in a blanket, and fastened by skewers upon the back of their papa, while the heir to the throne was accommodated in a separate cloth; and with this precious freight the curragh was launched upon the ocean.

Presently the wind freshened, the sea rose, and the frail bark was tossed upon the surface of an angry sea. In the fury of the gale the skewers that secured the blanket gave way; overboard went the progeny of the virgin body-

---

5.   A wicker boat covered with a horse-skin, much used by these islanders.

guard; and the young Mac Caunthca reached the mainland with a single son, the heir-presumptive to the throne of Torry.

It may be imagined that the care of an infant would have become a very troublesome charge upon the lover of the island princess; but here, too, the red man stood his friend. The dwarf volunteered to educate the child seven years, then hand him over to his father for seven more, when he, Red-beard, would again receive him for other seven; and thus the grandson of the three-eyed monarch would be disposed of, during nonage. It was done. The boy grew apace; and, indoctrinated at the feet of a gifted Gamaliel like little Red-beard, it is not surprising that the heir of Torry became a finished gentleman.

His first appearance in public is stated to have been at a country wedding; and there Ballar, attended by Mool and Mullock, and his customary suite, was punctual to claim his prerogative. Shocked at the immorality of his grandfather, the dwarf's protegé remonstrated with the old gentleman in vain; and, to strengthen his arguments, imprudently confessed the degree of relationship in which they stood.

Furious at the discovery, the ancient sinner determined on the youth's destruction; he raised his hand to uncurtain the third eye, but his grandson burst from the house, and ran for shelter to the forge of his relative, Gabshegonal. A hot pursuit took place. Ballar and his 'tail' pressed the fugitive closely; and the youth had only time to arm himself with a heated bar, when his truculent relation, with his train, rushed in. Before the eye could be uncovered, by one lucky thrust the heir of Torry annihilated its evil influence, and thus proved satisfactorily that the worst of eyes is no match for red-hot iron.

But, even in death, Ballar evinced no feelings of Christian forgiveness. Calling his grandson to his side, he requested that he would abridge his sufferings by cutting off his head; and then, by placing it upon his own, he assured him that all the knowledge he, Ballar, possessed, should directly be transferred to his grandson, and descend like an heir-loom in the family. With the first part of the request the young gentleman freely complied; but, being awake to the trickery of his grandsire, he prudently resolved to see what effect the head would have upon stone before he tried the experiment. The result proved that his suspicions were well-founded. A drop of poisonous matter fell from the head upon the rock; and a broken cliff is pointed out upon the island, said to have been disrupted by the head of Ballar resting on it.

The remainder of the legend is happy, as it should be. The princess in due time became a wife; her son danced at the wedding; and the maids of honour were provided with husbands, and, though rather tardily, were 'made honest women of' at last. No longer necessitated to commit their offspring to the ocean by the dozen, their progeny increased and multiplied; and from the

Danish princess, and the virgin train who 'bore her company', the present inhabitants of Torry believe themselves to be immediately descended."

* * *

PHELIM O'TOOLE'S NINE MUSE-INGS ON HIS NATIVE COUNTY[6]
Tune – "Cruiskeen lawn"

Co. Wicklow, the garden of Ireland, is situated about twenty miles south of Dublin. The principal towns of Wicklow and Arklow are old Norse settlements. The features of the county referred to in this poem – the brooks running from the Wicklow mountains, the hill of the Sugarloaf, the Dargle river, the corry lake of Luggalaw, the Devil's Glen, the vale of Avoca, Powerscourt Waterfall, the monastic settlement of Glendalough, the Scalp pass and Djouce mountain – are all notable beauty spots. From the top of the Sugarloaf one can see Wales on a clear day.

The beauties of Wicklow are recounted in these verses:

I

Let others spend their time
In roaming foreign clime,
To furnish them with rhyme
    For books:
They'll never find a scene
Like Wicklow's valleys green,
Wet-nurs'd, the hills between,
    With brooks –
    Brooks – brooks –
Wet-nurs'd, the hills between,
    With brooks!
Oh! if I had a station
In that part of creation,
I'd study the first CAWS like rooks –
    Rooks – rooks –
I'd study the first CAWS like rooks!

II

Oh! how the Morning loves
To climb the Sugar-Loaves,[7]

---

6.   *Bentley's Miscellany*, Vol. II, 1837, pp. 319-320.
7.   Two hills in the county of Wicklow, so called from their conical shape.

And purple their dwarf groves
    Of heath!
While cottage smoke below
Reflects the bloomy glow,
As up it winds, and slow,
    Is wreath –
    Wreath – wreath –
As up it winds, and slow,
Its wreath!
Oh! how a man does wonder him
When he 'as the big CONE-UNDER-HIM,
And ask'ed to guess his home beneath –
    'Neath – 'neath –
And ask'ed to guess his home beneath!

III

And there's the Dargle deep,
Where breezeless waters sleep,
Or down their windings creep
With fear;
Lest, by their pebbly tread,
They shake some lily's head,
And cause, untimely shed,
A tear –
Tear – tear –
And cause, untimely shed,
A tear!
Oh! my native Dargle,
Long may you rinse and gargle
Your rocky throat with stream so clear,
Clear – clear –
Your rocky throat with stream so clear!

IV

And there is Luggalaw,
A gem without a flaw,
With lake, and glen, and shaw,
So still;
The new moon loves to sip
Its dew with her young lip,
Then takes a ling'ring trip

O'er hill –
Hill – hill –
Then takes a ling'ring trip
O'er hill!
Oh! hungry bards might dally
For ever in this valley,
And always get their fancy's fill –
Fill – fill –
And always get their fancy's fill!

V

And there's the "Divil's Glin",
That devil ne'er was in,
Nor anything like sin
To blight:
The Morning hurries there
To scent the myrtle air;
She'd stop, if she might dare,
Till night –
Night – night –
She'd stop, if she might dare,
Till night!
Oh! ye glassy streamlets,
That bore the rocks like gimlets,
There's nothing like your crystal bright,
Bright – bright –
There's nothing like your crystal bright!

VI

And there's Ovoca's vale,
And classic Annadale,[8]
Where Psyche's gentle tale
Was told:
Where MOORE's fam'ed waters meet,
And mix a draught more sweet
Than flow'd at Pindus' feet
Of old –
Old – old –
Than flow'd at Pindus' feet

---

8.   The residence of the late Mrs Henry Tighe, the charming authoress of "Psyche".

Of old!
Oh! all it wants is whiskey
To make it taste more frisky;
Than ev'ry drop would be worth gold –
Gold – gold –
Then ev'ry drop would be worth gold!

VII

And there's the Waterfall,
That lulls its summer hall
To sleep with voice as small
As bee's:
But when the winter rills
Burst from the inward hills,
A rock-rent thunder fills
The breeze –
Breeze – breeze –
A rock-rent thunder fills
The breeze!
Oh! if the LAND was taught her
To FALL as well as WATER,
How much it would poor tenants please,
Please – please –
How much it would poor tenants please!

VIII

And if you have a mind
For sweet, sad thoughts inclined,
In Glendalough you'll find
Them nigh:-
Kathleen and Kevin's tale
So sorrows that deep vale,
That birds all songless sail
Its sky –
Its sky – sky –
That birds all songless sail
Its sky!
Oh! cruel Saint was Kevin
To shun her eyes' blue heaven,
Then drown her in the lake hard by –
By – by –
Would I have sarved her! – not I!

IX

And there's – But what's the use
Of praising Scalp or Douce? –
The wide world can't produce
Such sights:
So I will sing adieu
To Wicklow's hills so blue,
And green vales glittering through
Dim lights –
Lights – lights –
And green vales glittering through
Dim lights!
Oh! I could from December
Until the next November
MUSE on this way both days and nights,
Nights – nights –
MUSE on this way both days and nights!

Irish tales made a regular appearance, including this one by Waterloo.

* * *

THE TWO BUTLERS (OF KILKENNY)[9]

Theobald Fitzwalter, who accompanied Henry II into Ireland was created
Chief Butler of Ireland in 1177. His son, Theobald, assumed the surname of
Butler. Kilkenny Castle (when it was given to the State) was the chief seat of
the Butler Earls, Dukes and Marquesses of Ormonde. This Norman fortress
was Frencefied by the first Duke of Ormonde in the 17th century and extended into the 18th and 19th centuries. The castle has been completely
restored in modern times.

John Butler (1740-1795) ("Jack o'the Castle") 17th Earl of Ormonde,
to whom this story refers, was brother of Lady Elanor Butler, the older of the
two famous Ladies of Llangollen. He lived in Kilkenny Castle in utmost splendour and hospitality, hardly ever visiting Dublin and spending all his money
in local patronage. He was well read and friendly and was described as a
"hard-goer" and incessant talker.

He regularly adjourned to a city tavern referred to as "Hell-cat" where

9.   *Bentley's Miscellany*, Vol. I, 1837, pp. 306-312

"together with the best boozers and other gentlemen of Kilkenny" they devoured oysters and the best lobsters to be found and brought the company of the castle there.

"It is now almost a hundred years ago – certainly eighty – since Tom . . . emerged from his master's kitchen in Clonmell, to make his way on a visit to foreign countries...

His master was a very honest fellow – a schoolmaster of the name of Chaytor, a Quaker, round of paunch and red of nose . . . Summer school-vacations in Ireland occur in July; and Chaytor . . . gave leave to his man Tom to go wandering about the country. He had four, or perhaps five, days to himself. . . .

So he started for the land of Kilkenny . . . and, going it at a slapping pace, he made Kilkenny in six hours. I pass the itinerary. He started at six in the morning, and arrived somewhat foot-worn, but full not only of bread, but of wine (for the wine was to be found on country roadsides in Ireland in those days), in the ancient city of Saint Canice about noon.

Tom refreshed himself at the Feathers . . . and having swallowed as much of the substantial food and the pestiferous fluid that mine host of the Feathers tendered him, the spirit of inquisitiveness, which, according to the phrenologists, is developed in all mankind, seized paramount hold of Tom.

If there be a guide-book to the curiosities of Kilkenny, the work has escaped my researches. Of the city is is recorded, however, that it can boast of fire without smoke, air without fog, and streets paved with marble. And there's the college, and the bridge, and the ruins of St. John's abbey, and St. Canice, and the Nore itself, and last, not least, the castle of the Ormonds, with its woods and its walks, and its stables and its gallery, and all the rest of it, predominating over the river.

As the castle is the most particular lion of the city, it of course speedily attracted the attention of Tom, who, swaggering in all the independence of an emancipated footman up the street, soon found himself at the gave. 'Rearing himself thereat', as the old ballad has it, stood a man basking in the sun. He was somewhat declining towards what they call the vale of years in the language of poetry; but by the twinkle of his eye, and the purple rotundity of his cheek, it was evident that the years of the valley, like the lads of the valley, had gone cheerily-o! The sun shone brightly upon his silver locks, escaping from under a somewhat tarnished cocked-hat guarded with gold lace, the gilding of which had much deteriorated since it departed from the shop of the artificer; and upon a scarlet waistcoat, velvet certainly, but of reduced condition, and in the same situation as to gilding as the hat. His plum-coloured breeches were unbuckled at the knee, and his ungartered stockings were on a downward progress towards his unbuckled shoes. He had his hands – their wrists were garnished with unwashed ruffles – in his breeches pockets; and he diverted himself with whistling 'Charley over the water', in a state of quasi-ruminant quiescence. Nothing could be plainer than that he was a hanger-on of the castle off duty, waiting his time until called for, when of course he was to appear before his master in a more carefully arranged costume.

Ormond Castle was then, as I believe it is now, a show-house, and the visitors of Kilkenny found little difficulty in the admission; but, as in those days purposes of political intrusion might be suspected, some shadow at least of introduction was considered necessary. Tom, reared in the household of a schoolmaster, where the despotic authority of the chief extends a flavour of its quality to all his ministers, exhilarated by the walk, and cheered by the eata-bles and drinkables which he had swallowed, felt that there was no necessity for consulting any of the usual points of etiquette, if indeed he knew that any such things were in existence.

'I say,' said he, 'old chap! is this castle to be seen? I'm told it's a show; and if it is, let's have a look at it.'

'It is to be seen,' replied the person addressed, 'if you are properly intro-duced.'

'That's all hum!' said Tom. 'I know enough of the world, though I've lived all my life in Clonmell, to know that a proper introduction signifies a tester. Come, my old snouty, I'll stand all that's right if you show me over it. Can you do it?'

'Why,' said his new friend, 'I think I can; because, in fact, I am -'

'Something about the house, I suppose. Well, though you've on a laced jacket, and I only a plain frieze coat, we are both brothers of the shoulder-knot. I tell you who I am. Did you ever hear of Chaytor the Quaker, the schoolmaster of Clonmell?'

'Never.'

'Well, he's a decent sort of fellow in the propria quae maribus line, and gives as good a buttock of beef to anybody that gets over the threshold of his door as you'd wish to meet; and I am his man, his valley de sham, head gentleman . . . and butler. What are you here?'

'Why,' replied the man at the gave, 'I am a butler as well as you.'

'Oh! then we're both butlers; and you could as well pass us in. By coarse, the butler must be a great fellow here; and I see you are rigged out in the cast clothes of my lord. Isn't that true?'

'True enough: he never gets a suit of clothes that it does not fall to my lot to wear it; but if you wish to see the castle, I think I can venture to show you all that it contains, even for the sake of our being two butlers.'

It was not much sooner said than done. Tom accompanied his compan-ion over the house and grounds, making sundry critical observations on all he saw therein – on painting, architecture, gardening, the sublime and beautiful, the scientific and picturesque – in a manner which I doubt not much resembled the average style of reviewing those matters in what we now call the best public instructors.

'Have you anything to drink?'

'Plenty.'

'But you won't get into a scrape? Honour above all; I'd not like to have you do it unless you were sure, for the glory of the cloth.'

The pledge of security being solemnly offered, Tom followed his companion through the intricate passages of the castle until he came into a small apartment, where he found a most plentiful repast before him . . .

'By Gad! you appear to have those lads under your thumb – for this is great eating. I suppose you often rob my lord? speak plain, for I myself rob ould Chaytor the schoolmaster; but there's a long difference between robbing a schoolmaster and robbing a lord. I venture to say many a pound of his you have made away with.'

'A great many indeed. I am ashamed to say it, that for one pound he has lost by anybody else, he has lost a hundred by me.'

'Ashamed, indeed! This is beautiful beef. But let us wash it down. By the powers! is it champagne you are giving me? . . . By Gor! if you do not break the Ormonds, I can't tell who should.'

'Nor I. Finish your champagne. What else will you have to drink?'

'. . . Could you find us a glass of brandy?'

'Of course.'

By this time Tom was subdued by the champagne and the brandy, to say nothing of the hot weather; and the spirit of hospitality rose strong upon the spirit of cognac. His new friend gently hinted that a retreat to his gite at the Feathers might be prudent; but to such a step Tom would by no means consent unless the butler of the castle accompanied him to take a parting bowl. With some reluctance the wish was complied with, and both the butlers sallied both on their way through the principal streets of Kilkenny, just as the evening was beginning to assume somewhat of a dusky hue. Tom had, in the course of the three or four hours passed with his new friend, informed him of all the private history of the house of Ormond, with that same regard to veracity which in general characterises the accounts of the births, lives, and educations of persons of the higher classes, to be found in fashionable novels and other works drawn from the communications of such authorities as our friend Tom; and his companion offered as much commentary is is usually done on similar occasions. Proceeding in a twirling motion along, he could not but observe that the principal persons whom they met bowed most respectfully to the gentleman from the castle; and, on being assured that this token of deference was paid because they were tradesmen of the castle, who were indebted to the butler for his good word in their business, Tom's appreciation of his friend's abilities in the art of 'improving' his situation was considerably enhanced . . .

The Kilkenny man steadied the Clonmell man to the Feathers, where the latter most potentially ordered a bowl of the best punch. The slipshod waiter stared; but a look from Tom's friend was enough. They were ushered into the best apartment of the house – Tom remarking that it was a different room from that which he occupied on his arrival; and in a few minutes the master of the house, Mr. Mulvany, in his best array, made his appearance with a pair of wax candles in his hands. He bowed to the earth as he said,

'If I had expected you, my –'

'Leave the room,' was the answer.

'Not before I order my bowl of punch,' said Tom.

'Shall I, my –'

'Yes,' said the person addressed; 'whatever he likes.'

'Well,' said Tom, as Mulvany left the room, 'if I ever saw anything to match that . . . Och! then, what a story I'll have when I get back to Clonmell.'

'Well, Tom,' said his friend, 'I may perhaps see you there; but good-bye for a moment. I assure you I have had much pleasure in your company.'

'He's a queer fellow that,' thought Tom, 'and I hope he'll be soon back. It's a pleasant acquaintance I've made the first day I was in Kilkenny. Sit down, Mr. Mulvany,' said he, as that functionary entered, bearing a bowl of punch, 'and taste your brewing.' To which invitation Mr. Mulvany acceded, nothing loth, but still casting an anxious eye towards the door.

'That's a mighty honest man,' said Tom.

'I do not know what you mean,' replied the cautious Mulvany (for 'honest man' was in those days another word for Jacobite).

'I mane what I say,' said Tom; 'he's just showed me over the castle, and gave me full and plenty of the best of eating and drinking. He tells me he's the butler.'

'And so he is, you idiot of a man!' cried Mulvany. 'He's the chief Butler of Ireland.'

'What?' said Tom.

'Why, him that was with you just now is the Earl of Ormond'.

CHAPTER FIVE

Dickens and Thomas Moore

I n childhood Charles Dickens had a strong sense of "conviviality", as he recounted, and he sang songs at parties and at his own kitchen dramas. On occasion he was brought to the Mitre Inn in Rochester and would get up on the tables with his sister and sing the songs of Thomas Moore especially. Thomas Moore was born in Aungier Street, Dublin, in 1779 and his Irish Melodies were published in parts between 1807 and 1834. He was Dickens's favourite popular poet.

The following are two articles which appeared in *Studies* in 1948 written by Donal O'Sullivan:[1]

The Dancing Academy (*Sketches by Boz*)

---

1. *Studies*, Vol. 37, June–September 1948.

CHARLES DICKENS AND THOMAS MOORE

"Lovers of Dickens are familiar with the use he makes in his dialogue of the songs and poems that were popular in his time: sometimes by direct quotation, occasionally by allusion, but oftenest by a humorous perversion of the original. This applies particularly (but by no means exclusively) to his comic characters. Silas Wegg had a fondness for 'dropping into poetry', though he proposed to charge Mr. Boffin extra for reading it to him instead of The Decline and Fall because of its weakening effect on the mind. The governess to whom Mr. Richard Swiveller brought the little Marchioness to be educated was impressed by his 'prodigious talent in quotation'. Mr. Micawber was always liable to point his rotund periods by incorporating a few apposite lines from Byron or Burns or The Beggar's Opera. Among the treasured possessions of Captain Cuttle were 'The Little Warbler' and other cheap song-books, with extracts from which he would regale Sol Gills, puzzle Mr. Toots or comfort Florence Dombey as the case might require. And so one could go through the long list.

I had often noticed casually that Moore figured among the poets laid under contribution in this way, but precise references were lacking. However, I recently decided to spend the winter evenings in a complete re-reading of the novels and short stories for the pleasure that they always give me... and it then occurred to me that here was an opportunity of making an investigation of a kind that, so far as I am aware, has not been undertaken before. Using a blank sheet of paper as a bookmark, I noted the references and allusions to Moore's verses, and also to those of some others for purposes of statistical comparison. The result has been surprising. I came across five from Robert Burns: 'O'er the water to Charlie' (twice), 'My luve is like a red, red rose', 'We're a'noddin', 'Scots wha hae' and 'Auld lang syne'; about the same number from Gay; a couple of quotations from T.H. Bayly's beautiful but forgotten song, 'We met – 'Twas in a crowd'. Numerous authors contribute one or two apiece; and Byron's farewell to Moore ('My boat is on the shore', set to music by Bishop) occurs three times. Moore is responsible for about thirty, and so leaves all others far behind.

When due allowance has been made for the Irish poet's deserved ascendancy among the song-writers popular in the nineteenth century, it would seem from these figures that he held a special place in Dickens's affection. 'Tom Moore is my poet', says one of the characters in Sketches by Boz. 'And mine!' echoes a second. 'And mine!' add a third and a fourth. There can now be little room for doubt that he was the author's favourite also.

In assembling the instances below I have aimed at recounting sufficient of the circumstances to convey the point of the quotation or allusion in each case and also, it is hoped, something of Dickens's humour. The classification of the songs is that into which they naturally fall – 'Irish Melodies', 'National Airs' and 'Miscellaneous Songs'. A brief indication of the source of the music is given where I happen to know it; and the titles of the novels are followed by the chapter-references.

Moore's 'Irish Melodies' were issued in ten 'Numbers', the first in 1807 and the tenth (with a Supplement) in 1834. The airs, which were arranged by Sir John Stevenson, were mostly drawn from various published collections of folk-tunes, Edward Bunting's 1796 and 1809 volumes being the chief source. The 'National Airs', so called, range from 1819 to 1828, with arrangements by Stevenson and Sir Henry Bishop. Most of them profess to derive from the folk-music of various countries: thus 'Oft in the stilly night' is termed a 'Scotch air', 'Oh! come to me when daylight sets' a 'Venetian air', and 'The Vesper Hymn' a 'Russian air'. Such attributions, however, are without foundation, and the strong probability is that the majority of the 'National Airs' were composed by Bishop or Stevenson, though a few may have been written by Moore himself. For Moore combined the arts of music and poetry, and he composed the music for some of the pieces here classed as 'Miscellaneous Songs'. It is surprising that the authors of melodies of such beauty as the three just mentioned should have been willing to give them to the world under the cloak of anonymity.

Conscious though we may be of Moore's genius in the inexpressible magic of writing words for music, it is difficult for us now to realise the enormous popularity of his compositions throughout the Victorian age. However slight or obscure some of the allusions here given may seem to be, it is certain that they would have been instantly recognised and appreciated by all classes of the reading public for whom Charles Dickens wrote.

Irish Melodies

BELIEVE ME, IF ALL THOSE ENDEARING YOUNG CHARMS
("My lodging is on the cold ground": English folk-tune)

Bleak House, II, p. 18. Inspector Bucket happens to call on Mr and Mrs Bagnet on "the old girl's birthday", and he is asked to sing. "Not to be behindhand in the sociality of the evening, he complies, and gives them 'Believe me, if all those endearing young charms'. This ballad, he informs Mrs. Bagnet, he considers to have been his most powerful ally in moving the heart of Mrs. Bucket when a maiden, and inducing her to approach the altar. Mr. Bucket's own words are, to come up to the scratch."

Bleak House, II, p. 28. Inspector Bucket, engaged in solving the mystery of Lady Dedlock's disappearance, tackles the hostile Mrs. Snagsby, wife of the law-stationer of Cook's Court, Cursitor Street. Truculently persuasive as usual, he begins: "Now the first thing that I say to you, as a married woman possessing what you may call charms, you know – 'Believe me, if all those endearing and cetret' – you're well acquainted with the song, because it's vain for you to tell me that you and good society are strangers – charms – attractions, mind you, that ought to give you confidence in yourself – is, that you've done it."

The Old Curiosity Shop, p. 27. Mrs Jarley proudly displays to Little Nell the advertisements for her travelling wax-work show. These were "in the shape of hand-bills, some of which were couched in the form of parodies on popular melodies, as 'Believe me if all Jarley's wax-work so rare'."

DRINK OF THIS CUP

("Páidín O Raifeartaigh": from Holden)

The Old Curiosity Shop, p. 61. When Christopher Nubbles is arrested on a false charge trumped up by Quilp and his minion Sampson Brass, Dick Swiveller sends a pint of porter round to the gaol with the following note: "Drink of this cup, you'll find there's a spell in its every drop 'gainst the ills of mortality. Talk of the cordial that sparkled for Helen! Her cup was a fiction, but this is reality (Barclay & Co.'s). If ever they send it in a flat state, complain to the Governor. Yours, R.S." This passage gives the first four lines of the song, written as prose.

EVELEEN'S BOWER

("The pretty girl of Derby O!": English folk-tune)

Our Mutual Friend, I, p. 15. Mr. and Mrs. Boffin are about to remove to more aristocratic quarters in Cavendish Square, and the former interviews the rascally Silas Wegg with a view to installing him as caretaker at Boffin's Bower, where, as he points out, "a man with coals and candles and a pound a week might be in clover". "Now," says Wegg, "my independence as a man is again elevated. Now, I no longer

> Weep for the hour
> When to Boffinses Bower
> The Lord of the valley with offers came;
> Neither does the moon hide her light
> From the heavens to-night,
> And weep behind the clouds o'er any individual in the
>   present Company's shame."

"Thank'ee, Wegg," replies Mr Boffin, "both for your confidence in me and for your frequent dropping into poetry, both of which is friendly." The lines are a humorous perversion of the first verse of the song.

GO WHERE GLORY WAITS THEE
("Moll dubh and ghleanna": from Bunting)

Martin Chuzzlewit, I, p. 11. The two Miss Pecksniffs, on a visit to London, are staying with their father at Todgers's boarding-house, near the Monument. On the eve of their departure the young gentlemen of Todgers's assemble outside their bedroom-door and serenade them with "Go where glory waits thee". "It was very affecting – very. Nothing more dismal could have been desired by the most fastidious taste. The gentleman of a vocal turn was head mute or chief mourner; Jinkins took the bass; and the rest took anything they could get."

The Old Curiosity Shop, p. 58. Dick Swiveller finds himself alone with the small servant of Sampson and Sally Brass, whom he calls the Marchioness. "'The Baron Sampsono Brasso and his fair sister are (you tell me) at the Play?' said Mr Swiveller, leaning his left arm heavily upon the table and raising his voice and his right leg after the manner of a theatrical bandit. The Marchioness nodded." Dick then inquires: "Do they often go where glory waits 'em and leave you here?"

I SAW THY FORM IN YOUTHFUL PRIME
("Donald": from Thomson's Scotish Airs)

The Old Curiosity Shop, p. 27. Among the hand-bills advertising Mrs Jarley's wax-works was one inscribed "I saw thy show in youthful prime".

LOVE'S YOUNG DREAM
("An tsean-bhean bhocht": from Bunting)

The Mystery of Edwin Drood, p. 2. It is Rosa's birthday, and Edwin has been talking to Mr. Jasper about his present for her. Jasper murmurs "'Nothing half so sweet in life', Ned!" this is an allusion to the last lines of the first verse,

"Oh! there's nothing half so sweet in life
As love's young dream!"

WHEN FIRST I MET THEE
("O Patrick, fly from me": from an unknown Oxford correspondent)

The Old curiosity Shop, p. 23. Dick Swiveller is melancholy through losing Sophy Wackles. He meets Quilp, the author of his misfortunes, and addresses him: "Go, deceiver, go, some day, sir, p'r'aps you'll waken, from pleasure's dream to know, the grief of orphans forsaken." This is a humorous perversion of the chorus to the second verse.

WHEN HE WHO ADORES THEE HAS LEFT BUT THE NAME
("Codladh an tSionnaigh": from Bunting)

and

OH! BLAME NOT THE BARD
("Caitilín Triall": from Bunting)

The Old Curiosity Shop, p. 35. Dick Swiveller has been entertained by the mysterious Single Gentleman who has taken rooms over the office of Dick's employer, Sampson Brass. When he is leaving, the following conversation takes place:
  "'I beg your pardon', said Dick, halting in his passage to the door, which the lodger prepared to open. 'When he who adores thee has left but the name —
  'What do you mean?'
  'But the name,' said Dick ' has left but the name – in case of letters or parcels —
  'I never have any', returned the lodger.
  'Or in case anybody should call.'
  'Nobody ever calls on me.'
  'If any mistake should arise from not having the name, don't say it was my fault, sir,' added Dick, lingering. 'Oh blame not the bard -'
  "I'll blame nobody,' said the lodger, with such irascibility that in a moment Dick found himself on the staircase and the locked door between them."

THE YOUNG MAY MOON
("Irish tune" in Shield's Robin Hood)

Bleak House, I. p. 6. Esther, Richard and Ada are spending their first evening at John Jarndyce's place, Bleak House, where they meet Harold Skimpole. Esther writes: "It was late before we separated; for when Ada was going at eleven o'clock, Mr. Skimpole went to the piano and rattled, hilariously, that the best of all ways to lengthen our days was to steal a few hours from the Night, my dear! It was past twelve before he took his candle and his radiant face out of the room; and I think he might have kept up there, if he had seen fit, till daybreak." The passage embodies a quotation, slightly adapted, from the first verse of the song.

National Airs

FLOW ON, THOU SHINING RIVER
("Portuguese air")

Sketches by Boz. The Boarding-house. The lodgers are at tea in the drawing-room, and Mr Tomkins announces his intention of riding to Richmond and returning by steamer, remarking that "there are some splendid effects of light and shade on the Thames". Mr Wisbottle hums "Flow on, thou shining river".

OFT IN THE STILLY NIGHT
("Scotch air")

Little Dorrit, I, p. 23. Flora Finching, unable to forget her romance with him of a quarter of a century ago, moralises to Arthur Clennam: "So true it is that oft in the stilly night ere slumber's chain has bound people, fond memory brings the light of other days around people – very polite but more polite than true I am afraid." A humorous perversion of the opening lines of the song.

'TIS WHEN THE CUP IS SMILING BEFORE US
("Italian air")

Last half of second verse:

> "Though this life like a river is flowing,
> I care not how fast it goes on, boy, on,
> While the grape on its bank still is growing,
> And such eyes light the waves as they run."

The Old Curiosity Shop, p. 58. Dick Swiveller has spent the evening with the small servant in the dank basement, teaching her cribbage and regaling her with choice purl, ordered from the local public-house and "made after a particular recipe which Mr. Swiveller had imparted to the landlord". He now prepares to depart: "With which object in view, Marchioness," said Mr Swiveller gravely, "I shall ask your ladyship's permission to put the board in my pocket, and to retire from the presence when I have finished this tankard; merely observing, Marchioness, that since life like a river is flowing, I care not how fast it rolls on, ma'am, on, while such purl on the bank still is growing, and such eyes light the waves as they run. Marchioness, your health. You will excuse my wearing my hat, but the palace is damp, and the marble floor is – if I may be allowed the expression – sloppy."

THOSE EVENING BELLS
("The Bells of St. Petersburg")

David Copperfield, p. 38. It will be seen from the next entry that Julia Mills tried to maintain Dora's spirits by singing this song to her shortly after her father's death; but the words show the well-intentioned Julia to have been something of a Job's comforter, and the comment in her diary, "Effect not soothing, but reverse", causes no surprise:

> "Those evening bells! those evening bells!
> How many a tale their music tells,
> Of youth, and home, and that sweet time
> When last I heard their soothing chime.
>
> Those joyous hours are passed away!
> And many a heart that then was gay
> Within the tomb now darkly dwells,
> And hears no more those evening bells!"

Miscellaneous Songs

VERSES FROM "LALLA ROOKH"

The best-known lines in this long and once celebrated poem are the following two quatrains in "The Fire-Worshippers". They were set to music by Sir Henry Bishop:

> Oh! ever thus, from childhood's hour,
> I've seen my fondest hopes decay;
> I never loved a tree or flower,
> But 'twas the first to fade away.
>
> I never nursed a dear gazelle,
> To glad me with its soft black eye,

> But when it came to know me well,
> And love me, it was sure to die.

David Copperfield, p. 38. Mr Spenlow discovers through Miss Murdstone that David is in love with his daughter Dora and that the pair have been conducting a clandestine correspondence, with Dora's friend Julia Mills acting as go-between. He forbids David the house and is found dead the same evening. Grief-stricken at having been "a naughty and undutiful child", Dora retires to live with her aunts at Putney, accompanied by Julia and her pet dog Jip, and she refuses to see David. Julia keeps a diary for his benefit. Here is one of the entries:

> Wednesday. D. comparatively cheerful. Sang to her, as congenial melody, Evening Bells. Effect not soothing, but reverse. D. inexpressibly affected. Found sobbing afterwards in own room. Quoted verses respecting self and young Gazelle. Ineffectually.

Two days later, when Jip is temporarily lost:

> Search made in every direction. No J. D. weeping bitterly, and inconsolable. Renewed reference to young Gazelle. Appropriate, but unavailing.

The Old Curiosity Shop, p. 56. Dick Swiveller, lamenting the loss of Sophy Wackles, quotes both quatrains but alters the last line to "And love me, it was sure to marry a market-gardener."

Our Mutual Friend, IV, p. 16. On their way home from visiting her sister Bella (who, as Mrs. John Hamon, has made a glittering marriage), Lavinia Wilfer proceeds to "take it out of" her humble suitor, George Sampson. Stung to a retort, "'Oh yes!' cried Mr Sampson with bitterness, 'Thus it ever is. I never —' 'If you mean to say', Miss Lavvy cut him short, 'that you never brought up a young gazelle, you may save yourself the trouble, because nobody in this carriage supposes you ever did. We know you better.' (As if this were a home-thrust)."

FLY FROM THE WORLD, O BESSY, TO ME
(Composed by Moore)

Sketches by Boz. Scenes, 2. the scene is "a harmonic meeting", i.e., an old-style London music-hall. "The stout man is addicted to sentimentality and warbles 'Fly, fly from the world, my Bessy, with me'', or some such song, with lady-like sweetness."

FRIEND OF MY SOUL! THIS GOBLET SIP

Nicholas Nickleby, 41. The eccentric Gentleman in Small-clothes hails the susceptible Mrs Nickleby in these words (misquoted) over the garden wall: "Queen of my soul, this goblet sip!" "'Won't you sip the goblet?' urged the stranger, with his head imploringly on one side and his right hand on his breast. 'Oh! do sip the goblet!'"

HOLY BE THE PILGRIM'S SLEEP

The concluding lines of the second verse are:

> "Strew, then, oh! strew his bed of rushes,
> Here he shall rest till morning blushes."

(There is a similar couplet in "Oh, lady fair!" mentioned below).

The Old Curiosity Shop, p. 65. Dick Swiveller, recovering from brain fever, is being tenderly nursed by the faithful little Marchioness, who has run away from Sampson Brass's. "Having given Mr. Swiveller his drink and put everything in neat order, she wrapped herself in an old coverlet and lay down upon the rug before the fire. Mr. Swiveller was by that time murmuring in his sleep, 'Strew then, oh strew a bed of rushes. Here will we stay till morning blushes. Good night, Marchioness!'"

I KNEW BY THE SMOKE THAT SO GRACEFULLY CURLED
(Music by Michael Kelly)

The first two verses of this song are:

> "I knew by the smoke that so gracefully curled
> Above the green elms that a cottage was near;
> And I said, 'If there's peace to be found in the world,
> A heart that was humble might hope for it here.'
>
> It was noon, and on flowers that languished around
> In silence reposed the voluptuous bee;
> Every leaf was at rest, and I heard not a sound
> But the woodpecker tapping the hollow beech-tree."

Sketches by Boz. The Boarding-house. Mrs Tibbs, the boarding-house keeper, suspecting Tibbs of an intrigue with the servant Agnes, joins one of the lodgers in an attempt at eavesdropping but finds herself in a compromising position with him. "'Ah, you have done it nicely now, sir', sobbed the frightened Agnes, as a tapping was heard at Mrs. Tibbs's bedroom door which would have beaten any dozen woodpeckers hollow."

David Copperfield, p. 36. On the eve of their departure for Canterbury, the Micawbers are visited by David Copperfield and Tommy Traddles at their miserable lodging in the Gray's-Inn Road. Building castles in the air as usual, Micawber announces his intention of educating young Master Micawber for the Church. "He has a remarkable head-voice and will commence as a chorister. Our residence at Canterbury and our local connection will, no doubt, enable him to take advantage of any vacancy that may arise in the Cathedral corps." David comments: "On looking at Master Micawber again, I saw that he had a certain expression of face, as if his voice were behind his eyebrows; where it presently appeared to be, on his singing us (as an alternative between that and bed) 'The Woodpecker tapping'."

Martin Chuzzlewit, I, p. 25. Mr Mould the undertaker is sitting with his family in the parlour behind the shop, off Cheapside. "From the distant shop a pleasant sound arose of coffin-making with a low melodious hammer, rat, tat, tat, tat, alike promoting slumber and digestion.

"'Quite the buzz of insects,' said Mr Mould, closing his eyes in a perfect luxury. 'It puts one in mind of the sound of animated nature in the agricultural districts. It's exactly like the woodpecker tapping.'

"'The woodpecker tapping the hollow elm tree', observed Mrs Mould, adapting the words of the popular melody to the description of wood commonly used in the trade.

"'Ha, ha!' laughed Mr. Mould. 'Not at all bad, my dear. We shall be glad to hear from you again, Mrs. M. Hollow elm tree, eh? Ha ha! Very good indeed. I've seen worse than that in the Sunday papers, my love'."

Little Dorrit, I. p. 35. The heroine is working as a dressmaker at Mr. Casby's. Arthur Clennam pays an early call to convey the good news of her father's impending release from the Marshalsea. Mr. Casby's daughter Flora, still vainly thinking of "the dear dead days beyond recall", imagines that it is she that he has come to see. "'Papa', she said, all mystery and whisper, as she shut down the tea-pot lid, 'is sitting prosingly breaking his new-laid egg in the back-parlour over the City article exactly like the Woodpecker Tapping and need never know that you are here.'"

MARY, I BELIEVED THEE TRUE

First verse:

"Mary, I believed thee true,
And I was blest in thus believing;
But now I mourn that e'er I knew
A girl so fair and so deceiving!"

The Old Curiosity Shop, p. 8. Miss Sophy Wackles, with her widowed mother and two sisters, keeps a "Ladies' Seminary" at Chelsea. Being greatly attracted to Sophy, Dick Swiveller repairs thither to a dance, but withdraws in dudgeon because of Sophy's seeming to favour the attentions of Cheggs, the market-gardener. When departing, he addresses her in the above lines, written as prose and beginning, "Miss Wackles, I believed you true".

OH, LADY FAIR!
(A glee for 5 voices: composed by Moore)

First verse:

"Oh, lady fair! where art thou roaming?
The sun has sunk, the night is coming,
Stranger, I go o'er moor and mountain,
To tell my beads at Agnes' fountain.
And who is the man with his white locks flowing?

Oh, lady fair! where is he going?
A wandering pilgrim, weak, I falter,
To tell my beads at Agnes' altar.
Chill falls the rain, night winds are blowing,
    Dreary and dark's the way we're going."

Great Expectations, p. 13. Pip having been bound apprentice to Joe Gargery, the event is celebrated by a family party at the Blue Boar. "They were all in excellent spirits on the road home and sang 'O Lady Fair!' Mr Wopsel taking the bass, and asserting with a tremendously strong voice (in reply to the inquisitive bore who leads that piece of music in a most impertinent manner, by wanting to know all about everybody's private affairs) that he was the man with his white locks flowing, and that he was upon the whole the weakest pilgrim going."

WILL YOU COME TO THE BOWER?
(English folk-tune)

First verse:

> "Will you come to the bower I have shaded for you?
> Our bed shall be roses bespangled with dew.
> Will you, will you, will you, will you come to the bower?
> Will you, will you, will you, will you come to the bower?"

Our Mutual Friend, IV, p. 3. Wegg thinks he has got the upper hand of Mr Boffin, and on the latter's visit to Boffin's Bower he turns nasty, greeting his benefactor with:

> "If you'll come to the Bower I've shaded for you,
> Your bed sha'n't be roses all spangled with doo:
> Will you, will you, will you, will you come to the Bower?
> Oh, won't you, won't you, won't you come to the Bower?"

CHARLES DICKENS AND THOMAS MOORE

"In an article with the above title in the June issue of STUDIES, I assembled the allusions to Moore disclosed by a reading of Dickens's works. Mr. T.W. Hill, the distinguished Dickensian scholar, has kindly supplied me with certain further references, from which the information given below has been prepared.

OFT IN THE STILLY NIGHT –
Additional reference

The Uncommercial Traveller, XVI. Arcadian London. The theme is the emptiness of London in autumn, when society has for the most part left for the country or the seaside. "Soothed by the repose around me, I wander insensible to considerable distances, and guide myself back by the stars. Thus, I enjoy the contrast of a few partially inhabited and busy spots where all the lights are not fled, where all the garlands are not dead, whence all but I have not departed". Some of the lines of the second verse of the song are here adapted.

I KNEW BY THE SMOKE THAT SO GRACEFULLY CURLED –
Additional reference

Bleak House, 55. Inspector Bucket, after travelling through the night in pursuit of Lady Dedlock, arrives at Bleak House in company with Esther. "'Ah!' said Mr. Bucket, 'Here we are, and a nice retired place it is. Puts a man in mind of the country-house in the Woodpecker tapping, that was known by the smoke which so gracefully curled. They're early with the kitchen fire, and that denotes good servants'".

RICH AND RARE WERE THE GEMS SHE WORE
("Tá an samhradh ag teacht": from Bunting).

The Uncommercial Traveller, XVII. The Calais Night-Mail. This sketch deals in the author's jocose and breezy manner with the Channel crossing from Dover to Calais. The weather is bad, but Dickens is not much inconvenienced, "because I am under a curious compulsion to occupy myself with the Irish melodies. 'Rich and rare were the gems she wore' is the particular melody to which I find myself devoted. I sing it to myself in the most charming manner and with the greatest expression." A description of the discomforts of the passage is interspersed with humorous perversions of the first three verses, till finally: "So strangely goes the time, and on the whole so quickly, that I am bumped, rolled, gurgled, washed and pitched into Calais Harbour before her maiden smile has finally lighted her through the Green Isle, When blest for ever she she who relied, On entering Calais at the turn of the tide."

LINES TO THE HON. W.R. SPENCER

Martin Chuzzlewit, 16. Martin has just landed in New York. After being introduced to Colonel Diver, Jefferson Brick and other "worthies", he is fortunate to meet an American of a very different type in Mr Bevan. Dickens comments: "It was perhaps to men like this, his new companion, that a traveller of honoured name, who trod those shores now nearly forty years ago and woke upon that soil, as many have done since, to blots and stains upon its high pretension, which in the brightness of his distant dreams were lost to view, appealed in these words –

> 'Oh but for such, Columbia's days were done;
> Rank without ripeness, quickened without sun,
> Crude at the surface, rotten at the core,

Her fruits would fall before her spring were o'er!'"

The quotation is from Moore's Epistle to Spencer, in which the poet is severely critical of the United States."

Chapter Six

A Child's History of England
(and Ireland)

Charles Dickens published this history in instalments in *Household Words* between 1851 and 1853. Ireland does not fare well. A section of the history relating to Ireland and the Norman invasion is given here.

But first, Mr Murphy of the Honolulu branch of the Dickens Fellowship gave an outrageously funny paper in 1956[1] which the reader can judge for himself or herself.

A CHILD'S HISTORY OF ENGLAND BY THOMAS D. MURPHY[2]

"I did not, as a child, read Dickens's Child's History of England. Considering my paternal background, it would have been surprising if I had. My father

The making of Waxen Images (*A Child's History of England*)

1. Published in *The Dickensian*, Vol. 52, pp. 157–161; with Letter to the Editor, vol. 53, p. 59.
2. A paper read before the Honolulu Branch of the Dickens Fellowship.

had left Ireland at the age of seventeen to escape from under the hated Saxon yoke. He had had the choice of emigration or the probability of jail, for drilling secretly along with some other young patriots in preparation for the day when the English should be thrown out of the land. Someone had informed. Had he found me reading a history of England written by an Englishman, he would, I believe, have taken a very dim view of the matter.

During my formative years I did, however, though in somewhat oblique fashion, learn something about the English record. There were at least two large histories of Ireland (for adults) in our home library. On rainy afternoons, when I had exhausted my latest instalment of adventure stories from the public library, I sometimes dipped into these. They were at least as interesting as the collected works of Henry Bulwer, Lord Lytton, which also (unaccountably) graced our few shelves.

From the two histories of Ireland (written by Irishmen, of course) I derived the distinct impression that the English were cruel and tyrannous men of blood. I cannot recall that my father ever straightened out my thinking on this matter. Of course, had I possessed a copy of the Child's History of England, that would have set me right, for in the early pages it is boldly stated that the 'English-Saxon character' has been the greatest character among the nations of the earth, and that 'Wherever the descendants of the Saxon race have gone, have sailed, or otherwise made their way, even to the remotest regions of the world, they have been patient, persevering, never to be broken in spirit, never to be turned aside from enterprises on which they have resolved. In Europe, Asia, Africa, America, the whole world over; in the desert, in the forest, on the sea; scorched by a burning sun, or frozen by ice that never melts; the Saxon blood remains unchanged. Wheresoever that race goes, there, law, and industry, and safety for life and property, and all the great results of steady perseverance, are certain to rise.' According to Dickens, those who, like Alfred the Great, possessed the Saxon virtues, could not be subdued by misfortune, spoiled by prosperity, or shaken in perseverance. Lovers of justice, freedom, truth and knowledge, such men were hopeful in defeat, generous in success.

That certainly had not been what my Irish historians had written. True, they made no claim to the more stolid kinds of virtue which Dickens enumerates, but certainly no Irishman who read their works could doubt which was the noblest race of them all. (Of course, having read much American history since my early youth, I can now chuckle at all such outlandish claims.)

But suppose that I had indeed, as a child, had a copy of Dickens's History, and had read past his eulogy of the English character. Even my young mind would, I think, have noticed some inconsistency between his boasts of Saxon virtue and the rest of his story, which is that of a long, brutal, cruel, and generally purposeless scramble for power. Dickens certainly gives his young reader little reason to think that the long line of English monarchs contributed greatly to the blossoming of that English character which he so glowingly describes – and most of his chronicle is a record of the lives of kings and queens and of their intrigues and battles. With the shining exception of Alfred the Great, and those lesser lights William III, Anne, and Victoria (the latter briefly characterised as 'very good and much beloved') they generally appear as a pretty sorry set of characters. If I may illustrate, at random:

Henry IV is summed up as follows: 'Considering his duplicity before he came to the throne, his unjust seizure of it, and above all, his making of that monstrous law for the burning of what the priests called heretics, he was a reasonably good king, as kings went.'

As for the 'cold, crafty, and calculating' Henry VII, who 'would do almost anything for money,' he 'possessed considerable ability, but his chief merit seems to have been that he was not cruel when there was nothing to be got by it.'

In the first paragraph of two chapters on the career of Henry VIII our author says 'I shall take the liberty to call him plainly, one of the most detestable villains that ever drew breath,' and after much elaboration of this theme, ends the second chapter with the summation: 'The plain truth is, that he was a most intolerable ruffian, a disgrace to human nature, and a blot of blood and grease upon the History of England.'

Elizabeth Tudor fares somewhat better, for she 'was not half so good as she has been made out, nor half so bad as she has been made out.' She had her fine qualities, but was 'coarse, capricious, and treacherous, and had all the faults of an excessively vain young woman long after she was an old one. On the whole, she had a great deal too much of her father in her, to please me.'

James the First, 'his Sowship' was, we learn, 'ugly, awkward, and shuffling in mind and person. His tongue was much too large for his mouth, his legs were much too weak for his body, and his dull goggle-eyes stared and rolled like an idiot's. He was cunning, covetous, wasteful, idle, drunken, greedy, dirty, cowardly, a great Swearer, and the most conceited man on earth' – and a great deal more of the same.

I will forbear to tell you what Dickens thought of the vile reign of that 'miserable brute' John, or of the character of the wilful and untrustworthy Charles I, or that of the 'worthless' Merry Monarch, Charles II.

Now I am not sure how perspicacious a child I was, but it does seem to me that had I read Dickens simultaneously with my Irish historians, I might have found a good deal in his book to bolster the impressions of the English-Saxon character which I received from these other works.

Fortunately for the English people, however, their monarchs were not all as bad as Dickens painted them. In fact, our friend made no real effort to tell

England's story 'exactly as it happened'. The copy of the Child's History which I have just read has emerged from the perusal with a number of pencilled questions and exclamation marks on its margins. Andrew Lang, who wrote the introduction to this particular edition, states therein that he had originally intended to annotate the volume, but had decided that the result would be mere laborious pedantry. What he probably meant was that when he read the book the prospect of making all the necessary corrections had so appalled him that he had thrown up the sponge.

In addition to his failings in regard of accuracy and objectivity, Dickens makes no real attempt to deal with cause and effect relationships, or with the development of ideas. It may be that he thought children impervious to this sort of approach, and there will, of course, always be those – even now – even teachers – who will have a sneaking sympathy with this point of view. In any case, however, Dickens did not try.

But it really would be pedantic further to discuss our friend's shortcomings as a historian. That he was not. But he was a wonderful story teller; he had strong ideas as to how Englishmen should behave (and should have behaved); and he had the whole fascinating field of Albion's history with which to work his will. The result, though not always pure history, is always pure Dickens. That is why his book is such a joy. One does not always agree, but is never bored (I am sure that no child ever found this narrative dull), is often highly amused, and is frequently highly sympathetic to the author's point of view.

Let me illustrate by reference to some of the comments of this early Victorian middle class liberal, first on the matter of religion, and then on – well, let's call it the inhumanity of man to man – or, perhaps better, the inhumanity of Englishman to Englishman.

According to Dickens, the Druids probably kept the common people away from Stonehenge and other monuments when these were under construction so that after their completion the priests could tell the commoners that the new structures had been raised by their magical arts. He goes on to observe that it is 'pleasant to think that there are no Druids now, who go on in that way, and pretend to carry Enchanters' Wands and Serpents' Eggs and, of course, there is nothing of the kind, anywhere.' Oh Disenchantment!

The reader is assured that in Dunstan's time the priests were not only skilful in agriculture, medicine, surgery, and handicrafts, but could also, whenever they needed, make some piece of machinery with which to perform a miracle 'to impose a trick upon the poor peasants; they knew very well how to make it; and did make it many a time and often, I have no doubt.'

As to the great archbishop Dunstan himself, he was naught but an imperious, stern, artful, audacious, ill-conditioned juggler. At one time, it seems, there was a disputation between two church groups over some religious matter, and, as the opposed parties sat across from each other in a hall, Dunstan arose from among his supporters and exclaimed 'To Christ Himself, as Judge, do I commit this cause!' Whereupon the floor under the opposite party gave way, and many were killed and injured. 'You may be pretty sure that it had been weakened under Dunstan's direction, and that it fell at Dunstan's signal. His part of the floor did not go down. No, no. He was too good a workman for that.'

When this prelate died, the monks decided that he was a saint. Our author's comment: 'They might just as well have settled that he was a coach-horse, and could just as easily have called him one.'

One gets the vivid impression, after reading the account of Thomas à Becket's career, that this worthy's chief characteristic was that which had caused the downfall of the Archangel Lucifer.

We are assured, as concerns Joan of Arc, that she did, no doubt, believe she saw and heard heavenly beings. 'It is very well known that such delusions are a disease which is not by any means uncommon' and Joan had always been a 'moping, fanciful girl', a good girl, yes, but perhaps 'a little vain and wishful for notoriety.' But Dickens is not unsympathetic, and after describing the cruel manner in which she was hounded to the stake, he ends her story with a reference to the statue to her memory in the square at Rouen, and writes: 'I know of some statues of modern times – even in the World's Metropolis, I think – which commemorate less constancy, less earnestness, smaller claims upon the world's attention, and much greater impostors.'

England's Puritans were 'for the most part an uncomfortable people, who thought it highly meritorious to dress in a hideous manner, talk through their noses, and oppose all harmless enjoyments.' There were many of this sort in Oliver Cromwell's army, and they had 'such an inconvenient habit of starting up and preaching long winded discourses, that I would not have belonged to that army on any account.' So much for the Puritans.

On the other hand, their great enemy, Archbishop Laud, was one who thought bishops and archbishops 'a sort of miraculous persons' and 'brought in an immensity of bowing and candle snuffing.' A plague on both their houses!

In the time of James I 'it was comfortably settled that there was to be only one form of religion, and that all men were to think exactly alike. But although this was arranged two centuries and a half ago, and although the arrangement was supported by much fining and imprisonment, I do not find that it is quite successful, even yet,' says Dickens, triumphantly.

To turn to another part of the record as this author sees it. He is in complete sympathy with Wat Tyler and the oppressed common people who followed him during the Peasants' Rebellion. After describing the proposals for alleviation of their miserable lot which were presented to the 'deceitful' young Richard II, he exclaims 'Heaven knows, there was nothing very unreasonable in these proposals!' After describing Wat's death, and the dispersal of his followers, he remarks that 'the end was the usual end,' with some fifteen hundred of the rioters tried and executed with great cruelty, and many hanged on gibbets as a terror to their miserable friends among the country people. But we are assured that the deposed Richard, as he later languished in the Tower of London, made 'a far more sorry spectacle. . . . than Wat Tyler had made, lying dead, among the hooves of the royal horses in Smithfield.'

When William Fitz-Osbert had attempted to give the common men leadership he too had been cut down. 'Death,' remarks Dickens, 'was long a favourite remedy in silencing the people's advocates, but as we go on with this history, I fancy we shall find them difficult to make an end of, for all that.'

A thirteenth century battle between the French and the English ended, we find, in the usual fashion of those times, 'the common men were slain without any mercy, and the knights and the gentlemen paid ransom and went home.'

In a discussion of the Great Fire of London, it is remarked that this holocaust was, in a way, a blessing, because the burned sections were rebuilt more widely, more cleanly, and more healthily. In fact, the London of Victoria's day 'might be more healthy than it is, but there are some people in it still – even now, at this time, nearly two hundred years later – so selfish, so pigheaded, and so ignorant, that I doubt if even another Great Fire would warm them up to do their duty.'

Rumbold, the old Cromwellian soldier who was a partner in the Rye House Plot against Charles II, was apprehended and executed 'after defending himself with great spirit, and saying that he did not believe that God had made the greater part of mankind to carry saddles on their backs and bridles in their mouths, and to be ridden by a few, booted and spurred for the purpose.' And, says Dickens, 'I thoroughly agree with Rumbold!'

One could continue to illustrate our friend's passion for greater social justice than England's history had so far shown, but time does not permit. I must make an assessment. Let it be this – that had I read this 'history' as a child, I would have found therein no pretence of Olympian impartiality, but instead a burning hatred of cruelty and oppression, a love of human freedom, and a vivid hope for a better lot for the mass of men than that which they had suffered in the bad old past. It would have been good for me, as I am sure it has been for thousands of children. But I am just as glad I did not read the Child's History, for if I had, I would probably never have re-read it as an adult, and would have missed the vast entertainment it has so recently given me. . . . And, confidentially, after having read it, I now feel sure that if Charles Dickens had grown up in my father's village, he would have been out there in the pasture of a night with the rest of the boys, drilling for the day when the virtuous Saxons were to be tossed out of Erin! I am more fond of him now than ever I was."

*   *   *

An irate Edythe M. Glanville of London replied in the next edition of *The Dickensian*.

LETTER TO THE EDITOR

Sir,

I should like to protest strongly against the publication of the article on pp. 157 *et seq.* of the Autumn Number of *The Dickensian*. It is both offensive and absurd.

The author, Mr. Thos. D. Murphy, presumes to ascribe his own political views to the great novelist. In the concluding paragraph he says:

"I now feel sure that if Charles Dickens had grown up in my father's village, he would have been out there in the pasture of a night with the rest of the boys, drilling for the day when the virtuous Saxons were to be tossed out of Erin."

The implication is that the rescission of the twenty-six counties from the United Kingdom was gained by the military prowess of the "boys drilling in the fields". The fact is that the issue was determined by votes cast at a General Election. The "virtuous Saxons" were not "tossed out of Erin".

Dickens was far too shrewd an observer not to perceive that Ireland lost more than she gained by the change. Since the Act of Union, she was an integral and governing part of the world's greatest Empire – an Empire always foremost as the standard bearer of liberty. Now the Republic of Eire is a small and insignificant country – a good place to live out of as the population, ever dwindling by emigration, shows. Had her geographical position been on the east instead of on the west of the sister country, it is far from likely that even the most anti-British section would have advocated a break-away, exposing them to attack from bellicose Germans or Russians.

In conclusion, let me confess that I, your correspondent, am of pure Celtic stock and was proud of it although regarding British citizenship as my most blessed heritage.

Faithfully yours,

EDYTHE M. GLANVILLE
S. Kensington.

*   *   *

A CHILD'S HISTORY OF ENGLAND (AND IRELAND)

This history in simple and colourful language was serialised in *Household Words* over the three years 1851-53 and the rulers of England were presented very much as heroes and villains.

This extract, relating to Ireland, begins after the murder of Thomas à Becket, Archbishop of Canterbury, on the mistaken orders of King Henry II:

When the King heard how Thomas à Becket had lost his life in Canterbury Cathedral, through the ferocity of the four Knights, he was filled with dismay. Some have supposed that when the King spoke those hasty words, "Have I no one here who will deliver me from this man?" he wished, and meant à Becket to be slain. But few things are more unlikely; for, besides that the King was not naturally cruel (though very passionate), he was wise, and must have known full well what any stupid man in his dominions must have known, namely, that such a murder would rouse the Pope and the whole Church against him.

He sent respectful messengers to the Pope, to represent his innocence (except in having uttered the hasty words); and he swore solemnly and publicly to his innocence, and contrived in time to make his peace. As to the four guilty Knights, who fled into Yorkshire, and never again dared to show themselves at Court, the Pope excommunicated them; and they lived miserably for some time, shunned by all their countrymen. At last, they went humbly to Jerusalem as a penance, and there died and were buried.

It happened, fortunately for the pacifying of the Pope, that an opportunity arose very soon after the murder of à Becket, for the King to declare his power in Ireland – which was an acceptable undertaking to the Pope, as the Irish, who had been converted to Christianity by one Patricius (otherwise Saint Patrick) long ago, before any Pope existed, considered that the Pope had nothing at all to do with them, or they with the Pope, and accordingly refused to pay him Peter's Pence, or that tax of a penny a house which I have elsewhere mentioned. The King's opportunity arose in this way.

The Irish were, at that time, as barbarous a people as you can well imagine. They were continually quarrelling and fighting, cutting one another's throats, slicing one another's noses, burning one another's houses, carrying away one another's wives, and committing all sorts of violence. The country was divided into five kingdoms – DESMOND, THOMOND, CONNAUGHT, ULSTER, AND LEINSTER – each governed by a separate King, of whom one claimed to be the chief of the rest. Now, one of these Kings, named DERMOND MAC MURROUGH (a wild kind of name, spelt in more than one wild kind of way), had carried off the wife of a friend of his, and concealed her on an island in a bog. The friend resenting this (though it was quite the custom of the country), complained to the chief King, and, with the chief King's help, drove Dermond Mac Murrough out of his dominions. Dermond came over to England for revenge; and offered to hold his realm as a vassal of King Henry, if King Henry would help him to regain it. The King consented to these terms; but only assisted him, then, with what were called Letters Patent, authorising any English subjects who were so disposed, to enter into his service, and aid his cause.

There was, at Bristol, a certain EARL RICHARD DE CLARE, called STRONGBOW; of no very good character; needy and desperate, and ready for anything that offered him a chance of improving his fortunes. There were, in South Wales, two other broken knights of the same good-for-nothing sort, called ROBERT FITZ-STEPHEN, and MAURICE FITZ-GERALD. These three, each with a small band of followers, took up Dermond's cause; and it was agreed that if it proved successful, Strongbow should marry Dermond's daughter EVA, and be declared his heir.

The trained English followers of these knights were so superior in all the discipline of battle to the Irish, that they beat them against immense superiority of numbers. In one fight, early in the war, they cut off three hundred heads, and laid them before Mac Murrough; who turned them every one up with his hands, rejoicing, and, coming to one which was the head of a man whom he had much disliked, grasped it by the hair and ears, and tore off the nose and lips with his teeth. You may judge from this, what kind of a gentleman an Irish King in those times was. The captives, all through this war, were horribly treated; the victorious party making nothing of breaking their limbs, and casting them into the sea from the tops of high rocks. It was in the midst of the miseries and cruelties attendant on the taking of Waterford, where the dead lay piled in the streets, and the filthy gutters ran with blood, that Strongbow married Eva. An odious marriage-company those mounds of corpses must have made, I think, and one quite worthy of the young lady's father.

He died, after Waterford and Dublin had been taken, and various successes achieved; and Strongbow became King of Leinster. Now came King Henry's opportunity. To restrain the growing power of Strongbow, he himself repaired to Dublin, as Strongbow's Royal Master, and deprived him of his kingdom, but confirmed him in the enjoyment of great possessions. The King, then, holding state in Dublin, received the homage of nearly all the Irish Kings and Chiefs, and so came home again with a great addition to his reputation as Lord of Ireland, and with a new claim on the favour of the Pope. And now, their reconciliation was completed – more easily and mildly by the Pope, than the King might have expected, I think.

CHAPTER SEVEN

The Superiority of the Irish Penal System

Partly, no doubt, as a result of his boyhood experiences of visiting his father in the Marshalsea Debtors' prison, Charles Dickens was fascinated by prisons and imprisonment throughout his career. In "American Notes" he records his impressions of several US prisons including the Boston House of Correction. He participated vigorously in the fierce contem-

The Trial (*Pickwick Papers*)

porary debate over types of prison systems. He strongly favoured the so-called "Silent Systems" as practised, for example, at the Middlesex House of Correction, Coldbath Fields. Under this system prisoners could work together and use the same dormitories, but they were forbidden to speak to one another or communicate in any other way; they were, therefore, under constant close surveillance day and night. Charles Dickens bitterly opposed the rival "Separate System" as practised most notably at Pentonville "Model" Prison, London. Under this system prisoners were kept in perpetual solitary confinement, emerging from their cells only for brief periods of exercise, or for religious or secular instruction. They had to wear masks or veils on such occasions to prevent their recognizing each other. They were encouraged to profess repentance and contrition which in the view of Charles Dickens and others simply promoted hypocrisy, hence his satire on "Model Prisoners" in *David Copperfield*, chapter 61.

As Dickens published the following article in *All the Year Round* it has to be concluded that he approved of the new Irish system of penal reform to some degree, or was at least willing to consider its merits.

THE IRISH CONVICT'S PROGRESS[1]

"In one of the Louvre galleries is to be seen a grim and ghastly piece of painting, which is usually encircled by a throng of admirers of the morbid. It represents a murderer flying over the earth with his bloody knife displayed conspicuously in his hand, while, from behind, an avenging and supernatural spirit presses on him closely, waving a spectral sword. The allegory typifies Crime pursued by Justice. It is of the grand French school; was bought by the nation; and has, no doubt, considerable merit.

It is valuable, however, apart from its pictorial excellence, as illustrating the popular ideal as regards crime and punishment in their relation to the community. If it dwells on the disagreeable subject at all – always distasteful and unpalatable – it is only in company with its appropriate antidote – punishment, full, sound, satisfactory, and substantial. Crime is one of the necessary corruptions of society; but society has within itself the sure arm of chastisement, which shall be thus a vindication of its outraged laws. This is the popular notion of crime and its repression.

*   *   *

All are agreed that the mere infliction of pain upon the evil-doer, by way of retaliation for pain that he inflicted, is a very minor matter in a great scheme

---

1. *All the Year Round*, 20 September 1862, pp. 31-37.

for suppression of crime. Jails, too, are now universally reformed – classification has been introduced, so that the whole mass shall not ferment, and all particles become equally leavened with the one corrupt principle. In short, prisoners now are punished, and reformed – re-formed in its strictest sense – made into new men. The prison was not to be merely a place of pain, but a crucible in which criminal dross could be skimmed away, and an innocent precipitate left to be sent forth at the proper time.

There was a sound principle recommending itself by reason and common sense – by economy both of time, and money, and morals – and by a hundred other advantages so obvious that it is marvellous how it escaped notice centuries back. Rather it did not so much escape notice; it suggested itself to the thoughtful and the good over and over again. But there existed then, as there exists now, that disinclination in the administration of the country, to be moved by the advice of those in the crowd, and who are unaccredited by office. And those to whom the memory of one Oliver Goldsmith is dear, and to whom the story of his Vicar is the sweetest reading for simplicity, pathos, quaintness, poetry, and humour, will not be surprised to find that the wise and humane notions of our day in reference to prisons are distinctly set forth in this precious little romance. A century ago, all but three years...Oliver Goldsmith, whose serious speeches were a source of infinite amusement to his facetious friends, wrote the famous prison scene in the Vicar, wherein is set out what should be the principle for dealing with crime.

The true principle being at last recognised, some progress was made. But in England we were not yet even at the beginning. The best intentions will not alone ensure success. It was indeed decreed that criminals should be reformed; but the procedure for that purpose was a great science, in which it was fancied that we were skilled, but of which we did not know even the rudiments. The utopian idea of reformation began and ended with a perfect jail. The old cesspools were scavengered out and levelled. Enormous sums were sunk in costly prison palaces, and architects ran riot in ingenious devices of separate cells, galleries, lanes radiating from a centre like the spokes of a large wheel. Convicts were experimented on with ingenious devices – made into imitations of the misericordia society at Florence, by wearing caps with eye-holes in them, and were pampered in a substantial basis of good sound diet – the very best per contract. . . . And no doubt certain gross things being swept away did produce amelioration. The herding of criminal cattle together in one indiscriminate shed was no more; and thus those who were but partially tainted were prevented from becoming utterly rotten by contamination. But still, on looking for facts as a test of the efficacy of the new system in turning criminals into innocent members of society, it is ascertained beyond a doubt that a large proportion of arrested evil-doers, are old offenders. There is a suspicion abroad that tickets-of-leave are no more than letters of marque.

This is scarcely cheering as the result of a system on which enthusiasm, earnestness, money, and the labour of good men, have been lavished. And yet it is a little remarkable that in a contiguous island there has also been at work a new prison system, in which costly jails, separate systems, galleries, wheel-spoke promenades, and the rest, have their place; but with this difference: that these elements are not considered the reform of the prisoners. They are not the system, but adjuncts of the system. And the remarkable result of the practice in the island alluded to, is this:

That out of every Hundred Criminals discharged as reformed, only ten return on a Fresh Conviction

This comes of no other than the famous Irish convict system, worked and perfected on the basis of Captain Machonochie's plan, by its zealous prophet Sir Walter Crofton, of which shall be given a detailed account.

We may suppose for a moment that the English judges of assize are on their rounds. We will suppose, also, that Messrs. Sheppard and Wild, two professionals of eminence, have been satisfactorily convicted, and just 'put forward' to hear their respective sentences. Mr John Sheppard has entered a house 'burglariously', and is 'impressively' sentenced to seven years' penal servitude. Mr Wild, who has beaten a fellow-creature with a bludgeon to within a hair's-breadth of murder, is also impressively consigned to fifteen years' penal servitude – a sentence acknowledge by that gentleman with an easy and familiar leer.

About the same time we may assume that the Irish judges are busy with their task of sifting and filtering the calendar, and that Messrs. Murphy and Callaghan, two offenders, are 'set forward' to receive sentence. Mr Murphy is consigned to a duress of seven years, like his English brother, but in the case of Mr Callaghan, even at this early stage, something testifies to the excellence of the Irish system; for the jail governor steps forward with a tabulated form, which states that Mr Callaghan has been a previous offender, and in consequence receives the severe penalty of fifteen years. This profitable result, the true test of gauging the punishment by the offence, has been arrived at through the machinery of the perfect Irish police organisation; for, on the arrest of every prisoner who has the slightest appearance of familiarity with his calling, either a photographic portrait, or a sort of 'signalement' of the minutest description, is forwarded to Dublin Castle, and by careful indexes the offender is hunted down in the books of the convicts' prisons . . .

We shall first trace the progress of Messrs. Murphy and Callaghan through their various stages of reformation; and it will be seen whether, without any reference to results, the system recommends itself.

Messrs. Murphy and Callaghan are presently brought to Dublin, from whatever quarter of the country they may have had their trial in, and are conducted to a huge fortress-like building, situate in a healthy suburb, and whose quality is marked out with a fatal distinctness by the huge tower-like pair of chimneys which rise in the centre of every model jail. This is the Mountjoy Prison, where, what may be called, the annealing process takes place. It is felt that, with the criminal native fresh from crime, and inflamed and resentful at the punishment just inflicted, it would be idle attempting any experiments through mere moral appeals; and this, too, becomes precisely the time when the penal portion, or physical suffering with which to a certain degree every crime should be visited, may be fitly applied. Accordingly, here the wholesome terrors of the silent system, and the separate system, are put in force. It is conceded even by its most determined opponents, that the effect of this treatment, if not efficacious for reformation, is at least sure and certain as a terrible deterrent – if anything, almost too severe: setting into operation, even at this gloomy stage of this famous Irish system, the secret and power of which lies not in this special point or that, but in a general leaven through the whole, seasoning every portion. The mystery lies in treating each prisoner as though he were the solitary tenant of the prison; and not as a vile single cast from a corrupt matrix, which has cast a thousand others precisely similar to himself. He is not held to be a number, or a name, an abstraction in pen and ink on the books of the establishment. But he is held to be a living man, with a soul, and with reason.

The ground being thus got ready by a very rude diet, and an utter deprivation of all interesting employment during the first three months, the system comes into play; and this, curiously enough, by explaining the system to him. It is impressed upon him – not in a cold, official fashion, but in free personal interviews, and by the means of lectures over and over again repeated, like a course of scholastic training – that the length or shortness of his imprisonment is to depend upon himself; that his prison existence is not to be one weary blank of monotony – the cheerless, unchanged interior of cell from the first day to the last – but a progressive ascent, marked by change and variety, improvement, moral and physical, encouragement and co-operation from superiors, and, finally, as just mentioned, an early and speedier enlargement. These advantages are enforced on him as entirely depending on his own conduct – not merely a negative observance of prison rules or sanctimonious demeanour – but a positive good behaviour under probation and trial and different circumstances. Daily it is instilled into him that there are to be stages in his probation, that it is actually possible for him to improve his condition – not at the end of six years' time, which would be so remote as to have, practically, little or no influence – but within the next eight or nine months, which is a point near enough to be a sufficient spur to hard labour. Thus, though Messrs. Murphy and Callaghan may have entered their separate cells full of a dogged scowling hostility, and a rooted conviction that governors and jailers were their natural enemies, it must gradually break on them that these odious officials are (for whatever object) strangely anxious to co-operate with them in improving their condition and shortening their imprisonment...

In their separate cells, then, Messrs. Murphy and Callaghan are yet to pick oakum for the first three months of their term. This labour is chosen as being of a monotonous and unintellectual sort. The diet is rough and low. After the three months the labour is changed to something of a sort where the mind can find some variety and a little interest, such as boot-closing, and the diet is improved. All, too, look forward to the shortening of that nine months into eight; and the result of this appeal either to the interest or better feelings of the criminals in the year eighteen hundred and sixty was, that out of two hundred and thirteen tenants of the prison, no fewer than one hundred and seventy were found not to have committed even the slightest breach of the rules, and thus shortened this portion of the punishment by a month.

Mr Murphy has possibly been refractory, and is, perhaps, detained to work out his ninth month. Mr Callaghan has been docile, possibly hypocritical, or has, perhaps, shrewdly seen that a change would be for his advantage. He is, therefore, removed after only eight months' residence. He has been in early life a labourer in the fields before he took to evil courses, so he is despatched to Spike Island. Or, he has been a skilled handicraftsman, and is sent to Philipstown – the tradesman's prison.

Spike Island is a huge convict depôt which, a few years back, was bursting with nearly three thousand convicts. Nature has bountifully laid it out, especially for prison treatment, and the Royal Engineers have made extensive fortifications heartily co-operate with nature. Mr Callaghan and Mr Murphy are set busily to work – quarrying, trimming and chipping stone, in excavations, and other severe 'hodman's work'. They are also put to carpenter's and smith's work, if they have any skill in that way. They are, moreover, taught the various trades of masons, carpenters, smiths, shoemakers – a practice common enough in other convict prisons; but which is here made an element of the system by being held out as a reward to the deserving and well conducted.

At this stage, sets in the 'mark' system on which it is scarcely necessary to dwell, being a matter of pure detail. The principle of a steady and gradual promotion – marked by nice shades – is carried out, and the convict is made to perceive the advantage by small but perceptible advantages, and is stimulated by a little personal distinction in the shape of badges, which proclaim his progress conspicuously. If he attain the highest number of marks – which is nine each month – twelve months successively, he steps into a superior class of this Spike Island stage – is kept apart from the common and more degraded herd, which is an appeal to his self-respect and pride, as though they were not worthy to associate with him; thus, in spite of himself, there is a sort of emulation excited, the fruits of which may at once be realised, in the shape of presents and tangible rewards – which, too, at the same time are helping him on to an abridgment of his term. . . .

With common criminals, when the day of enlargement arrives, the doors are flung open, and they are plunged again into the free world, as into the open sea. The shock must be about as sudden; especially after a long confinement of seven or fifteen years. The change from restraint to perfect liberty is enough to dislocate even better balanced organisations; and though perhaps the terrors of their late place of abode may be fresh, still it is found on experience that they are not sufficient. In the way of these is a Discharged Prisoners' Aid Society, which interposes between the late convict and these new dangers.

In the Irish system it is arranged, that the prisoner shall not be rudely plunged into freedom; but shall climb by graduated steps into that happy condition. So that almost before Messrs. Wild and Sheppard shall have been formally set free, they shall be actually enjoying – under certain precautions – a sort of liberty; a sort of amphibious state, where the good and well conducted shall be, practically speaking, almost as free as labouring men are, and where for those only who are inclined to be troublesome does anything like restraint arise. Such a place of probation may be accepted at once as eminently rational, but at the same time considered as utopian. On the wild common of Lusk, some twenty or thirty miles from Dublin, in view of a boisterous sea, is to be seen this strange spectacle of a prison which is yet no prison, and of physically free men who are yet morally prisoners.

On this wild common are the prisoners doing battle, and severe battle it is, with a stubborn soil. . . . Very different, too, this open-air husbandry to that prison work within the walls of a jail. For here there is no jail in sight, neither are there jailers. There is, indeed, an iron sleeping room not far away which may be moved about, and the workmen are watched over by one or two officers. Above all, they feel that they are earning their bread as day labourers, for they are paid by the week the sum of two shillings and sixpence. In the evenings, after the hard day's toils, some strange spectacles are witnessed on that wild bleak common. The men are seen gathered in one of the large huts round an intelligent lecturer, who twice a week gives them entertaining lectures on useful topics. To reading, which has been previously learnt, writing and arithmetic are now added; prizes are given; and such is the taste acquired, that the sixpence per week he is allowed out of his earnings often goes in a book.

Finally, Messrs. Murphy and Callaghan, having served in this intermediate stage, the one for two years, the other for fifteen months, and having conducted themselves with propriety, are informed that the glad day of their liberation is come, and are set free. Mr Murphy's term is thus shortened by twenty-one months, and Mr Callaghan's by five years. This is a result they have known from the beginning; they have worked their way to it, not through any grace or favour from authority, but through their own hard exertions, now creeping forward a little, now thrown back, but making steadily all the while for a fixed goal.

Though the fall has been broken, and we may reasonably conclude that our two enlarged convicts will do nothing to discredit their training, still it is felt that the public generally have a certain claim to protection, and that the institution which is so confident in its own results as to set prisoners free, should give some guarantee to the public for its safety: most of all, if that public be so confiding as to take these enlarged convicts into its service. Theoretically, then, we suppose them still in prison, and the excellent police organisation of Ireland keeps its eye upon them anxiously; yet not so as to harass. It is one of the strangest things in the world to walk round the great thoroughfare of Dublin and to hear whispered, by one in the secret, 'that man so busy scavengering is a fifteen years' convict; that man trowelling so neatly is a seven years' convict;' or to be taken through a great workshop and pointed out this man and that, of innocent and honest expression, as criminals whose sentences are not yet expired. Such the police note carefully. These 'leavers' must report themselves at stated intervals... So when any symptoms of back-sliding are visible – and these usually manifest themselves in no worse shape than a little drink – the offender is sent before one of the directors, who firmly but kindly admonishes. Finally, Messrs. Murphy and Callaghan being really and genuinely free, it will be found that their score of punishment stand thus:

> Mr Patrick Callaghan, 15 years.
> 8 months separate system.
> 7 years 4 months Spike Island.
> 2 years Intermediate P.
> 5 years at large under surveillance.
> So with Mr Murphy in proportion to his term.

CHAPTER EIGHT

Stories from around Ireland

Dickens's journals contain many articles of stories from around Ireland. This chapter contains three: Frank Finlay's 'A Deadly Mist', 'Irish Constabulary Constitution' and 'Clonmel Assizes' by anonymous authors.

A DEADLY MIST[1]

Frank Finlay was proprietor and editor of the Belfast *Northern Whig* – a leading Irish newspaper noted for its strong Unionist policy.

When Dickens, in August 1858, paid his first visit to Ireland Finlay was one of the prominent citizens of Belfast who welcomed the great novelist to the city and helped to make his readings there a success. From that time a cordial friendship was established between the two men and, for the next

The Ferry (*Little Dorrit*)

---

1.   *All the Year Round*, 13 November 1869, pp. 564-566.

eleven years, Finlay was a frequent guest at Dickens's Rochester home, Gad's Hill Place. Dickens published this short account of a strange, frightening experience which Finlay sent to him.

"Sunday morning by the sea. The early church bells going. A close sea-mist hanging heavily over the sands, and a baffled sun trying to make light of it, and failing. My window wide open, though sere October is growing old, and one long melancholy ripple of smooth sea wailing slowly along the shore. I have had a good breakfast, a fine romp with my children, and my wife is dressing for church. Everything with me is very calm and very happy; but only an hour ago I was in mortal peril of my life, and, instead of being in this pleasant room, with the voices of my little children outside breaking on my ear, and with the wash of the wave on the beach below my window setting a bass to their sweet treble, I might have been at this moment floating white and stiff on the still sea, with the thick mist hanging around me, and this world's loves and cares over with me for ever.

One hour ago, only an hour, I went out, as usual, to bathe. The sands run up to my very windows, and the high tides sometimes touch the little wall that stands in front, so that I can often walk from my own hall-door into the water at a few yards' distance. But this morning the tide was dead out, and a heavy sea-fog was lying all over the sands, so that I could not see where the water and the land joined. I had not gone twenty yards until, looking back, I saw my house looming through the fog, quite altered in appearance, and, though much larger, still much more distant than usual. In a few more steps I lost it altogether. I soon came to the water's edge, took off my overall, and laid it on a flat stone: the only stone I could see, for there are no rocks. The sea was dead calm and I had to wade a long way out before I got deep enough for a plunge, after which I began to swim. The water was not too cold, there was not even a languid heave on its surface, and I struck out, enjoying the free motion, until I began to feel tired. I am a bad swimmer, and had never knowingly gone out of my depth. Dropping my feet I found myself up to the neck, and I then suddenly perceived that I was closely encircled by a dense mist, and was utterly at a loss to know which way the shore lay. The tide, I knew, was rising fast. I could not trust myself to swim, lest I should be swimming out to sea, instead of towards the land. I made a step or two in one direction, then in another, but always seemed to be getting deeper. Then, like a sudden blow, came upon me the full sense of my situation. here I was, opposite my own door, where my wife and little children were waiting for me, within perhaps two hundred yards of dry land, dangerously deep in the water, and helplessly unable to find my way out.

The peril was imminent. I must have been, I now think, on the top of a low bank of sand, and, though shallow water and safety must have been within twenty yards of me, I could not, to save my life, tell which way to turn. It flashed on me that I should be drowned: drowned quietly and surely, within gun-shot of my home; and that the flowing tide, there being no current and no wind, would float my dead body up, and leave it on the sands before my door. The danger was terrible: yet there was no hurry. The tide was rising fast, but I could not be drowned for at least ten minutes, and I had that time before me to do what I could with. . . .

I stood quite still, and looked to see if there were any ripple of current against my neck that would show the inflow of the tide. There was none. I held up my wet arm to feel for a wind. There was not a breath. I strained my ears to hear any noise – the barking of a dog, voices on the land, the crowing of cocks, anything that would answer the, to me, tremendous question, Where is the shore?

Not a sound. The stillness was awful and horrible. To shout for help was the last resort; but I would not spend my strength in that, until I had tried everything else; and I knew, besides, that being a Sunday morning, and the sands deserted, there would be neither boat nor boatman on the shore. I remembered, too, that voices in a fog almost always seem to change their direction, and that they mislead those who come in search. Steadily and without noise the tide rose up, until the water reached my chin. I was perfectly collected, and endeavoured to recall all I had read of similar emergencies, tried back in my memory to find, if I could, some chance for life that some one else in deadly peril had risked and won. Holding my breath, and laying my ear close to the water, I strained every nerve of hearing in vain; but where the one sense on which I was depending failed me, another came to my rescue. Between the dense mist and the water, there seemed to be about an inch of interval, and through this chink, as it were, I saw the dusky base of a stone beacon which I knew stood out in the sea, nearly opposite my house... I struck out and swam to the beacon, where I laid hold of an iron bar which served to stay it to the rock below.

When the momentary exultation was over, I found I was not much better off than before. I had the beacon to hold to, and could even climb to the top, which was still a foot above the surface of the sea; but I know it would be covered deep at half tide. Still here was more time gained; and the fear of death, or I should rather say, the settled assurance without fear, passed from me. Climbing to the top of the beacon, I tried if I could look out over the mist, but it was thicker than ever. Now came a curious illustration of the extraordinary closeness together of what we are accustomed to consider as our most opposed mental and moral emotions . . . I had been as near my death as ever I shall be until the end does come; yet I was so suddenly struck with the absurdity of my appearance – a naked man perched like a crane on a stone beacon in a white fog – that I burst into a roar of laughter.

Like an arrow through the mist came the quick bark of a terrier, followed by a cry of 'Papa!' It was my little daughter's voice. She and Snap had gone down to the beach to look for me, had found my overall, and were quietly waiting beside it. . . . With a glad heart I dropped off the beacon, and, after swimming a few strokes, found my feet on firm land once again."

*   *   *

IRISH CONSTABULARY CONSTITUTION[2]

The Irish Constabulary (Royal Irish Constabulary from 1867) was established by Sir Robert Peel between 1812 (when he was Chief Secretary for Ireland) and 1836. "It became the blueprint for later colonial police forces throughout the British Empire" (Foster).

"The Irish constabulary force is entirely recruited from amongst the peasantry of the country – chiefly from the farming classes. If a small farmer have three or four sons – too many ever to make a comfortable living off the few acres of land – one or more of them arranges to enter the constabulary. Many features connected with the force tend to make it exceedingly popular. There is always at least one married man at each rural station, or barrack, whose wife and family, mixing with the peasantry, in reality form a portion of it. The younger men are general favourites with the farmers' daughters of the district, and to marry a constabulary private is no sinking of caste. The life of a constable is, on the whole, attractive. There is all the military paraphernalia which turns the heads of many of both sexes, and none of the drawbacks attending a solder's life. There is no fixed term of service – every man can resign on giving one calendar month's notice; there is no absence from home and country; no mixing with the scum of society.

I joined the force when I was but nineteen years of age. At the time I was private tutor to a magistrate's family in the west of Ireland, and had before me prospects of doing much better than any profession of arms could offer. But drilled I must be, and enlist as a private soldier I would not. Without the knowledge of my parents or of the gentleman whose sons I was instructing, I proceeded to the county town, armed with testimonials as to character and respectability from the parish clergyman and a deputy-lieutenant of the county. I repaired with these necessary documents to the office of the county inspector of the constabulary in my native county. I was not long delayed in the office. I was asked to read and write, and only a few words were required of

---

2.   *All the Year Round*, April 15, 1867, pp. 375–377.

me in either case – though my handwriting would not now pass muster in a solicitor's office. But the only ordeal which I dreaded came at length. It was necessary that I should be five feet eight inches in height, and, although I had measured myself repeatedly before I left for the county town, yet I feared I would fall short... I divested myself of my shoes and stockings at the bidding of a sergeant, who acted as clerk to the county inspector, and I then stepped lightly under the standard. What with stretching my neck and straightening myself up as well as I could, the standard ran up to five feet eight and a quarter inches. The inspector good humouredly remarked that I had 'a whole quarter of an inch to spare, and a young man who had just gone out would gladly buy it from me, if it could be readily disposed of.' My predecessor had proved a quarter of an inch short, and was sent home to 'grow it'. . . .

On the first of the ensuing month I presented myself at the Phoenix Park, Dublin, to undergo four or five months' drill, with the following regulation outfit: two suits of plain clothes, with a sufficiency of shirts, socks, boots, and other garments. I was duly sworn in as a sub-constable, or 'full private', engaging to belong to no secret society, except the society of Freemasons. This latter clause is as a special protection against Orangeism, Ribbonism, Fenianism, and all illegal secret organisations.

The department in the Phoenix park is a large military institution. It is under the supreme command of a colonel from the army... The department is beautifully situated in the vicinity of the vice-regal lodge in the park; which forms one of the most splendid drill-grounds in Europe or perhaps in the world. The cavalry and infantry departments are in the same barrack. All the proceedings in connexion with the department are exactly the same as in any large military barrack. . . . There is only this difference between the constabulary department and the military department, that the greatest stranger to Ireland will be the first to observe, that while the occupants of the barrack in Phoenix Park look like the 60th Rifles in dress and drill, and will be taken at first sight for light infantry of the line, yet their manner, their language, and their intelligence in conversation, remove them far above the standard of the ordinary soldier.

The period of drill having expired, the effective men are told off to different counties; one strict rule being observed, that no man is to be sent to his native county, lest there might be local temptations to breaches of the 'no favour' clause of the constabulary oath. The training of the whole force in one central department, from which they are scattered north, south, east, and west, and to which they occasionally return on receiving promotion, and under other circumstances, tends greatly to foster an esprit du corps amongst the thousands of which the force is composed. The four constables that the traveller meets with in an isolated roadside barrack in the mountains of Ireland do not feel that there are only four of them. They hardly ever fully realise this. They are four of a great force of between eleven thousand and twelve thousand well-disciplined men, under the command of one inspector-general, and with one great drill-centre in the Phoenix Park and commanding centre in the Castle of Dublin. The four apparently isolated men know where every station, or barrack, in their own and the adjoining counties, is situated, and that even in times like the present they could not be long left without relief, if able to hold out for but a short time against an attacking force...

The chief office is in the Lower Castle Yard, Dublin, and between it and the department in the park hourly intercourse is kept up by mounted order-lies, and between it and the counties by daily despatches. Each county inspector is responsible for the discipline and good order of the force in his county, or riding of a county, and he only communicates direct with The Castle.

The duties of the constabulary are multifarious. They act as an ordinary police force throughout the country. They attend elections, assizes, races, fairs, and markets, to preserve the peace. In cities and towns like Cork, Limerick, and Belfast, they perform regular police duties, singly on beats. They also dress in 'plain clothes', to act as detectives. They arrest criminals. They collect agricultural statistics. They suppress illicit distilleries. They look after poachers of game and salmon. They take the census at each decade. They deliver and collect the voting-papers for the elections of poor-law guardians annually. In fact there is scarcely an act of parliament in reference to the civil government of Ireland with which the constabulary have not some duty to perform. They are, besides all this as civil servants, an admirable military force, as their actions prove in suppressing Smith O'Brien's 'rebellion of '48' and their most recent discharge of military duties in suppressing the Fenian rebellion. Their courage and skill at Tallaght, eight miles from Dublin, with fourteen men, under Sub-Inspector Bourke, dispersed five hundred or more armed Fenians, and actually captured sixty-five stragglers in flight; their spirited defence at Kilmallock, under Head Constable Adams, when the same number of men kept a barrack under a three hours' fire from a Fenian force commanded by the officer of the late army of America, and when the barrack contained three women and thirteen children – the wives and children of the constables – prove them to be no mean soldiers.

When the loyalty, or disloyalty, of Ireland is discussed, it would be well to bear in mind that the constabulary fairly represent the great mass of the populace of the country. The force is about divided into two-thirds Roman Catholic and one-third Protestant: this again truly represents the country. I have myself been the only Protestant in a party of six in a country station in a parish in Connemara. With all these matters I never knew religious difference to exist amongst this force; although the men are individually strict observers of their own religious duties, and the most regular attendants at church. They thus set an example to their countrymen, who are too often found to quarrel about creeds. . . .

Many of the constabulary improve themselves greatly in education after they leave the department. In country stations they frequently study closely in leisure hours. They are, as a rule, well read in the current literature of the day, and I knew several fair classical scholars in the force . . . and others who understood more than one continental tongue.

How are these men paid? When I joined, I received one pound nineteen shillings a month for the first six months, and two pounds five shillings a month afterwards, with an increase of three-halfpence a day when I had served two years. This, with barrack accommodation and uniform, formed my entire remuneration. The pay of the non-commissioned officers and officers was in proportion. Last year an act of parliament was passed to increase their pay; but as the cost of living has greatly increased of late years, I do not think the men are better off than in my years of service. The promotion is slow, because of the sub-inspectors not being taken from the ranks of the force. To make the constabulary still more effective, officers ought to be promoted from the ranks, and not have, as at present, raw cadets placed over experienced first-class head constables."

* * *

CLONMEL ASSIZES[3]

Clonmel ("meadow of honey") in Co. Tipperary is situated in the Golden Vale on the River Suir valley in southern Ireland. It developed as a Norman town in the 12th century. Laurence Sterne (1713-1768) author of *A Sentimental Journey* was born there.

Agrarian unrest and outrage were a dominant feature of Irish civil and political life in the 19th century until Gladstone's Land Acts of the 1880s.

"The Clonmel assizes opened in the spring of 1828, with the usual ceremonies. Till half a century before, the Irish Bar, when on circuit, travelled on horseback. The crown prosecutor, rejoicing in a good jailful; the leading chiefs, their saddle-bags brimming with record briefs; the gay and sanguine juniors, reckless and light-hearted, came riding into the town the day before the assizes, in as close order as a regiment of cavalry, holsters in front of their saddles, overcoats strapped in tight rolls behind, mounted servants following with saddle-bags full of black gowns and law-books, barefooted suttlers tramping behind with stores of wine and groceries. A mile or so from the town, the gentlemen of the grand jury came riding out to vociferously welcome the new-

---

3.   *All the Year Round*, "Notable Irish Assizes", Vol. 30, 1867, pp. 595–600.

comers. But in '28 the barristers stole down in the mail one by one, and the picturesqueness of the old entry had all disappeared.

The principal trial of the assize of 1828 was that of the assassins of Daniel Mara, a man who had been condemned to death by the secret societies that were then, and still are, the curse of Ireland, for having brought to justice the murderer of a land-agent named Chadwick. . . .

Mr. Chadwick was the collector of rents or steward for an influential family who had property near the old abbey of Holy Cross. He was not peculiarly hard or rigorous with the smaller holders, nor was he a hard-hearted man; but he was overbearing and contemptuous to the peasantry, and used to tell them boastingly that he 'fattened upon their curses.' The country-people, while brooding over their hatred for this man, used to craftily reply on such occasions that 'his honour was mighty pleasant; and sure his honour, God bless him, was always fond of his joke.' The poor oppressed people had acquired the Indian's craft and the Indian's unrelenting thirst for revenge. At last Chadwick, who feared nothing, carried his repressions to too daring a pitch. He began building a police-barrack at Rath common, that was to be a sort of outlying fort to repress the insolence and turbulence of the disaffected people. The secret tribunal of the Tipperary village then resolved that he should die. A reckless, handsome lad, named Patrick Grace, offered himself as the executioner, and was accepted. Relying on the universal sympathy, the lad came to Rath Common, in open day, on the public road, and close to the barrack, where passengers were perpetually passing, he shot Mr. Chadwick dead, and left him weltering in his blood. This murder spread dismay and horror throughout Ireland, showing as it did the daring ferocity of the secret tribunals and the sympathy shown their agents by the great mass of the peasantry. All this time Grace remained bold and careless, conscious of the sure secrecy and power of the confederacy to which he belonged, and whose murderous work he had done. But he miscalculated, for a worthy man, named Mara, who saw the shot fired, and who stood near Chadwick at the time, gave immediate information, and Grace was at once arrested and tried at the Clonmel summer assizes of 1827. . . . The gibbet for Grace was erected close to the abbey of Holy Cross, and near the scene of the murder. Patrick was escorted to the last scene of his short life by a body of troops, and fifteen thousand awe-struck people assembled round the scaffold. To the surprise and disappointment of the peasantry, their martyr, though showing no fear of death, expressed himself contrite, and implored the spectators to take warning by his example. While the body of the poor lad still swung in the air, his gloves were handed by one of his relations as a keepsake to an old man, a friend of Patrick's, named John Russell, who, drawing them on, swore at the same time that he would never take them off 'till Paddy Grace was revenged.'

Philip Mara, knowing his life would certainly be taken, was sent out of

Tipperary by the government; but the peasantry, true Arabs in revenge, then resolved to exterminate his kindred. His three brothers, all masons working at the new barrack, were doomed to death. . . . On the 1st of October, 1827, the three brothers struck work about five o'clock, and descended from the scaffold to return homeward. Suddenly eight men rushed upon them, and fired a volley. The guns were old, and the volley did not take effect. Two of the brothers and an apprentice escaped in different directions, but Daniel Mara, the third brother, lost his presence of mind, and ran for shelter into the house of a poor widow. He was hotly pursued. One murderer got in after him through a small window; the seven others burst open the door, and savagely put him to a cruel death. This crime caused a greater sensation than even the death of Chadwick, and struck a deep terror through the length and breadth of Ireland. The government instantly offered a reward of two thousand pounds for the assassins; but of the hundreds of accomplices none would betray the eight murderers.

At last, through the personal exertions on the spot of Mr. Doherty, the solicitor-general, a highway robber named Fitzgerald, who was cast for death in the Clonmel jail, offered to furnish evidence to government if his own life was saved. Two men, named Patrick Lacy and John Walsh, were at once arrested, and on the 31st of March, 1828, tried at the Clonmel assizes for the murder of Daniel Mara.

The prisoners, careless of the evidence of a mere 'stag' or informer, always regarded by juries with suspicion, remained firm and composed. Lacy was a tall handsome young man, with a good colour and a clear calm eye. He was dressed with extreme care, his white hands were loosely bound together. Walsh, a far more harmless man, was a sturdy, square-built fellow, with firm and rather a fierce look. The prisoners seemed to entertain little apprehension till Mr. Doherty suddenly rose, turned to the dock, shook his lifted hand, and called 'Kate Costello.'

This woman was the witness on whose reluctant evidence the whole case for the prosecution turned. The case up to her appearance stood thus: Fitzgerald and Lacy had been sent for from a distance by Paddy Grace's relatives to do 'the job'. The band was formed, and the ambuscade laid; but something defeating their plans, the murder was adjourned for another week. On Sunday, the 30th of September, another band of assassins was collected, and they met at the house of a farmer, named John Keogh, living near the barrack on which the Maras were at work; here they were waited on by Keogh's poor relation and servant, Kate Costello. On the morning of Monday, the 10th of October, the conspirators proceeded to a wooded hill, called 'the grove', above the barracks, where their fire-arms had been hidden. There fresh men joined them, and Kate Costello brought them food and whisky. They remained hiding there till five o'clock, when it was announced that the Maras were coming down from the scaffolding and going home. The men then came down from the grove and murdered Daniel Mara, as we have seen. With their hands still red with an innocent man's blood, these ruffians went to the house of a respectable, orderly farmer, named John Russell. He gave the red-handed men welcome, and placed food before them. . . .

The first witness that leaped on the table was Fitzgerald, the robber, a fine athletic young men of about three-and-twenty. . . . He proved a most methodical and exact witness, detailing his actions for a whole month with great accuracy. This man had been in the habit of robbing by night the very peasants, whose outrages he at other times put himself forward to redress. He entered farm-houses armed, and demanded board and lodging. By day he would often compel passing travellers to kneel down to him while he presented a musket at their heads. Yet with all this he was chivalrous in many things, and was a favourite with the peasantry. He was especially anxious to assure the spectators that he had not sold the cause for gold, but simply to save his own neck.

When Fitzgerald had finished, there was a great anxiety in the court about the appearance of Kate Costello. The friends of the prisoners began to believe 'that she would never turn against her people'; but suddenly the door of the witness-room opened, and a little withered woman entered, and tottered to the table. Her hands were white and clammy; her eyes closed; her long black hair was dishevelled; and her head drooped on her shoulder. Her voice was an almost inarticulate whisper, and she almost swooned and could not be recovered till she was sprinkled with water. The rod used to identify prisoners was then put into her hands, and she was desired to turn to the dock, and to point out the murderers she had seen in the grove.

Walsh, one of the prisoners... begged the judge to allow other prisoners to be put with him and Lacy in the dock, in order to test the witness more severely. The judge instantly acquiesced in this demand. The jail being at some distance, some time was lost in this delay, and during this time Kate Costello sank back in her chair apparently almost lifeless.

It was about four o'clock in the morning, and the candles were burning low in their sockets, when the band of prisoners entered the court, astonished and alarmed at the sudden summons. The only sound was the clank of the fetters and the grounding of the soldiers' brass bound muskets on the pavement. Again Kate Costello rose with the fatal index-rod in her hand. The face of Walsh was wrung with the intensest anxiety, and some women among the spectators exclaimed: 'Oh Kate!' – a passionate adjuration that seemed to thrill her to the heart. It was not Walsh or Lacy that she cared for, but her own kinsmen, who were also accomplices, and shortly to be tried. She herself had been threatened with death unless she disclosed the truth. If she did disclose it, her life was also in peril. Terrible alternative! At last she advanced towards the dock, raised the trembling rod a second time, and laid it on the head of Walsh. . . .

Walsh, who, while there was hope, had been convulsed with agitation, now became calm and composed as his landlord came forward and gave him a high character for integrity and good conduct. Both prisoners were at once found guilty.

Kate's relations, Patrick and John Keogh, were tried a few days after the execution of Lacy and Walsh. It was rumoured that John had been Kate's lover, and that, though he had deserted her, she would not take his life away or betray 'her people.' The Keoghs had been the chief planners and actors in the murder of Mara, with whom they had been intimate... This time Kate Costello's manner was entirely changed; she had taken the first step, and now she did not falter. She kept her quick shrewd eyes wide open and fixed upon the counsel, and she watched the cross-examination with a keen wary vigilance. She exhibited no compunction, and without apparent regret laid the rod on the heads of her relative and her lover. Early on Sunday morning the verdict of guilty was brought in. The prisoners, the day before blooming with health, were now white as shrouds. The judge told them that, as it was Easter Sunday, he should delay passing sentence.

Old John Russell pleaded guilty at the bar, in the hope of saving his sons, lads of fifteen or sixteen. 'Let them,' he kept saying, 'put me on the trap, if they like, but do let them spare the boys.' These assizes lasted three weeks, nearly all the cases being connected with agrarian outrages. There was scarcely one example of a murder committed for mere gain.

It was at these same assizes, at which three hundred and eighty persons were tried, that one of the murderers of the Sheas was tried. This outrage was one of the most inhuman that ever took place in Ireland, and is still talked of in Tipperary with peculiar horror. The crime dated back to the year 1821. In November of that year, a respectable farmer, named Patrick Shea, who had lately turned out of his farm an under-tenant, named William Gorman, came to live in the house left vacant by the eviction. It was situated in a dark gloomy glen, at the foot of the misty and bleak mountain of Slievenamawn, and, on a clear day, it was just visible from the high road through the narrow defile of Glenbower.

On Saturday, 18 November, a man of evil character, named William Maher, came to a low shibbeen near the mountain, kept by a man and woman named Kelly, of infamous character. These people sold spirits without a licence, and their house was a well-known resort of bad characters of both sexes. Maher, who was the paramour of Kelly's wife, retired to a recess in the house (probably that used for secret distilling), and melting some lead, ran it into musket bullets. The woman, having heard the 'boys' were going to inflict summary justice on the Sheas, for being so harsh to Gorman, whom they had driven out penniless, and without covert or shelter, and being sure Maher would be in the business, taxed him with it, and, having some good instincts left, besought him not to take away life. Maher answered with equivocations. The bullets were scarcely finished before a newly married servant of the Sheas, Catherine Mullaly, a cousin of Mary Kelly, came in. Maher, who knew Catherine, began bantering her in the Irish way, and the girl joined heart and soul in the repartees. Maher's aim was to discover if the Sheas' house, which was well garrisoned, contained any store of firearms.

The girl, pleased with his attentions, gradually disclosed to Maher the fact that the Sheas had a great many muskets and pistols, and when she left Maher put on her cloak for her, and bade her farewell as a friend. Mary Kelly, who knew the wretch better, the moment the door closed on Catherine, implored Maher whatever was done, not to harm that poor girl. He promised, and soon after quitted the house with the bullets, leaving Mary Kelly confident of the safety of Catherine. But, nevertheless, the next day her fears revived when she heard Maher and some mysterious whispering men, who dropped into the shibbeen that day after mass talking under breath.

Mary knew that 'a word would have been as much as her life was worth,' so she did not speak of it even to her husband; but on the Monday night, when he was asleep, stole out of bed, slipped on his coat, and made her way cautiously and slowly under the loose stone walls and hedges to the vicinity of Maher's house. She stopped, for she could hear voices. At length the door opened, and she hid herself behind some brambles as the murderers came out. They passed her, armed and in file; eight faces and eight voices she recognised. One of the eight carried two long lighted sods of turf which he kept alive by his breath. They did not see her, and passed on. Trembling and terror-stricken, but still magnetically drawn, she followed them from hedge to hedge, till they outstripped her on the path to the Sheas' house. From where she stood the farmhouse was visible. As she looked, a fire leaped out of the roof, ran over the thatch, and instantly rose into a pyramid of flame, for the wind was high that night; the whole glen grew crimson. The door was barricaded by the murderers. Not one of the Sheas escaped. Shrieks and cries for mercy rose from the seventeen burning wretches within. The conspirators yelled with laughter, whooped for joy, and discharged guns and blunderbusses to celebrate and announce their triumph. Then came a silence, and after that, when the wind abated for a moment, Mary Kelly could hear the deep groans of the dying, and low moans of agony, as the fire spread fiercer to complete its horrible task. At every fresh groan the monsters discharged their guns in fiendish jubilee.

A friend of the Sheas, named Phillip Hill, who lived on the opposite side of the hill adjoining the house, heard the guns echoing in Slievenamawn, and, arousing his friends, made across, if possible, to save the Sheas. These men arrived too late; nor did they dare to attack the murderers, who drew up at once to meet them. . . .

John Butler, a boy who had a brother in the Sheas' house, had accompanied Hill, and, eager to discover the murderers, approached nearer than the rest to the fire, and by its light recognised William Gorman. The murderers returned by the same way as they came, and were again observed by Mary Kelly from her hiding-place. The wretches as they passed her were rejoicing over their success, and William Gorman, with detestable and almost incredible inhumanity, was actually amusing the party by mimicking the groans of the dying, and mocking the agonies he and his comrades had inflicted.

The morning beginning to break, Mary Kelly, haggard and affrighted, returned home with her terrible secret; but she did not breathe a word either to her husband or her son, and the next day, when taken before a magistrate, denied all knowledge of the crime.

John Butler also went back to the house of his mother – an old woman – and, waking her, told her that her son had been burnt alive with all in the Sheas' house. The old woman uttered a wail of grief, but, instead of immediately proceeding to a magistrate, she enjoined her son not to ever disclose the secret, lest she and all their family should meet the same fate.

The next day, all that side the county gathered round the ruins. Mary Kelly was among them, and no doubt many of the murderers. The sight was a fearful one, even to those innocent of the crime. Of the roof only the charred rafters were left; the walls were gaping apart; the door was burned to its hinges, close by it lay sixteen corpses, piled together: those who were uppermost were burned to the very bones; those below were only partially consumed. The melted flesh had run from the carcases in black streams along the scorched floor. The first thought of all had been to run to the door.

Poor Catherine Mullaly's fate was the most horrible and most touching of all. In the midst of the flames she had been prematurely delivered of a child – that unhappy child, born only to instantly perish, was the eighteenth victim. In trying to save her child, she had placed it in a tub of water, where it was found, with the head burned away, but the body perfect. Near the tub lay the blackened body of the mother, her skeleton arm hanging over the water. The spectators beheld the sight with dismay, but they were afraid to speak...

For sixteen months Mary Kelly kept the secret. She did not dare to reproach Maher, who constantly visited her house, and yet she shuddered at his approach. Gradually her mind began to yield to the pressure. She became incapable of sleep, and used, in the dead of the night, to rise and wander over the glen, remaining by the black ruins of the Sheas' house till morning, and then returning, worn and weary, to her home. . . . At length conscience grew stronger and drove away fear. She revealed her secret in confession, and the priest, like a good and honest man, prevailed upon her to give instant information to Captain Despard, a justice of peace for the county of Tipperary.

It was not till 1827 that William Gorman was apprehended and put upon his trial. There is no doubt that Shea, the middleman, had been cruel and oppressive to Gorman, his under-tenant. He had retaliated upon him the severities of the superior landlord. Gorman had been distrained, sued in the superior courts, processed by civil bill, totally deprived of his farm, house, and garden, and then driven out, a disgraced beggar, to brood over vengeance.

A keen observer (we believe, the son of the celebrated Curran), who was present at this remarkable trial, has left a terrible picture of Gorman's appearance and manner as he stood at the Clonmel dock. 'He was evidently,' he says, 'most anxious for the preservation of his life; yet the expression of anxiety which disturbed his ghastly features occasionally gave way to the exulting consciousness of his revenge. As he heard the narration of his own delinquencies, so far from exhibiting contrition or remorse, a savage joy flashed over his face; his eyes were lighted up with a fire as lurid as that he had kindled in the habitation of his enemies; his hand, which had previously quivered and manifested, in the peculiar movement of his fingers, the workings of deep anxiety, became for a moment clenched; and when the groans of his victims were described, his white teeth, which were unusually prominent, were bared to the gums; and though he had drained the cup of vengeance to the dregs, still he seemed to smack his lips and to lick the blood with which his injuries had been redressed.'

Immediately after the conviction and execution of this monster, a large meeting of Roman Catholics was held at Clonmel to express horror at his crime, and to consider some means of removing the causes of such outrages. Mr. Sheil's speech to the peasantry produced an enormous sensation. 'How deep a stain,' he said, eloquently, 'have these misdeeds left upon the character of your country! and what effort should not be made by every man of ordinary humanity to arrest the progress of villainy which is rolling in a torrent of blood, and bearing down all the restraints of law and morality. Look, for example, at the murder of the Sheas, and tell me if there be anything in the records of horror by which that accursed deed has been excelled, and say, you who know it best, you who are of the same sex as Catherine Mullaly, what must have been the throes with which she brought forth her unfortunate offspring, and felt her infant consumed by the fire with which she was surrounded. We can but lift up our hands to the God of justice and ask Him why He has invested us with the same forms as the demons who perpetrated that unexampled murder!. . . .' "

* * *

LOUGH DERG[4]

Lough Derg ("the red lake") is a small, lovely lake in the mountains of south Donegal in the northwest of Ireland. Lough Derg was internationally celebrated in the later Middle Ages as the place of St Patrick's Purgatory, a cave where Patrick was said to have fasted for 40 days and to have had a vision of the Otherworld. It was believed that any properly disposed pilgrim entering the cave might, by St Patrick's help, himself behold the horrors of purgatory and hell. Pilgrims came to Lough Derg for this purpose – even from distant lands. After the cave was blocked up in the 17th century the site of the pilgrimage was moved to Station Island (a half mile offshore in the southern part of the lake).

If you wear a handkerchief tied on your head, you'll be able to pass everywhere without question.

"I declining, however, to adopt this counterfeit presentment of a pilgrim, my companion resumed, 'You will at least be careful not to show any disrespect, nor pry too much into what you may see going on around you?'

I assured him, that to insult my neighbours in their conscientious observances, was what I should be sorry to do, and, furthermore, promised to restrain my curiosity within moderate bounds; whereupon we made arrangements to visit together that celebrated place of Roman Catholic pilgrimage existing on an island in Lough Derg, County Donegal, Ireland; to which as many as fifteen thousand people are said to have repaired to do penance in a season (extending from the first of June to the fifteenth of August in each year), though it is calculated that the numbers of pilgrims, during the season of 1850, is not likely to exceed six thousand.

After a drive of about two hours' duration, chiefly along the shore of Lough Erne... we turned northwards, and, passing through the village of Pettigo, entered upon a bleaker region, where the road became gradually worse, the huts poorer and less frequent, the patches of oats more scraggy and unfenced, and the land boggier and browner; until at last the view on every side presented nothing but dark stony hills, with marsh at their feet, and rough heather on their sides, among which lay here and there a very few miserable cottages, scarcely distinguishable from the weather-beaten rocks and crooked clumps of turf which were scattered about these cheerless uplands.

Leaving our jaunting-car at a hovel by the road-side, we proceeded on foot towards the Holy Lake, which was about a mile distant.

---

4. *Household Words*, "The Irish Stationers", October 5, 1850, pp. 29–33.

We had previously passed many pilgrims going to, and returning from, it, and now soon fell into company and conversation with three women, each barefoot and carrying the usual staff in her hand and small bundle on her shoulders. They had walked about sixty miles, performing on their way part of the required penance, as is permitted in certain cases. Those who do thus are said to 'bring their fast in with them.' These pilgrims, however, had made but a short journey in comparison with others; some of whom reached the Lough from the remotest southern corners of Ireland, others (but these of course not on foot) from various parts of England and Scotland, and some even from America. It was by no means an unusual thing, I was assured, that a person should cross the broad Atlantic for the single purpose of 'making the stations' here. In most of such instances, and indeed in many of the others, the pilgrimage is undertaken in discharge of vows made during sickness.

The Lough soon unfolded itself to our sight; an irregular sheet of water that seemed about two miles across, surrounded by a waving circle of wild brown hills. Several green islands were strewn on its surface; but a small fleet of whitewashed houses, jumbled together 'stem and stern,' which appeared to float on the water about half-a-mile from the shore where we stood, soon monopolised our attention. These edifices are, in reality, built upon the Station island, almost hiding it from view (its dimensions being probably no more than one hundred yards by forty), and comprise two Chapels, the Prior's house, and five lodging-houses. At the end of the pilgrim-season the island is altogether deserted.

On the small scrap of ground unbuilt upon near the centre of the Island rose a solitary tree; and round this, and across by the wall of one of the houses, and disappearing behind its gable, we could see a constant succession of figures moving in Indian file.

After satisfying our first curiosity with this prospect, and learning that it would probably be a considerable time before the appearance of a boat to ferry us across, we joined (with some consciousness of an un-pilgrim-like exterior) a party of pilgrims who were lolling on the grass beside a boat-quay of rude stones, and not far from a building resembling a coach-house, inscribed 'Pilgrim Lodge,' which had a third of its length inside cut off by a wooden partition, and a slit in this with 'Tickets' written above. . . .

Two wrinkled old women, who had made the pilgrimage many times before, conversed earnestly about the picture of the Virgin at Rimini, said to have lately become endowed with motion; repeatedly ejaculating their praises and thanks in reference to the miracle; though as to whether its direct object was the cursing of Protestants or the blessing of Catholics, they were unable to form a conclusion. A stout, middle-aged woman, with a Louth brogue, who sighed frequently, confessed that she felt 'greatly through-other, surely,' at the thought of what might be before her on the Island, it being her first visit;

upon which she received encouragement from the rest, and information as to how she ought to proceed. An indulgence is promised to those who guide others; and from this, added to the natural disposition of the people it results that information is most readily given to the newcomers by those who have been already initiated.

An old bugle sounded from Pilgrim Lodge not having succeeded in calling to us the attention of those on the Island, the conversation, at least in the knot of Stationers with which I consorted, gradually dropped, and I was left to muse in silence over the many strange facts and traditions connected with the lake, whose clear water was rippling over little pebbles up to the grass on which we lay, while its hills were now cheered with sunshine amid the breadths of shadow thrown on them by a circle of great white clouds ranged at their backs. Fionn-lough, the Fair Lake, was its name, say the old legends, until baptised Lough Derg, the Red lake, in the blood of a monster who inhabited it, slain by Saint Patrick. Whether the island 'purgatory' was established in the fifty century by the saint himself, or in the ninth, or the twelfth, its origin runs back far enough into the night of time to be invested with all the mystery of those strange indefinite years of the past. . . .

By this time a concourse of between thirty and forty pilgrims have arrived at the shore; some of them, to my comfort, well-dressed. All the women, rich and poor, are barefoot, but not all the men; for it is not absolutely necessary to take off the shoes until the duties of the penance be commenced. At last the boat, a large clumsy one, with an awning over the stern-sheets, quits the Island and slowly nears the quay. . . . It comes alongside; and the passengers, chiefly women, disembark and exchange greetings and blessings with those who are about to take their places. The latter obtain tickets, price sixpence-halfpenny, from the Lessee of the island, a short stout jovial man, wearing a glazed hat, who attends on every trip, and has a good-humoured word for everybody; the boat gets gradually filled with passengers; the rowers place themselves two or three to each of the heavy oars; the rope is cast off, and we crawl away from the shore, impelled with short splashing strokes, and steered by the Lessee himself, seated beneath the awning among the 'decent' minority of the company, who pay a shilling each for this distinguished position on board.

At the Island quay many of both sexes are waiting to receive the new arrivals. We disembark as quickly as may be, and pass up at once along the lane formed by houses from the water's edge, which opens into a small, irregular space of craggy ground, with a chapel (the principal one) at its extremity; and this space is alive with people pursuing one another barefoot along a course, marked out by rough stones, which leads them in regular succession round a series of little circles, called Saints' Beds. Each is absorbed by his or her own set of beads; though not so much so as to hinder here and there some peripatetic of delicate feet from making an effort to pick and choose among the sharp-cornered stones which beset the journey; while those who have gone shoeless all their lives, have clearly the advantage, and step along carelessly over rough and smooth; nor is more or less suffering in this respect, said to make any difference in the merit of the station; though some, I believe, think otherwise. What adds to the peculiarity of the scene is, that the head-dresses of the men consist of tightly-tied handkerchiefs of various colours, with a sprinkling of woollen night-caps.

The circuit is performed in the following manner:– Starting from the broken stem of an ancient stone cross, about four feet high, and carved with a spiral embellishment, each Stationer goes seven times round the chapel, repeating a decade each time; after the seventh, he stands with his back against a cross cut into one of the stones of the chapel, and stretching out his arms, declares his renunciation of the World, the Flesh, and the Devil. His next movement is to the furthest Bed, consisting of a circle of perhaps nine feet in diameter almost surrounded by an uneven grey wall about three feet high, an opening in which gives access to the interior, where stands a time and lip-worn cross of stone; and here he goes round outside the wall three times, saying three Paters and Aves; kneels and says three more; rises and walks round inside the wall three times, saying three Paters and Aves, kneels and says three more, and then kisses the central cross. After this he passes to the next Bed, where the same formula is observed; thence to another; and thence to a fourth; after which comes the 'Big Bed,' resembling two of the others placed side by side, over which spread the leaves of a dwarf sycamore, almost the only bit of vegetation on the island. This bed must be encircled nine times without, and six times within. The next stage is to the water's edge on the eastern shore, where ten Paters and Aves are repeated standing, and as many kneeling. The practice of wading into the lake, which existed not long ago, has been forbidden, as well as that of carrying stones away as memorials. This latter prohibition, by the way, may have arisen out of no unreasonable fear that the island, being small, and composed chiefly of stones, would, by degrees, be completely carried off by the pilgrims. From the shore the stationer proceeds to a rock on a rising ground, and there repeats two more Paters and Aves standing, and two kneeling; after which, returning to the twisted cross whence he first set out, he kisses it, and repairs to the western shore to wash his feet; so finishing one Station, during which one full Rosary has been repeated. A Stationer who is experienced in his duties, makes his tongue and feet move so harmoniously together, that each prayer comes in at precisely the proper part of the journey, without either hurry or delay. A Station ended, the pilgrim is at liberty for a time, in some instances spent in meditation or grave discourse; in others, in chat, smoking, and idleness.

After looking as closely as we might, without seeming too curious at the never-ending, still-beginning procession round the Chapel and the Beds, we entered one of the lodging-houses, where we were comfortably served with tea and bread and butter. We might have had meat too, for the asking; all things being lawful before the commencement or after the termination of one's penance, except intoxicating drinks; the tasting of which within three miles of the Lake is strictly prohibited.

While enjoying our cup of tea (though the beverage has, I fancy, a smack of the peculiar water which forms its diluent,) we may try to get a definite notion of a pilgrim's routine from first to last. It is, we find, usually as follows: – Say that he enters the Island on Monday evening; he secures a lodging consistent with his means, – the lodging-houses ranging from a snug slated house to a hovel, and the number expected to sleep in one bed, bearing an inverse proportion to the cost, – takes care to eat a hearty meal, and then repairs to evening prayers at the Chapel. . . . After a night, probably, of sound repose, in spite of all inconveniences, he is roused at four on Tuesday morning by the bell which summons him to join the multitude about to flock to the Prior's morning mass; that over, he is likely to set himself to make his first station round the Chapel and the Beds. Three of these stations must be accomplished during the day, but the time when is left to his choice: some perform all the three without interruption.

On Tuesday evening, having eaten nothing since the preceding evening, he is allowed to refresh himself with some bread and wine, and then goes into 'Prison.' It is necessary for the true appreciation of the nature of his fare to understand that the wine is the boggy-flavoured water of the lake, drank hot. The pilgrims speak loudly of its wholesome qualities, as well as of its rich and nutritious flavour; but on the second point, at least, my opinion is distinctly opposed to theirs. They certainly, however, give the best proof of their sincerity by drinking it in large quantities, and sometimes almost scalding out of the kettle. About seven o'clock, then, our Stationer goes into 'Prison,' that is, into the Chapel, as substitute for the now obliterated purgatorial cave; to stay without food or sleep until the same hour on the following evening. He is not, however, obliged absolutely to remain within the doors of the Chapel during the whole of the time, but has liberty to pass in and out, under certain restrictions.

In the Chapel, the men are gathered on one side, the women on the other, – some of them on a bench that runs round the wall, some on the altar-steps, but most on the ground, seated or kneeling. . . .

About midnight, some one well acquainted with the ritual, and who not unproudly assumes the office of temporary leader, commences the rosary aloud, and is followed by all present; the responses being audibly repeated by them in the proper places. They are now performing one Station of the

prison-day, with the same prayers as are used on the other days in performing the Stations out of doors; and to mark their progress the more plainly, the
leader calls out at intervals from his place on the altar-steps, 'Now the Bed on
the top of the hill;' 'Now the Big Bed;' 'Now the Stone;' and so on, assigning
the proper prayers to each stage of the imaginary perambulation.

Three Stations have thus to be gone through occupying, perhaps, from
four to five hours; at the end of which time the candles have burnt and gut-
tered away, and the new daylight looks in through the Chapel windows on a
hot, sleepy, and most uncomfortable crowd; some of whom begin to stretch
their cramped limbs and seek the refreshment of open air, even at the risk of
an increased appetite, – under the circumstances a most undesirable ac-
quirement; for the consumption of as much as a crumb of bread would cause
them to 'lose the benefit of their Station'. . . .

In the course of this day the Prisoner is examined by a priest on the
leading points of his creed, and if his answers be satisfactory, he is inducted
into the Confessional by means of a ticket, for which the Prior receives tenpence,
and which the holder may present to any of the four priests on the island.
This sum, and that paid at the ferry, are the only charges incurred by the
pilgrim, in addition to those for his board and lodging.

On Wednesday evening (having gone into prison on Tuesday evening) he
is present at evening prayers, though whether in a state of very vigilant attention may be doubted; after which he is released; and returning to his
lodging-house, refreshes his exhausted frame with the stated allowance of
bread, oaten or white, and the usual unlimited flow of wine. In a great many
cases, however, tea is permitted. His next step, it can scarcely be doubted, is
to bed; where he sleeps soundly till roused at four. . . . The rain, perhaps, is
battering fiercely at his window. No help – he must brave it; and as he casts
a shuddering look out into the dim, miserable morning, he sees a string of
drenched figures already crouching along the prescribed course, tracing their
'rough road returning in a round,' who have probably been so engaged during the greater part of the night; for pilgrims commence their penances when
they choose, and all the various stages are going on in the Island simultaneously.

This third day, Thursday, the Stationer 'receives' (the Communion), makes
three Stations, and attends evening prayers; immediately after which his penance is at an end. He may be supposed to eat a hearty meal (the first since
Monday), and either quits the Island that evening, or remains until the following morning.

Whilst we were at tea in the lodging-house, pilgrims were constantly swarming in and out, like bees in a hive; one asking another if he were 'in Prison,'
or 'going out' (*i.e.* of the Island); or what Station he was in; or mentioning that

he had just made his third in fifty-one minutes (implying, by the way, the possession of a watch); in all the motley crowd, however – there and else-where – every one appeared to me to behave with great seemliness and consistency.

About six o'clock in the evening, we went to the Chapel, and heard the Prior preach. His sermon was an excessively strange one to unaccustomed ears; for he addressed his audience in the most familiar conversational tone, and even translated the language of Scripture into the humblest and most modern vernacular. Yet, doubtless, this is the right way to preach to the understandings and hearts of the uneducated, and the Prior spoke like a man who took an interest in what he was talking about; while his language, though so unadorned was always correct and forcible. . . .

Leaving the Chapel, we repaired to the quay, and embarked in a small boat, anticipating the large one, which speedily restored us to the mainland. A new group of Stationers were here awaiting transportation, and I confess I felt somewhat ashamed to receive various blessings from these as a faithful son of the holy Catholic Church."

CHAPTER NINE

Household Words

Charles Dickens edited the weekly magazine *Household Words* from 1850–1859 and *All the Year Round* from 1859 until his death in 1870. None of the articles are ascribed to any author. One day in the office this matter was raised with Dickens, as recalled by Percy Fitzgerald in a memoir of the novelist, as it was felt that the career of established writers would be adversely affected unless recognition was given to their works or that the efforts of struggling young writers to gain recognition would be equally thwarted. However Charles Dickens said he would insist on anonymity. 'Anonymity Sir?' remarked one of the journalists 'do you mean mononymity, with the name of Mr Charles Dickens printed at the top of every page, for indeed 'Conducted by Charles Dickens' were so printed at the top of every page. The articles of specific Irish interest from these journals are contained in this chapter.

SAINT PATRICK[1]

Ireland's national day is March 17 to honour Ireland's patron saint, Saint

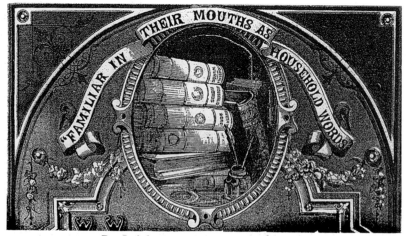

Part of the cover of *Household Words*

Patrick. The occasion was celebrated in many parts of the world. Here is an account of the national holiday in the home country.

"Saint Patrick's Day in the morning, in our village, is ushered in by our amateur band, who played the tune so called through the streets for several hours after midnight, scaring the slumbers of the more orderly portion of the community, and accompanied by a mob of the less orderly. Whoever has lived near the practising-room of an amateur band knows that he might as well have a menagerie for neighbour; and now, when they burst out publicly, each making his brazen utmost of noise, the effect is tremendous. The clamour preserves some faint appearance of unanimity only through the exertions of two or three old militia bandsmen – the civilised allies, as it were, of this regiment of musical Bashi-Bazouks. Several times the din approaches; now up the street; now down; blares under the window, and withdraws – the drum's everlasting cadences vanishing last and returning first upon the auricular horizon. . . .

I can perceive by the moonlight that our big drummer has already been doing honour to the day. Overcome with libations, he has now laid his huge instrument horizontally on the ground, and himself in the same position beside it; and in that difficult attitude plays out his part. . . .

Now it is the day itself. Men and boys of the Roman Catholic faith wear bits of shamrock in their hats, and the little girls have each a cross on the shoulder; that is, a round of white paper three or four inches broad, with bits of ribbon of various colours stretched across it like the spokes of a wheel. The chapels are crowded at morning mass; and, at the mid-day ceremonial, the chapel-yards are filled with the overflow of worshippers, who catch a faint murmur through window or door, and stand or kneel outside with due regularity. A little later, the streets have frequent groups of country folk in their best attire – the girls with sleek hair, bright ribbons, and gay shawls, the matrons with snowy-bordered caps and cloaks of blue cloth, and every man and boy of the rougher sex garnished with his sprig of shamrock. . . .

Every public-house counter is thronged with noisy customers, so is the dark little back-room, so is the room up-stairs. . . . In this apartment the élite take their refreshments – which consist of raw whiskey, whiskey toddy, temperance cordial, a little porter and ale of bad quality, and tobacco smoke. How this and the other pretty girl, who are being treated by a friend or lover, can sit with complacence in so stifling a climate, or bear to swallow even a glassful of such flaming usquebaugh, is difficult to understand. Down-stairs, the calamity-water (an expressive name for it) is usually tossed off neat, and abominable stuff most of it is – the worst new grain whiskey, with its fieriness heightened by poisonous chemicals. . . .

The song tells us it was St. Patrick himself who

> Taught our Irish lads
> The joys of drinking whiskey;

but nothing can be more calumnious. The saint was a man of the most abstemious habits, and his teaching of a very different kind from that just mentioned. The genuine life of St. Patrick, as far as we can make it clear to us at a distance of fourteen centuries, is remarkably interesting; and though many points remain doubtful or in dispute, the main facts seem to be well established. We need not pause to weigh the claims of Ireland, Scotland, Wales, Cornwall, and Brittany to the honour of giving him birth – the evidence appears to favour Scotland – and among half-a-dozen dates we may be content to accept Anno Domini three hundred and eighty-seven as the year in which he came into the world, and four hundred and sixty-five as that of his death, at the age of seventy-eight, and on the day answering to our seventeenth of March. In the language of martyrologists, the day of a saint's nativity is that of his quitting earth and entering into the higher life. His father was Calphurnius, a deacon, who was the son of Potius, a priest. It is asserted by those who maintain the necessity of clerical celibacy, that they took orders after their children were born. The future saint was baptised with the British name, Succoth. . . . At the age of sixteen, having accompanied his parents, brother, and five sisters, to Armoric Gaul – since called Lower Brittany – to visit the relatives of his mother, Conchessa, he was in that country made prisoner by a piratical expedition commanded by the banished sons of a British prince, and, with many fellow prisoners, carried to the north of Ireland, and there sold into slavery. . . . Thus the youth became slave to Milcho, the petty prince of a district now included in the county Antrim, and his three brothers – receiving the name of Ceathertigh, because he served four masters; but Milcho, noting his diligence and probity, bought the others' shares and made him wholly his own, sending him to tend cattle on the mountain of Slieve-Mis.

* * *

In the seventh year of his slavery, he heard one night, in a dream, a voice telling him that he was soon to be restored to his native country; and, again, that a ship was prepared for him. 'Whereafter,' says he, 'I turned me to flight, and left the man with whom I had lived for six years, and in the strength of God, who would guide my steps aright, went, fearing nothing, until I had found that ship.' He reached a haven, and found there a ship, unmoored and just ready to sail. . . .

After many adventures he reached his home in Britain, and embraced his parents; who entreated him, after the tribulations he had endured, never to leave them. But, after some time had passed, he saw one night, in a vision, a man – as if coming from Ireland – whose name was Victoricius, who carried a great number of letters, and gave him one, in the beginning whereof he read – The Voice of the Irish People. 'And whilst I was reading the letter,' says the saint, 'me-thought I heard the voice of those who dwelt beside the forest of Foclute, which is nigh the western sea, and they exclaimed, 'We beseech thee, holy youth, to come and walk amongst us!' And I was greatly touched in heart and could read no further, and so I awoke, and thanked God that after so long a time he had approached them according to their cry.' 'And another night (whether within me or beside me, I know not, God knoweth), I heard most learned words, which I could not understand, only this, at the end: 'He that gave his life for thee;' and then I awoke, rejoicing.'

After these visions, though dissuaded by parents and friends, he gave himself up to the Church, and to study; beginning under his mother's uncle – St. Martin – Bishop of Tours. On being priested he received the new name of Magonius, and studied in various places on the continent. . . .

In the year four hundred and thirty-one, Pope Celestine sent Bishop Palladius on a mission to preach to the Irish, amongst whom Christianity had already taken some hold, but Heathenism was still so dominant that Palladius, after less than a year's sojourn, found himself forced to fly to North Britain, where he died soon after. Then Pope Celestine, considering the eminent piety, learning, and other gifts of Magonius, resolved to send him upon the Irish mission, and therefore consecrated him bishop; at the same time re-baptising him with the honourable name of Patricius, which carried its dignity from the ancient times of Rome (meaning Pater Civium, Father of the People), and was afterwards given to kings of France. . . .

In the year four hundred and thirty-two – Bishop Patricius then forty-five years old – landed on the coast of Wicklow; but, being driven to the ship by the Pagan population, he sailed northward to a bay in what is now called the County of Down. Here the lord of the district hastened to attack the strangers as pirates, but was arrested by the venerable looks of the bishop, listened to his preaching, and was baptised with all his family. There Patricius immediately established his first church, which was called simply, Sahal Phadrig – Patrick's Barn – whence the parish of Saul, in Down, derives its name. When he re-visited the scene of his youthful captivity, a strange event occurred. Two daughters of his old master, after hearing him preach, were baptised and became nuns; whereupon Milcho, strongly attached to the ancient traditions, and perceiving that his former slave was now in authority as their successful antagonist, made a great fire of the house and goods, and consumed himself therein; the news of which, coming to St. Patrick, caused him to stand for three hours silent, and in tears.

Having learned that the time was approaching when King Leoqhaire would hold on Tara Hill a great triennial convention of tributary princes, nobles, and Druid priests, St. Patrick resolved to come and preach to them, at all hazards, knowing the importance of influencing the great people of the country; so, on Easter Eve, four hundred and thirty-three, the next day being that appointed for the opening of the convention, he raised his tent on the north bank of the river Boyne, and kindled a fire before it. Now, it was a penal act for any one to light a fire in the province at the time of the convention of Tara, until the king's bonfire had first indicated the opening of the solemnities; and when St. Patrick's fire shone through the vernal night, and was seen after by the court and multitude encamped on Tara Hill, the utmost astonishment prevailed among them, and the Druids told the king that this fire must be speedily extinguished, or else the man who had kindled it, and his successors, should rule Ireland for ever. The king instantly sent messengers to drag the culprit to his presence, but when Patrick appeared within the circle of the court, so noble and venerable was his aspect, that Erc, son of Dego, instantly rose and offered him his seat. St. Patrick was permitted to preach, and Erc and Dubtach, the poet laureate, were his first converts, along with Fiech, a young poet under the instruction of Dubtach, and who is judged to be the author of a certain poem extant in praise of the saint. The queen and others followed their example, and at last the king himself. It is on this occasion that St. Patrick is said to have successfully used the trefoil or shamrock, growing at his feet, as an illustration of the doctrine of the Trinity; whence this herb came to be assigned to the patron saint of Ireland, and raised into a national emblem. . . .

In his peregrinations, he founded several churches and made many converts; and having been thirteen years in Ireland, he established himself in Armagh (the High Place), and on that hill founded a city and cathedral, with monasteries, schools, and other religious edifices. In that place, chosen fourteen hundred years ago by Saint Patrick, the cathedral, several times re-edificated, stands firm at this day, and his archiepiscopal successor retains the dignity then established, of Primate, and Metropolitan of All Ireland; while, by a curious etiquette, the Archbishop of Dublin is styled Primate of Ireland, without the All.

He travelled continually – a winged labourer, as Chrysostom terms St. Paul – until too old; when he spent his last years in retirement and contemplation, though not neglecting to hold synods and councils, and rule the affairs of the church. The latest part of his life was passed alternately in Armagh, and in the Abbey of Sahal; and in the latter place, where he had adventurously founded the first of several hundred churches, he expired, full of good works and honours, on the seventeenth of March, four hundred and sixty-five, aged seventy-eight.

St. Patrick is said to have been a man of small stature, but of great energy and activity of mind and body, and we have some proofs that his very aspect must have inspired regard and submission. He was truly humble, wore coarse garments, and worked cheerfully and stoutly with his own hands.

Self-denying, humble, fearless, diligent, religious, in a wide and difficult field of action; his life was noble, and his memory is worthy of reverence. Yet certain of the rites with which his day is kept and honoured in Ireland have little reverence in them. St. Patrick's Chapel of Ease, by excise consecration, so crowded today, is a small, dingy, strong-smelling place, where, before the wooden altar, over-huddled with foul glasses and battered pewters, in a plash of whiskey, the devotees hiccup and yell the venerable name of their country's apostle as an incentive to debauchery and madness.

The tradesman or artisan who six months ago registered a vow against drinking, formally excepted the season of the Saint, and, after an interval of hopeful quiet, his family are now again to endure the horrors and miseries inevitably brought on by a drunken father, or son, or husband, who, for his part, shall waken to find the path of reformation vanished from under his foot, and harder to regain than ever. The youth, the tender girl, are half-persuaded, half-forced into their first visit to a tavern, in honour of the day. The experienced toper deliberately, and freed from the last lingering touch of shame (sure it's St. Patrick's Day), wallows into the deepest mire of helpless sottishness. Quarrels rise; oaths and foul words, fists and cudgels, in motion; shrieking wives, weeping sisters and daughters vainly interfering. Then come the efficient green-coated men, truncheons in hand, who, bursting into the thickest of the row, haul off sundry torn, bloody, and foaming creatures, scarcely recognisable as human, to the lock-up. . . .

Alas! the good Patricius! practically invoked as Saint of Sots, Patron of Publicans, Defender of National Drunkenness! What can we say, but that people often use their saints (alive or dead) unreasonably enough – and their sinners too?"

* * *

THE IRISH UNION[2]

The new Poor Law Act enacted in England in 1834 was extended to Ireland in 1838. Union workhouses were established all over the country for indoor relief. They were notorious places for harshness and deprivation. Charles Dickens often satirised them in his novels, most notably in the first seven chapters of *Oliver Twist*. In Ireland the network of such institutions was just in place to receive the full shock of the Famine of 1845–1847, although inadequate to absorb that shock.

---

2.   *Household Words*, 6 November 1852.

"There was a time – even until very lately – when almost any child in Ireland would understand the parable of the house built upon the sand better than an English reader of the New Testament; for, until lately, houses as fragile as any mud dwelling in Palestine, and far more wretched than Jew or Arab ever lives in, were exceedingly common in Ireland. There are some now, but so few that travellers point them out to one another as they pass. I do not mean – I wish I did – that wretched dwellings are few in Ireland. They are fearfully common still; but that particular sort of house – the mud hovel of the lowest order – has nearly disappeared. Wrecks and ruins of such huts, not quite melted away, remain, as mournful objects in the landscape; and it is but too well known what would be found under the rubbish of some of them, the bones of families who died in the famine, and who were buried – no other burial being possible – by tumbling down the roof upon them. But to scores of these there may be only one such now tenanted.

Where do the people live who once lived by thousands in hundreds of such hovels?

They live in the handsomest, and certainly the very cleanest abodes in Ireland; so clean that one might eat one's dinner off the floors, and look long for a speck on the window-panes, or a spider in the sleeping-rooms; mansions of greystone, of the domestic-gothic style of architecture, with lofty ceilings, vast kitchens, and some acres of ground round the walls; and usually, a blooming garden in front, with bushes of roses and fuchsias, and plots of balsams, with tall evergreens intermixed.

What can this mean? It means that, set down thickly all over Ireland, there are now refuges for the poor, called Workhouses.

The time is past for all argument as to whether there ever should have been these workhouses in Ireland. There they are: and if they had not been there, the greater part of the poor of Ireland would have gone, long ago, into the narrowest house of all – underground.

At first, the people objected vehemently to go into the house. The large class of roaming beggars, accustomed to whiskey, tobacco, gossip, and idleness, could not bear the confinement to a settled home, where there was work to do, and no pipe or grog; and they cursed the system which drew off so much charity as to compel them to work for their whiskey and tobacco, if they must have them. . . . Some were sure they could not live upon any diet but potatoes; and all shrank from the necessity of being washed on entering the place. The bath was the grand horror. It was a warm bath; pleasant and comfortable, one would think; but the inmates said – and say to this hour – that the washing is like stripping them of a skin, or a suit of clothes; the feel of the air directly meeting their skins is so new and strange!

All balancing between begging and the workhouse was, however, put an end to when the potatoes failed.

When the traveller sees a palace of grey stone, which might be a college, or a national museum – with an edifice in front, and another at hand or behind, of the same stone, connected with the larger building by walls – he knows that he is not far from a town; for this is a Union Workhouse. He feels some wish to explore the interior of this vast mansion; and he probably employs his first leisure hour – if he is stopping, at the town – in walking up to it. At least, I did; and, finding a ready and ever eager admission everywhere, I inspected a good many, and found each more interesting than the last.

What a pleasant flower-garden this is! gay and bright with flowers. Everybody in the house has access to this garden; and it is plain that nobody does any harm. Ring the bell. The porter opens to us; and when we ask whether we can see the house, replies eagerly, 'O yes, to be sure!' He takes our cards to the Master, but intimates that we are welcome any way; and that perhaps we will write our names in the Visitors' Book before we leave. On one side of the entrance-hall is a room where applicants are received and first spoken to; and on the other, is the room where the surgeon examines them, to ascertain their state of health; and especially, whether they have any infectious disease. If they are healthy, they have only to cleanse themselves thoroughly in the warm bath in the next room, and put on the dress of the house; and then they are ready for admission. Their clothes are seldom worth preserving – being mere strings or bundles of tatters. . . .

The master appearing, we exchange greetings, and ask him how he is satisfied with the state of the house now. He tells us that it is a very different affair now from what it was. There are not, at present, many more inmates than the house was built for, and two out of five auxiliary houses are closed. In two of the wards, they are still obliged to put two in a bed; but it will not be for long. At one time, when all the auxiliary houses were open, and the deaths were twenty-five in a day, it yet was necessary to put three into a bed; and, in regard to the children, even four.

Mounting the steps of the house, we see on the right hand a pleasant parlour, with the remains of dinner on the table. These are the apartments of the master and mistress. Their rooms open into the school-rooms – the lofty, light, spacious apartments, with their rows of benches, and the platform at one end for the teacher, and the great black board, with its bit of chalk lying ready at hand. These schools are under the system of the National Board, and here may be seen the pleasant sight of Catholic and Protestant children sitting side by side, without any thought of quarrelling on theological subjects. However it may be hereafter, one cannot but suppose that they will be the happier and the more amiable for having thus sat together now.

At an angle of the boy's school-room is the work-room. A steady-looking man is walking about, from loom to loom, seeing how his pupils get on. That little fellow, who is leaning so anxiously over his web, has learned weaving only four days.

The women and girls bring their crochet-work up to the likeness of point-lace with very little teaching; finding out for themselves how to execute any pattern that may have met their eye. One of these girls, who had puzzled over such a pattern, saw in a dream how to do it, and got up in the night to put it down, that she might not lose it again. And these novices are weaving – rather slowly, perhaps – but without fault, as far as we can see.

What is this furthest room? Oh! here are the aged men sitting in a room which is not a thoroughfare, and where there is no draught. They cower over the fire, even in warm weather. But, these are only a few of them; more are out in the sun, and some are in bed upstairs. The aged women are in a corresponding apartment at the other end; and we go to see them. On our way we find the nursery. It answers to the boys' work-room. What a strange sight it is – such a crowd of infants. Some can run alone; and they play bo-beep behind the old women's aprons. Some sit on the floor sucking their thumbs; two or three dozens are in cradles, asleep, or staring wide awake. . .

We have now seen the whole width of this ground-floor. Next we must see the length. We pass through a yard, and glance into the wash-house, where women and girls are busy and merry among the suds, and managing the great boilers. In the adjoining laundry, there are large hot closets, where heaps of clothes are drying in a trice. Answering to these places are the kitchen and shed. In the kitchen, there are large boilers to manage, and a girl, mounted on a stool, is wielding – not the washing staff – but a kind of oar. This is soup she is stirring, with such an exertion of strength. It is the soup that the people have every day for dinner. No – there is no meat in it. They have never been meat eaters. Milk is their only animal food – now, as always. The soup is made of meal, with a variety of vegetables shredded in, and salt and pepper. This, with a loaf of bread made of mixed Indian meal and rye, is their dinner. It is near four o'clock now; and we may see them at dinner presently. Four is their dinner hour; and they have nothing more, unless they like to keep some of their bread for supper: but they go to their beds at seven. Their other meal is breakfast, at nine. For this they have porridge made of Indian meal, very thick and nourishing... They are soon to have potatoes again – just twice a week; and greatly they are reckoning on this: but they may find themselves more fond of the meal than they are aware of. They are now entering the dining-hall. Let us see them take their places.

This room is the chapel as well as the dining-hall. It is spacious and lofty, and the tables and benches standing across the room instead of lengthwise, give a sociable appearance to the dining... What a change it must be to most of these people to sit down to a clean table, on a clean bench, and with clean hands; instead of huddling round the pot, on a clay floor, half full of stinking puddles.

* * *

What a strange company it is! – what odd infirmities, and what a gradation of ages brought together! Did you ever see a clumsier or shorter dwarf than she who is filling the pans? And the young man without a coat, who has lost his right arm – he is not a pauper, surely – seeing his moustache. No, he is employed in the yards; that is all; though he looks as if he fancied himself the master of all and everybody. Looking along the tables, however, and passing over the cases of personal injury from disease or accident, a fine state of health seems to be the rule.

The infirmary is at the further end of this hall, divided from it only by a vestibule, so that the convalescent may attend chapel without going out of doors. At first we see only a sprinkling of sick people; a room where the extremely aged are in their comfortable beds; their palsied heads shaking on their pillows, and their half-closed eyes looking as if the sleep of death were visibly creeping over them: and another room where three or four young mothers are recovering from their confinement. These, we are told, are, like many whom we saw below, 'deserted women.' their 'desertion,' however, turns out to be a smaller affair than the sad word would convey. These women are all wives; and they are, for aught that anybody knows, loved by their husbands. The husbands are gone to earn money for them, and will come back, or send money for their families to follow them. Some who are in England for the harvest, will return, with the funds for winter subsistence: but more will spend the money in going to America, from Liverpool or Bristol, where they will earn more money still, and send for their wives, after a year or two. . . .

And now we come to the strangest suite of rooms of all. At the first glimpse, it is like entering an arbour. The walls are coloured green, and all the window-blinds (which are down, although the windows are open), are green also. There is a green tinge, from the reflection, on all the white pillows and sheets, and on the faces of all the patients, who are lying in precisely the same posture, and as if asleep – all those scores and hundreds of them, from end to end of all the wards. They are 'down in the ophthalmy.' The only difference, except in age, in any wardfull of patients is, that some have wet rag laid across their eyes, and others have the rag on the pillow ready to be put on at any moment. It is a very mournful sight. That little boy of four years, admitted into the female ward for convenience – the beautiful child with the long lashes lying on his blooming cheeks, – is he to be blind? Or the delicate-looking girl of twelve, with her bright hair lying all about her head in thick waves; or those mothers who listen for their children's voices from the playground, and will soon have them in their arms, but may never see their faces again – are these likely to be blind? The medical officer, who approaches our party, makes a sign, to intimate that although all eyes are closed, these people are not asleep. . . . As soon as we are in a white light again, the surgeon says that he hopes he has turned the corner now: he is dismissing his patients by fifties at a time, and fewer are falling into the disease.

The proportion of those who lose both eyes is very small. Of the forty-six thousand cases of ophthalmia which occurred in the Irish workhouses last year, only two hundred and sixty-three resulted in total blindness; and above forty thousand were cured. Six hundred and fifty-six lost one eye each. These facts seem to show that there must be a lamentable amount of disease of the eyes out of the workhouses; for the large number of one-eyed persons whom we met in all the towns makes such a number as the above appear a mere trifle among the whole population. The doctor cannot at all explain the prodigious extent of the disease. Dirt, crowding, and foul air will account for a good deal of it... It is strange and sad; but we are comforted by hearing from the doctor that the little boy, and the young girls, and those indispensable mothers, are likely to be as well as we are, very soon.

The Matron produces a key. We are to see the dormitories, which are kept locked after the morning sweeping and airing. They are curious places; long rooms, with an aisle or gangway along the middle, left by platforms on either hand, about ten inches high. On each platform lies a row of bundles, each bundle being a bed for one person – unless a pressure of numbers compels crowding. The mattress is tied in the form of an arch; and resting upon it is a smaller arch, composed of the tug and blankets neatly folded and set up in that form. The beauty of the platform is that it can be kept perfectly and constantly clean, which is more, I believe, than can be said of any bedstead whatever, liable to promiscuous use. The beds being lifted away, the platform can be swept and scoured like a floor, and it everywhere looks like a new deal table. In three hours' time the people below will come up in detachments, be told off into their wards, untie each his or her bedding, and go into a bed as clean as in a gentleman's house. Ah! how unlike the sleeping accommodation I have seen in many a better cabin than these people came from – bedsteads standing in a slough of mud, with potatoes stowed away underneath, the turf-stack within reach, the hens perched on the tattered counterpane, and little pigs rubbing their snouts against the ricketty headboard!

Before departing, we go to the Board-room, where the guardians meet. It is in the entrance building, over the hall. Here was planned that strange proceeding, the clearing of the workhouse of the able-bodied, or a certain number of them, without distinction of sex, whereby upwards of twenty girls were thrust out into the world without protection or resource... As if by mutual agreement, the guardians of several unions did this; and all have been visited with such censure from the Poor Law Commissioners, as well as their neighbours, that such a piece of profligate tyranny is now likely to occur again. We look at the very instructive documents which stud the walls of this solemn room, where the fates of so many human beings are decided; we receive the statistical memoranda we petitioned for, and in return write our names, addresses, and a remark or two in the Visitors' Book.

As we go away, we stop a minute to see the boys at work in the sloping fallow which descends to the meadow. That bit of ground – somewhere about two acres – has been all dug by the boys, and now they are trenching it, in a style of thoroughness which one would like to see throughout their country. They are regularly taught by a qualified agricultural instructor; and certainly that field of turnips, and the mangold wurzel beyond, clean and strong, do credit to his teaching. It is incredible that the agriculture of Ireland can long remain in its present disgraceful state, when thousands of boys like these go out into the world as able-bodied labourers; and it is incredible that the many thousands of orphan girls who are brought up in habits of cleanliness, thrift, and industry in these refuges, should not produce some effect upon the comfort and household virtue of the next generation. They may not be having the best possible education, but they are receiving one which is wonderfully good for their original position and circumstances."

* * *

STONING THE DESOLATE[3]

The Curragh of Kildare comprises 5000 acres of flat, fertile land. It was an ancient meeting-place and commons from at least the 12th century. The area is renowned for horse breeding and with the foundation of the Irish Turf Club at Kildare in 1790, the status of the Curragh as the premier racing venue in Ireland was established.

It was also noted from 1646 as a military training centre and was the largest military barracks in Ireland. During the Crimean War the camp was rebuilt in 1855. The camp-following prostitutes referred to in this article were known as the "wrens of the Curragh" from their abode.

"There are, in certain parts of Ireland and especially upon the Curragh of Kildare, hundreds of women, many of them brought up respectably, a few perhaps luxuriously now living day after day, week after week, and month after month, in a state of solid heavy wretchedness, that no mere act of imagination can conceive. Exposed to sun and frost, to rain and snow, to the tempestuous east winds, and the bitter blast of the north, whether it be June

---

3.   *All the Year Round*, 26 November 1864.

or January, they live in the open air, with no covering but the wide vault of heaven, with so little clothing that even the blanket sent down out of heaven in a heavy fall of snow is eagerly welcomed by these miserable outcasts. The most wretched beings we profess to know of, the Simaulees and Hottentots of Africa, have holes whereinto they may creep, to escape the heat of the sun or the winter's rages, but the women-squatters of the Curragh have no shelter, there is no escape for them but to turn their backs to the blast, and cower from it. The misery that abounds round our large camps in England is a load heavy enough for us to bear, but it is not at all to be compared to what can be seen daily in Ireland. If one of these poor wretches were to ask but for a drop of water to her parched lips, or a crust of bread to keep her from starving, Christians would refuse it; were she dying in a ditch, they would not go near to speak to her of human sympathy, and of Christian hope in her last moments. Yet their priests preach peace on earth, good will among men, while almost in the same breath they denounce from their altars intolerant persecution against those who have, in many cases, been more sinned against than sinning. This is not a thing of yesterday. It has been going on for years, probably fifty, perhaps a hundred.

Twenty years ago, in eighteen forty-four, I remember the priest's coming into the barracks at Newbridge, with a request that the commanding officer would grant him a fatigue party of soldiers to go outside and pull down a few booths which these poor creatures had raised against the barrack wall. The priest, I am sorry to say, had his request granted, and at the head of the soldiers, on a cold winter's day, he went out and burned down the shelter these unfortunates had built. At this time it was quite common for the priest, when he met one of them, to seize her and cut her hair off close. But this was not all. In the summer of 'forty-five, a priest, meeting one of the women in the main street of Newbridge, there threw her down, tearing from off her back the thin shawl and gown that covered it, and with his heavy riding-whip so flogged her over the bare shoulders that the blood actually spirted over his boots. She all the time never resisted, but was only crying piteously for mercy. Of the crowd which was formed round the scene, not a man nor a woman interfered by word or action.

I will speak only of what I have seen. Last year I was in Mr. Tallon's shop in Newbridge, when one of these girls came in and asked for half an ounce of tea. She was cleanly and respectably dressed – was perfectly sober and quiet in her demeanour; in fact, from her appearance I should never have guessed her position. The shopkeeper had weighed the tea and was about to give it, when, stopping short, he threw it behind him, saying, 'No! I'll not serve you.' To this she made no reply, but meekly turned and walked away. Surmising what she was at once, I could not help saying, 'Good God, do you refuse to sell a fellow-creature the necessaries of life?' 'Yes,' was the answer; 'were she dying, I would not give it to her, or any like her.' I attempted to argue with him, reminding him that it was only those without sin themselves who should cast the first stone or trample upon the fallen; but he would not listen. I called for the half ounce of tea, paid for it, and following her up the town, gave it the poor creature. Her look of thankfulness more than repaid me.

Yet in Newbridge these people are better off than in any other part of the country; for a charitable farmer who owns some small fields near the barracks, has allowed them the use of a deep dry ditch by the roadside. This they have covered over with some hay and branches of trees, which forms for them a kind of shelter from the weather.

Vastly different is it, however, in other parts of Ireland, where they can get no better shelter than a hedge affords. On the Curragh, for instance, the only protection they have from the pelting rain, the driving sleet, or the falling snow, is a furze bush; and this they are not allowed to erect or prop up by any means into a kind of covering. The moment they attempt to make a roof of it, it is pulled down by the police or under-rangers... I remember one morning when I was on pass, making my way across the Curragh. Going down from the Grand Stand towards the Camp Inn, I passed a rising piece of ground on my left, under the brow of which the sheep and lambs were cowering together for shelter from the sharp north wind which was then blowing bitterly. I did not observe four women lying in a bit of a hole they had scooped out, until one called after me, and asked me to give her a shilling for God's sake, as they were starving. The sight of them, wet, cold, and perishing from want and exposure, caused me to turn back and give the shilling; and I own that my remonstrance was very feeble even when she to whom I had given it jumped up, saying, 'Long life to you! this will get us a drop of whisky,' and ran off to get it. The mere prospect of the drink seemed to impart new life to two of them, but the other evidently cared nothing about that which gave her companions so much pleasure. Her eye was languid, her skin hot and dry, her head ached; she was suffering from an attack of fever. I left her, and walking back towards the station, met a policeman, whom I informed of her state, and he promised to get her taken to the workhouse if he could. I discovered afterwards that an under-ranger had reported this woman's case to the police, and that information of her illness had been forwarded to Naas, when the policeman was told to apply to the relieving-officer at Newbridge. On looking for him, the constable learnt that the relieving-officer came only now and then to Newbridge, and that to find him he would have to go to Milltown. Thither the kindly man did not grudge going, and there he was told by the official that 'he would see about it.' Next day, finding the poor wretch still neglected, and sinking fast, he had her conveyed in a car to the Naas workhouse, where she died in a few hours after her admission.

Thus they are exposed all the year round: if it rains for a week they have to remain in it, having the wet ground for a couch, and a few wet rags for a covering. No refuge for them; no pity; no succour. In England the publicans will suffer them to remain by their firesides while their money lasts; landlords will let them rooms while they pay rent; shopkeepers will supply them with goods while they can find money for the articles: but here, in Ireland, they are outcasts in the fullest sense of the term, abandoned, persecuted, spurned. I am well aware that these women are the dregs of society, also that some mistaken Christians will say that 'any pity shown to them is at best an encouragement of vice,' while others, like Scrooge, will inquire 'whether the workhouse and prisons are not still in operation?' To such it is useless to make any appeal. But to those who can feel for the poor and homeless, who, to the best of their ability, attend to the Divine commands to feed the hungry, clothe the naked, visit the sick, and raise the fallen, I appeal for at least a thought of Christian mercy towards the wretched outcasts, who exist on the Curragh, and around our barracks in Ireland.

It is the old story – a poor girl is attracted by a soldier when the troops come to her town. When he marches away, she leaves all – friends, fortune, and good name – to follow him; little recking of the pains that lie before her. Soon the trifle of money is spent, and then the clothes go piece by piece. When money and clothes are gone, what shall she do? She cannot dash through the ring of scorn already surrounding her, to go home and drink the bitterest dregs of her cup in the rebuke of her own kindred. The man she has followed lovingly and unwisely, had not means to support her; yet she cannot starve. Gradually the outcast sinks lower and lower, till she probably ends her days by the side of a barrack wall, or on the leeside of a bush at the Curragh. Of the soldiers who should share the blame of this, men are ready enough to remember how they are in a manner cut off from all domestic joys or pleasures, and have as a class very little forethought. Their daily bread is always found them; whether in sickness or in health they need never know what a sharp thorn hunger is. And so, being thoughtless, the soldier does not prevent women from following him from town to town, and from barracks to camp. . . .

In India these camp-followers are placed under the care of one of their own sex – a female muccadum, or overseer, who is paid so much a month out of the canteen fund... The women themselves are comfortably housed; they are obliged to keep their huts in good order, and themselves clean and well clothed; if they misbehave they are punished; in case of disease, they are sent to a native hospital till they recover. This system modified to suit home moralities might be advantageously introduced at our barracks and camps, and would go a great way to stay the spread of disease which fills our army hospitals, and ruins the health of our soldiers. As the hour before the dawn is the darkest, so I trust that, upon the night of these unhappy squatters, the first glimmering of dawn is soon to break."

THE SPADE IN IRELAND[4]

"In the 'famine year,' of 1846, an application was made to the benevolent public for food and seed by the Irish Presbyterian Home Mission, on behalf of the peasantry of the West of Ireland, and particularly of those in a remote district in the county of Mayo. The usual practical shrewdness of Scotchmen suggested to some gentlemen of Edinburgh the uselessness of aggravating the future destitution of the Irish people, by merely squandering money in doling out rations; which, when exhausted, would leave the recipients more destitute, and with weaker habits of self-reliance than before the period of relief. . . . An experienced agriculturist from the South of Scotland was dispatched to the proposed scene of operations. From his representation it appeared that the people inhabiting this district, being found to be of a peaceable and industrious character, and little acquainted with the common practice of systematic husbandry, it was afterwards thought, that in place of continuing the temporary assistance which was still required, the money to be so expended, might be thrown into a channel of a more permanent character, by renting a few hundred acres, for the double purpose of introducing an improved system of cultivation, and of affording profitable employment to the destitute. . . .

A lease of Castle and Parkmore farms and the Townland of Ballinglew for twenty-one years, and three lives, has been taken. The land is two miles from the sea-coast, nine from the sea-port of Killala, and sixteen from the market-town of Ballina. It has good roads, abundance of lime and freestone peat for fuel, and sea-weed for manure. It is three hundred and seventy-four statute acres in extent, the rent is only sixty-four pounds, and that rent (only three shillings and sixpence per acre) is higher than that of the surrounding holdings. Although the tenants were greatly in arrear, the lessees wisely procured a remission of the landlord's claims, and paid the holders a handsome premium in consideration for the tenant right, to maintain the policy of conciliating, and giving confidence to the 'natives.' Useless fences and roads were removed, unnecessary hedges and ditches rooted out and filled up, fields put into convenient shape and dimensions, an immense quality of surface stones removed from the soil, buildings repaired, proper housings and cattle sheds erected, and a thrashing mill, to be driven by water power, is constructed. At the end of the first complete year (1849), sixty-five acres of oats, potatoes, barley, vetches, carrots, parsnips, and turnips, of considerable yield and excellent quality, were gathered, and employment afforded for forty men at sixpence per day, and as many women and children at from threepence to fourpence; thereby securing subsistence to upwards of two hundred individuals.

---

4. *Household Words*, 26 April 1851, pp. 114-115.

Scotchmen can do nothing without schools, and the first building which the subscribers erected was a school-house. They had great difficulty in procuring a teacher, being generally told by those to whom they applied, that they declined being shot by wild Irishmen. They, at last, secured the services of an able and enthusiastic Scotch schoolmaster, who understands and can direct all country work, and who finds not only his pupils apt and docile, but his full grown neighbours peaceable and friendly.

The chief burden of the success of the experiment has devolved upon a hard-headed Caledonian farm overseer, one James Carlaw, who has not only the faculty of farming skilfully, and making every one about him work efficiently, but whose natural tact and knowledge of human nature have made him universally acceptable to his labourers, and placed him on the highest terms with his Catholic neighbours, including the priest. . . . After due probation, he imported his wife and five children to Ballinglew . . . and now Mrs. Carlaw manages the dairy, and her children attend the school with the infantry of the district.

The entire Townland of Ballinglew, on which the farm is situated, is to be exposed for sale, under that invaluable measure, the Encumbered Estates Act. The rental, at present, is three hundred and ten pounds; it consists of nearly one thousand five hundred acres; it is tithe and land-tax free; and it is expected that the whole will go for three thousand five hundred, or four thousand pounds! ... No agriculturists in Europe have the advantages of such cheap land and labour as are offered to our bucolic Britons in Ireland. Able-bodied labourers at sixpence; and useful weeders and hoers at threepence per day; with land, bearing fine crops of oats, barley, turnips, and potatoes, at four shillings and eightpence per acre; and to be had, prospectively, at less than three shillings, with a profit to the landlord of five per cent. on a price of four thousand pounds!

We feel convinced that an interview with James Carlaw would soon reassure an English farmer that he may devote his energies to the cultivation of Ireland, without any fear of being 'shot from behind a hedge.' The vast tide of emigration which is flowing from that country to this island, of the labouring poor – and to the Colonies and United States, of the small farmers – indicates a voluntary relinquishment of the soil by the native occupiers, which may satisfy the reflective that a clear stage is left in the Sister Kingdom for British agricultural enterprise, which could not fail to be crowned with success. Sir Robert Peel suggested the plantation of Ireland, which means its settlement, not by isolated emigrants, but in such numbers as to constitute a neighbourhood; an aggregation of English and Scotch in a district, such as would keep each other in countenance, and cheer their hearts by co-operation. Ireland is yet destined to be our right arm, in place of being our wooden leg; she may be regenerated by green hearts and cheerful hopes, throwing off her leprosy, and recovering her elasticity, 'so that her flesh shall become as the flesh of a little child.' She has been bled and blistered, sweated, and drugged, to no effect, but to reduce her strength, and aggravate her symptoms. It is time rulers should be asked – as the proprietor of the sorry nag was, under similar circumstances – 'Have you ever tried him with oats?' The first trial of the experiment has succeeded at Ballinglew. We hope it will not be the last."

* * *

IRISH STREET SONGS[5]

'It has long been known by all persons acquainted with Ireland and the Irish, that Tom Moore's songs, charming and musical as they are, never acquired any real popularity with the large mass of the people, especially that large section who still speak the Celtic Language, and for the most part the Celtic language only. The men in frieze very soon discovered that there was something wanting in the lyrist of Holland House. Irish poets, too, complained that the fine old melodies of Erin were corrupted, tinkered, and often spoiled by the bard of Paternoster-row. They found, they said, a want of earnestness and patriotism, worst of all, a deficiency of Irish feeling, character, and local colour.

The Irish class themselves, in songs, as equal to the Germans, inferior only to the Scotch, and superior to the Italians, the Spaniards, and the English. It might, perhaps, lessen the value of this assertion to remark that Mr. Thomas Davis, of the Nation (who made it), did not know much of either German, Italian, or Spanish; but still the assertion remains as a standard for future Irish writers equally qualified to pronounce a judgment. While the Irish allow Burns to be a poet of a higher class than Moore, they envy France B,ranger. But the Englishman, the poor, absurd, wrong-headed Saxon, they say, is nowhere among the lyrical poets. The Jacobite risings moved the heart and brain of Scotland, as profoundly as if the return of the scurvy Stuarts would have secured a pot of money to every Scotchman; but even the civil wars did not inspire England with a single ballad that has lived.

The old Irish bards, whose works even Spenser found to savour 'of sweet wit and good invention,' and to be 'sprinkled with some pretty flowers of natural device, which give good grace and comeliness,' delighted in metaphor. In their poems Erin figures as Ros geal Dove or Droimann Donn; she is an enslaved virgin who leads the poets through Fairy land, to dismiss them at last with a prophecy of the day when her warriors shall set her free. . . .

---

5.   *All the Year Round*, 28 May 1870.

One of the earliest of the patriotic songs still popular, is the Ros gal dubh (the white-skinned, black-haired Rose). The poet typifies Erin as a beautiful maiden in distress, hints at Rose's dangers, and at mysterious help from Italy and Spain, and ends with a fiery outburst of passion over the bloody struggle that must take place ere his Rose shall be finally torn from him. This poem dates from the time of Elizabeth.

The Jacobite troubles were sources of inspiration to the Irish song-writers, whether hiding in Wicklow, or starving at St. Germains. Many a pining exile, faithful to Erin as the banished Israelite to Judaea, poured forth his soul in passionate longings for Erin Ogh. One of the most beautiful of these laments is the Ban-Chnoic Erin Ogh (the fair hills of Virgin Ireland). This plaintive song commences:

> Beautiful and broad are the green fields of Erin,
> Uileacán dov O.
> With life giving grain and golden corn,
> Uileacán dov O.
> And honey in the woods with the mist wreaths deep,
> In the summer by the paths the high streams leap
> At burning noon rich sparkling do the fair flowers steep,
> On the fair hills of Erin Ogh!

It is said to have been written by an Irish student at St. Omer. The Irish Jacobite songs are seldom gay or hopeful, as Over the Water to Charley, Charley is my Darling, or Hey, Johnnie Cope, are ye Wakin' yet? There are a few exceptions, and the most remarkable of these is the White Cockade, which Mr. Callanan has translated with spirit. . . .

The poet begins:

> King Charles he is King James's son,
> And from a royal line is sprung;
> Then up with shout and out with blade,
> And we'll raise once more the white cockade.
>
> O! my dear, my fair-haired youth,
> Thou yet hast hearts of fire and truth;
> Then up with shout and out with blade,
> We'll raise once more the white cockade.

* * *

Another of these Jacobite minstrels (and the writers of street songs are so seldom known that it is interesting to trace the patriarchs), was John M'Donnell, surnamed Claragh, a native of Charleville, in the county Cork. He was the contemporary of a celebrated Limerick poet, whisky-drinker, and wit, John Toomey. M'Donnell began at least, even if he did not finish, a History of Ireland, and had the intention of translating the Iliad into Irish. He was a staunch Jacobite. In his Vision, a patriotic song, a beautiful Banshee (not the weeping and wailing hag of modern Irish legends), is supposed to lead him through the fairy haunts of Ireland. The song ends with a dubious prophecy almost worthy of the great Zadkiel, or a Derby Day prophet:

'Say O say, thou being bright!
When shall the land from slavery waken,
When shall our hero claim his right
And tyrants' halls be terror shaken?'
She gives no sign – the form divine
Pass'd like the winds by fairies woken;
The future holds in Time's dark folds,
The despot's chain of bondage broken.

* * *

M'Donnell died in 1754, and his brother poet, John Toomey, wrote his elegy. Some time after these men came Owen O'Sullivan (Owen the Red), a native of Kerry. This eccentric bard was a reaper, and in the off season an itinerant hedge schoolmaster, whose wandering disciples learnt from him to translate Homer and Virgil into Irish. He is a favourite poet of the Muster peasantry. Like Burns, he loved not wisely but too well; like Burns, too, he drank himself to death in his prime. O'Sullivan's great drinking song begins almost fiercely, and with the poet's usual irrestrainable dythrambic vehemence:

This cup's flowing treasure
I toast to that treasure
The brave man whose pleasure
Is drinking rich wine.
Who deep flagons draining,
From quarrels abstaining,
The morn finds remaining,
All joyous, divine.
It ne'er shall be mine
To gather vile coin,
To fools at life's waning,
For age to resign.

* * *

In the troubled times, when the French Revolution gave false hopes to the disaffected in Ireland, the song-writers' hearts began again to stir with wild impulses. It was in 1797, when the French tricolor was waving in Bantry Bay, and the moment of the expulsion of the hated Saxon seemed at hand, that that fine song, The Shan van Vocht (the poor old woman), was written: the refrain sounds like the advancing march of armed men. The poor old woman named in the song is, we need hardly say, a seer or prophetess, who foretells the speedy gathering of the pikes 'in good repair' on that noble battle-field not unused by the Danes and Milesians of old – the Curragh of Kildare. At many a rebel camp on the green hills of Erin have these words been shouted:

> Oh, the French are on the sea,
> Says the Shan van Vocht,
> The French are on the sea,
> Says the Shan van Vocht.
> Oh! the French are in the bay,
> They'll be here without delay,
> And the Orange will decay,
> Says the Shan van Vocht.

This martial song has one especial and unusual merit among songs, that the last verse rises to a climax, and expresses a higher thought than those preceding it. The final words rush on with the irrestrainable velocity of an avalanche. Pity they were so mischievous and so fallacious!

> Will Ireland then be free?
> Says the Shan van Vocht.
> Yes! Ireland shall be free,
> From the centre to the sea.
> Then hurrah for Liberty!
> Says the Shan van Vocht.

*   *   *

The troubles of '98 and of Emmet's time were commemorated in that fine lyric, The Wearing of the Green, by Henry Grattan Curran. Mr. Boucicault's picturesque paraphrase of the song, or even more than paraphrase of it, in Arrah-na-Pogue, has made it almost as well known in London as it is in Dublin. As in most Irish rebel songs, and, indeed, most Irish lyrics that are not mere tipsy praises of whisky, there is a tone of sorrow and despair; as Tom Moore says beautifully in his Dear Harp of my Country:

> So oft has thou echoed the deep sigh of sadness,

That e'en in my mirth it will steal from thee still.

Curran's finest verse is the following:

> O, I care not for the thistle,
> And I care not for the rose,
> For when the cold winds whistle,
> Neither down nor crimson shows.
> But like hope to him that's friendless,
> Where no gaudy flower is seen,
> By our graves with love that's endless,
> Waves our own true-hearted green.

The so-called Irish patriot is never tired of singing of the green flag, the green immortal shamrock, and the green hills of Erin. In the Up for the Green: a song of the United Irishmen of '96, the chorus ends:

> Then up for the green, boys, O up for the green,
> Shout it back to the Sassanach, 'We'll never sell the green;
> For our Tone is coming back, and with men enough, I ween,
> To rescue and avenge us, and our own immortal green.'

A notice of Irish street songs would be incomplete that did not treat of the convivial as well as the patriotic songs. High in this class stand those two jovial reckless lyrics, Garryowen, and the Rakes of Mallow. The first is very old; the most lively verse runs:

> We are the boys that delight in
> Smashing the Limerick lamps when lighting,
> Through the streets like porters fighting,
> And tearing all before us.
> Chorus:
> Instead of spa we'll drink brown ale,
> And pay the reckoning on the nail;
> No man for debt shall go to jail,
> From Garryowen in glory.

It is not easy to beat this song for tipsy jollity and headlong Celtic 'devilment,' but it must be confessed that in the Rakes of Mallow the two first verses sound like the bangs of a drunken man's shillaleh:

> Beauing, belling, dancing, drinking,
> Breaking windows, cursing, sinking,

Ever raking, never thinking,
Live the rakes of Mallow.

Spending faster than it comes,
Beating waiters, bailiffs, duns,
Bacchus' true-begotten sons,
Live the rakes of Mallow.

* * *

The finest song relating to the Shamrock, is the Green little Shamrock of Ireland: written by Cherry, the actor, for Mrs. Mountain, who sang it in a monopolylogue in the Little Opera House, Capel-street, Dublin, in 1806. The first verse is very pretty and fervid:

There's a dear little plant that grows in our isle,
'Twas St. Patrick himself sure that set it,
And the sun of his labour with pleasure did smile,
And with dew from his eye often wet it.
It thrives through the bog, through the brake, through the mireland,
And he called it the dear little shamrock of Ireland:
The sweet little shamrock, the dear little shamrock,
The sweet little, green little shamrock of Ireland. . . ."

CHAPTER TEN

Dickensian Dublin

Mr John Ardagh wrote that Dublin boasted two streets named after Dickensian characters at one time, "Nickleby" (78–79 Lower Tyrone Street, north Marlborough Street, 1840) and "Pickwick Place" (Great Strand Street, 1839), but both have long since vanished.[1]

The articles about Dublin describe the many facets of the city in Dickensian time, from the grandeur of a Castle levée to the rag and bone shops of the Coombe, from the fine arts of Hutton's coach-building factory to a spectacular production of the Colleen Bawn in the Royal Liffey Theatre.

THE CASTLE OF DUBLIN[2]

"The cheerful city which stands of the banks of the Liffey has special features and attractions of its own, and which almost take it out of the uniform pattern which belongs to most cities of the United Kingdom. It has architectural pretensions of no mean order, all its public buildings being in the same style, and almost of the same era. . . .

How then does a city, without trade, manufactures, or law, look as gay . . . as if it were fattening on trade, and manufactures, and wealthy citizens? We may put all this down to the presence of a Court – a Court which has been called 'Brummagem', 'a sham,' and a hundred such contemptuous names. . . .

At the proper time in 'the season' . . . the grand rooms are thrown open, the Viceroy and the Vicereine are ready to see their subjects, to feast them in their halls.

For a 'sham,' and a thing that we are taught Brummagem, the matériel for a 'sermony' is very complete. Peeping into this Throne-room, which is all a-blaze with gold, with a coved ceiling, which has rich amber hangings and furniture to match, and which recalls a state-room in the palace of St. Cloud, we can see a throne with a handsome canopy, and for a matter of spectacle, a very glittering pageant indeed. . . . the Viceroy himself, who may be assumed

---

1. *Dickensian*, Vol. 23 (1927).
2. *All the Year Round*, 26 May 1866.

The Valentine (*Sketches by Boz*)

to be that genial, gracious, pastime-loving and Irish-loving nobleman, the late Earl of Carlisle, whose strangely heavy white hair, rosy full face, and gartered knee make a picture that will be long recollected. On each side, in a semicircle, are his 'staff,' the dozen or so of 'aides,' the 'master of the horse,' 'comptroller,', 'chamberlain,' 'gentlemen at large,' 'state stewards,' 'private secretaries,' 'physicians to the household,' 'surgeons to the household,' make up a respectable and showy gathering. But opposite them, thus making a sort of semicircular lane, is a yet more effective crowd, the dignitaries and persons of quality of 'the Court,' who have been privileged with what is called the 'private entrée.' Here we have archbishops and primates, and lord chancellors and lords justices, chief justices, lord mayors, deans, chaplains, heralds in gorgeous tabards, knights of St. Patrick, commanders of forces, privy councillors in profusion, earls, marquises, barons, and all the 'ladies' of these illustrious persons. When we think that every one looks their best and wears their best, and that every family diamond is put on to the best advantage, the whole must be a rather dazzling sight. But for them the whole spectacle must be a show of great interest and amusement. For here, now, the pages are letting down the agitated little Glorvina's train, and the dreadful moment is at hand. Her stately mamma, well accustomed to such a process, has stalked on majestically, undismayed if a whole regiment were drawn up there. Already the officials have got the little girl's card, and are passing it on from hand to hand, and the last has chanted it aloud: 'MISS GLORVINA SARSFIELD!'

with the addition, 'TO BE PRESENTED!' which, translated into English, means a vice-regal privilege consecrated by immemorial usage. . . . The charming little Glorvina – a Connemara rosebud – now making her curtsey . . . is drawn over, and the osculatory tribute exacted in a half paternal fashion. . . .

This ordeal passed through, Miss Glorvina's train is carefully gathered up and restored to her, and she emerges into the long room or gallery, where there is the crowd who have successfully passed through. One of the most entertaining things in the world is to stand at this door and study the play of human female expression as each emerge – the satisfaction, shyness, and complacency, which all struggle in the one face.

Next we troop into ST. PATRICK'S HALL – the grand ball-room – with the painted ceiling and the galleries, where the musicians play, and the mirrors and the scarlet tiers of seats. Here, too, is a dais, and another throne. And down this room when the drawing-room is done, and the thousand or so of ladies, gentle and simple, have passed by, there is 'THE PROCESSION,' and vice King and vice Queen march solemnly and stately down to the drumming and trumpeting of music in the gallery. By one o'clock all have departed; and in the next morning's papers we have the 'correct list' in due order of precedence, and, more pleasant reading still, a minute account of the jewels, dresses, laces, lappets, 'bouillons,' 'buffons,' and the rest.

Almost next day set in the dinners and balls. Country paterfamilias with his wife and daughters – a staunch supporter of government – is bidden. The late Lord Carlisle dispensed an almost sumptuous hospitality. Those weekly 'banquets' as they were called, where a hundred guests were entertained in the large St. Patrick's Hall as elegantly and as perfectly as if it were a dinner of twelve, will not be soon forgotten. This amiable nobleman delighted in having 'his friends about him.' He loved everything that the Irish would call 'sport', and was never wanting where 'sport' called for him. It was worth seeing this Viceroy at the curious ceremony on St. Patrick's-day, when the guards were relieved at the Castle, and the bands played Irish airs, and the Viceroy appeared on his balcony literally loaded with shamrocks. A mass of the great unwashed below, crowded densely, listening to their national airs; and when some stirring jig struck up, the charm became irresistible, a number of rings were instinctively formed, and then was Pat and Andy 'footing it,' regardless of all proprieties. Police rushed up to avert the profanation; but the good-natured Viceroy was seen protesting as furiously from his balcony, and the odd morning entertainment proceeded. As the fun waxed furious the contagion spread, more circles broke out, and presently the great yard was a mass of human beings dancing like dervishes."

* * *

TRIUMPHANT CARRIAGES[3]

"After much consideration, we have come to the conclusion that there is less wear of shoe-leather in Ireland than in any Christian country in the world. In Ireland, when a man ceases to go barefoot, he somehow or other rides. This is a curious and a rather serious matter, which may be looked at in more ways than one. The deficiency of a middle class in Ireland is a solemn and mournful truth, on which it is not now our business to enlarge. We do not mean, of course, that there is no middle class; nor that it is much smaller in the half-dozen chief towns of Ireland than in considerable towns elsewhere. In fact, a town is impossible without a broad middle-class stratum on which to found its institutions. What we mean is, that over the greater part of the surface of Ireland there is spread a thin population of uncomfortable people (as we should think), with a nobleman's seat, and the mansions of a few gentry somewhere near; and very few shopkeepers, or farmers, or merchants, to transact the business of those above and below them. My lord's family and the gentry ride and drive, of course, as lords and gentry are wont to do: and the poor people walk – without shoe-leather.

If you travel near a bog in autumn – and that is a thing sure to happen to the tourist in Ireland – you will occasionally see a dingy procession on the road before you, which looks, from a distance, like a small brown funeral. When you come nearer, you see a dozen or so of large hampers, without lids, filled and piled up with dried peat, in the shape of bricks; each hamper being mounted on a rude sort of truck, and each truck being drawn by a small donkey. On the truck is somewhere perched a boy, man, or woman. . . . This is, we believe, the lowest order of Irish carriage. Then comes the superior sort of turf-car, made of upright slips of wood, sloping outwards, so as to look like a square basket of rails upon wheels. This is light and pretty, and serves well for carrying peat, hay, animals, and whatever the farmer has to convey that is solid. Our substantial country cars and waggons are rarely seen – and still more rarely the farmers' gigs which abound on English roads. Besides that, there are few men in Ireland answering to our farmers; they prefer their 'outside car' to our gig – and very reasonably. That 'outside car' is the most delightful vehicle we know of – so light and well-balanced, that a horse can draw a greater load for a longer distance than an Englishman can believe, until he sees it: so safe, that it is scarcely possible to apprehend an accident: so convenient, that it has been praised till people are tired of hearing of it; wherefore we will say no more about it. After this come the handsome carriages, made in Dublin, which are much like the handsome carriages seen in

---

3.   *Household Words*, 23 October 1852.

London and Paris, and New York, and other places where an aristocracy has
to please itself about its means of conveyance.

Made in Dublin, we say. Thereby hangs a tale, which has, for years,
interested us, whenever we have thought of Dublin and the Irish, and which
may, therefore, interest others. So we will briefly tell it.

In the last century, we must remember, Ireland did not belong to England as she does now. She was yoked to England, but not incorporated with
her. There was then no United Kingdom, such as we speak of now. Ireland
was subject to our monarchs, and had a Viceroy living in Dublin, as representative of the Sovereign; but she had her own Parliament, managed her
own affairs, and had much less claim on the aid, fellow-feeling, and co-operation of England than now, when the representatives of the whole people of our
islands sit in the same legislature, and become more united in their real
interests, year by year. In those days it was all-important to Ireland to have
flourishing branches of industry of her own. One of the best illustrations of
the wisdom and folly of that day is the coach-making business, for which the
Messrs. Hutton have made Dublin famous.

In 1779, Mr. John Hutton, a worthy citizen of Dublin, set up a coach-
manufactory in Great Britain Street. All that we know of his business during
the first ten years is that it was successful. There was no doubt about that: but
his friends believed his success to be owing in part to the central situation of
his factory, while he knew it to be owing to the goodness of the work done
there. When, in 1789, he removed to Summerhill, where the factory now is,
he was told that he was going out of the way of the great thoroughfares, and
that the citizens would desert him. His reply was, that if his carriages were
good, people would come to Summerhill for them; and so they did, for the
business became a very fine one, employing a large number of men.

The Irish rebellion – one of the most mournful events in history – took
place; and then the flag with the united arms of Great Britain and Ireland,
floated from the Tower of London and the Castle at Dublin, on the first day of
the century; and Mr. John Hutton went on growing rich, and his men went on
making coaches in the old way, never imagining that anything could be better. The coaches were eminently good, certainly; and Mr. Hutton chose that
they should continue to be so. More Irish gentry now went to London, and
they saw and valued all recent improvements in carriages. In 1806, one
young son came into the business, and in 1811, another; and it may fairly be
supposed that these young men might introduce some new ideas, and infuse
fresh spirit into the business. However this may be, it is clear that the men –
some few of them – at this time made up their minds to manage the business
in their own way, and allow none but friends of their own to be employed.

One April afternoon in that year (1811), they waylaid and cruelly beat a
fellow-workman, named Davis, on the ground that he had been a saddler

originally, whereas he was now foreman of the harness-makers in the factory. The folly of this act presently appeared. Owing to Davis's ability, the firm had been able to make some harness at home which had before been imported from England. When Davis was disabled, the importation was renewed, and several men lost their employment, – none of them being qualified to fill the place of the injured man. On the twenty-seventh of the same month, some of the malcontents concealed themselves in the factory, instead of going home from work and in the course of the night they destroyed the linings of several new carriages, and cut and defaced the panels, carving on them the names of obnoxious persons, and threats to their employers.

It was now time for Government to interfere. A reward of two hundred pounds was offered for the apprehension of each of the first three persons who should be convicted of either of the offences which signalised that unhappy month. As for the Messrs. Hutton, they were fully aware of the importance to their country of sustaining such a manufacture as theirs; and they knew that it could be done only by their conducting their own business in their own way. They reasoned kindly with their men, even affectionately, showing them the true state of the case, while they declared that they would submit to no dictation, but conduct their manufacture in their own way, or retire from business. By this time, the manufacture was so large, that the whole city was interested in its continuance.

In 1812, it was found to be desirable to bring over an accomplished coach-painter from London. No man was removed to make way for this Richard Couchman. The benevolent employers hoped to provide work for new men by every improvement they introduced; but some few of their people were rather muddle-headed – confounding the employment of an Englishman in Ireland with sending over Irish work to be done in England; which last was exactly the misfortune which the Messrs. Hutton were striving to avert. They knew that the Irish gentry would buy carriages in London (now that every body was frequently going to London), unless they could have them at least as good for the same money in Dublin. Richard Couchman gave a supper to his fellow-workmen on his arrival, according to custom. On that night (in December, 1812), one of his guests, Arthur Conolly, told him that the Irishmen did not want any Englishmen among them, and that he, for one, would not have his work found fault with. This man had been originally a labourer in the yard, at eight shillings a week. He had been taught a branch of the business by Mr. Hutton; and was now receiving excellent wages as a painter. After this supper, he became so morose and sullen, that his employers, at the suggestion of Couchman himself, raised his wages to twenty-eight shillings per week, to remove from his mind any notion that he was supplanted, or out of favour. Nothing would do, however; and he so conducted himself, that it was necessary to discharge him the next June.

On the twenty-seventh of August, as Couchman and another workman were going home in the evening, and just as they had parted, Couchman was felled by a blow on the head. He was not at once perfectly insensible. He felt many more blows, 'as a sort of jar,' saw many legs, the glittering of weapons, and the ends of bludgeons. He saw also the face of Conolly and of one Kelly; and so did the comrade he had just parted with, who was also struck, and had a narrow escape. It seems to carry us back to a very old time, to read that these two men – Conolly and Kelly – were pilloried. They were imprisoned for two years, and pilloried three times.

And now came out the civic heroism of the benevolent employers. They were very rich, and they might have withdrawn from business. But they knew the worth, both of the principle for which they were contending, and of the maintenance of such a manufacture as theirs. They knew themselves to be in peril of their lives. They went out to their country houses every evening well armed. But they issued addresses to their men, brave as benevolent, – in which they avowed that they knew the guilty ones among their people, and had their eye upon them; that they would not yield a single point on any compulsion whatever; and that they preserved their sincere attachment to the faithful among their work-people, to whom they would be faithful in return. They escaped attack. . . .

In 1824, there was another conflict; but it was much less serious. The coach smiths of the city of Dublin complained of the importation, by the firm, of certain articles of wrought iron, different from what they were accustomed to make; which was, of course, the reason of the importation. . . . Some of them refused to touch the iron work imported from England. This stopped the manufacture, of course, as far as the new material was meant to be applied. The firm issued an admirable address to the rest of their people, promising to employ them as long as it was possible to do so; but showing that this could be but for a short time, if the carriages could not be finished. They had already offered to set up in business two of their own smiths, to copy the English patterns, supplying them with capital, material, and apparatus, and paying the same price as in England: but the refusal of the offer showed that the aim of the men was to preclude recent improvements, and compel their employers to make coaches in the old way, and in no other. On this occasion, there appeared to be very great danger that the firm would be obliged to close their manufactory. . . .

It will have been observed that none of the conflicts, during all this long course of years, had been about wages, or hours of working. There had been no possible ground for it; for the firm had never been in combination with other employers against the men; although the men had been in combination with others against the introduction of English improvements. The practice of the firm had always been to pay liberal wages, in order to secure the best work. They hired the labour which suited them, – which was always of the highest order that could be obtained. If the men were satisfied, they supported them against all encroachment and injury. If the men were not satisfied, they let them go in all good will, and, if it was possible, helped them to settle themselves more to their minds. There was little of this parting, however; for the best men knew when they were well off. They were maintained in sickness, pensioned after long service, watched over with vigilant good-will; and wise men were in no hurry to throw away friends who would do this.

The time came when the advantage of such an understanding was put to the proof. In times of distress, the carriage is the first luxury laid down by those who must economise, and it is the last thing to be purchased by those who can do without it. We all remember the years of distress from 1836 to 1843. At that time the younger of the two brothers was alone in the business, – the father having died long before, and the elder brother being at that time the member for Dublin, with O'Connell for his colleague. It had long been foreseen that there must be some decline in the business from the increase of railroads. To this was added the seven years' distress. Mr. Hutton stood between his men and utter ruin as long as possible. His large capital enabled him to allow his stock to accumulate: but the time came, towards the close of 1842, when he was compelled, in order to keep on his men, to reduce their work and wages slightly. There were persons who endeavoured to make mischief between him and his people on this occasion; but he easily made himself understood by giving his reasons, and the facts of the case. After that came the famine, and with it, of course, a prodigious falling off of business. The Irish gentry could not buy carriages while the people were starving, and the rates were heavier than many could pay. And when affairs began to come round, and there seemed to be a prospect of better days, a terrible accident happened. His family being absent, Mr. Hutton was sleeping in town, when a servant rushed into his room in the middle of the night, crying out, 'O, sir! the factory is on fire!'. He was on the spot instantly, in time to save the Lord Mayor's grand carriages, which were wanted the next day, and which were worth many hundred pounds. The timber-yard was safe, happily; a circumstance of great importance, as it takes some years to season the wood properly. But the loss was very great – many thousands of pounds over and above the insurance. It was a melancholy sight to the gazing crowd, to see the carriages brought out – some of them on fire inside, and others cracking and warping, and to know how many more were destroyed. And there was the fear that Mr. Hutton would now retire. He was rich; his brother had retired; and he might be supposed to have had enough of it, considering what the last few years must have been. Happily, he has not retired. He has rebuilt his factory, and very nearly brought everything round to its former state of order; and, as there are sons in the business, it may be hoped that the establishment may continue to be the blessing to Dublin that it has been for nearly three-quarters of a century.

There are no heart-burnings there now; – no dispute – no mistrust. The principle of the firm is, at length, understood, so as never to be mistaken again. To make the best possible carriages, in order to secure this fine business to Dublin, is the aim; and to use their own judgment as to how this is to be done, is the determination of these gentlemen. Their fellow-townsmen now see what a blessing it is that they have been so resolute in holding to their determination. Any stranger in Dublin, who mentions their names, is sure to hear what is now thought of them and their kindly victory."

* * *

THE LENGTH OF THE QUAYS[4]

"To an Englishman whose chief knowledge of Ireland has been confined to what he has been able to glean from books and newspapers, and what he has gathered from the testimony of travellers, and from the conversation of Irishmen themselves, the first sight of the city of Dublin cannot fail to awaken in him an emotion of agreeable disappointment. From all he has read, and all he has heard of the misery and destitution of Ireland; of her squalid poverty and utter prostration, physical and moral; of the decay of her commerce, the stagnation of her inland trade, the grovelling poverty of her people, the neglect of her aristocracy, and the mismanagement of her rulers; of the lamentable and pitiable state indeed to which she has been reduced by much misgovernment and more national indolence – from what, in fine, he has seen and may inductively argue from the raggedness and wretchedness of the teeming Irish colonies in London, and Liverpool, and Glasgow, he may expect, on landing on Dublin Quay, to find himself in a metropolis of hovels occupied chiefly by beggars and slaves, trampled upon by a few foreign tyrants, and priest-ridden by a rampant clergy. He may expect to see such nobles as are not absentees in second-hand attire; the ruined gentry growing and selling potatoes for a subsistence; he might look in every street for a repetition of Church Lane, St. Giles's, or Fontenoy Street, Liverpool, with tattered mendicants in every street, a pig in every parlour, and a whiskey shop at every corner.

He lands. A magnificent city, numbering more than two hundred and fifty thousand inhabitants, stretches along the two banks of a bright and unsullied river, in the midst of some of the most beautiful scenery in the world. Two magnificent lines of quays, broken by bridges (of which there are

4. *Household Words*, Vol. 7, 1853, pp. 582–586.

seven within the municipal boundary), and which equal in architectural elegance, though of course not in size, anything we can show on the River Thames; streets of palaces; a bank which is amongst the finest architectural monuments in Great Britain; a splendid palace of justice (the Four Courts); a sumptuous Custom-House; a noble university; two venerable cathedrals for the Protestant form of worship and one for Catholic rites, together with a crowd of churches and chapels for every species of religious denomination. Were I to state that he may walk miles without being solicited for alms: that he may peep into scores of parlours without catching the remotest glimpse of a pig wrestling for potato-parings with ragged children: that he may sojourn in Dublin for days without seeing a drunken man: that no blackguard boys pursue him with ribaldry, or fling mud at him, or tilt tip-cats in his eyes: no gents puff cigar-smoke in his face: no man curses him for a Saxon, or insults him for a heretic: that the people are civil and obliging: that there are shops which would put the glories of Ludgate Hill and Regent Street to shame: hotels that for magnitude and splendour vie with the Adelphi at Liverpool and the Bedford at Brighton: and when I state that to crown all this there has been built in Merrion Square, on the lawn of what was once the Duke of Leinster's palace a Palace of Art and Industry, elegant and tasteful in construction, vast in extent, and magnificent in contents, due solely to the genius and patriotism of Irishmen, and to which more than ten thousand persons resort daily: – were I to declare so much, I should be enumerating what may or may not happen to a stranger in Dublin. . . .

So many things that he expected to see the traveller does not see, that he is fairly puzzled and amazed. The pigs and the drivers whooping after them; the excited Hibernians brandishing shillelaghs and whisky bottles, and entreating passers-by to tread on the tails of their coats – where are they? Are the colonists in England more Irish than Ireland? I came to behold looped and windowed raggedness, and, behold! I find luxury and splendour.

The Dublin quays are nearly three miles long. The pretty little river Liffey, for its whole course throughout the city, is not hidden, like the Thames at London, by houses and wharfs. No hideous seven-storied warehouses, no rubbish crowded wharfs, no Phlegethonian fleets of frowning coal-barges, no factories with tasteless chimneys twisting out black smoke, no piles of rotting timbers, or dismantled half broken-up ships, or unpicturesque stone-yards, or uncouth ship-building sheds, or tumble down crazy houses, or slimy stairs, line the banks of Dublin river or obstruct the spectator's view. The stream is visible throughout; and you may travel on either bank by a broad well-paved road, running immediately between the houses and the river. In this and in numerous other instances there is a striking and agreeable resemblance between the quays of Dublin and the quays of Paris. The long unbroken lines of parapets and balustrades, and the shining river rippling and glistening at

their feet. The numerous watchmakers, knick-nac, toy and curiosity or bric-
...-brac shops, with the good humoured throng of well-dressed loungers – (it
is astonishing what a number of persons in Dublin, male as well as female,
seem to have nothing to do) – peering at watches, toys, and jewellery, turning
over shells and bog-wood bracelets, and thrusting their fingers into parrots'
and macaws' beaks. The numerous shops for the sale of fishing tackle, devo-
tional books, and queer little pictures of the Virgin and saints, rosaries,
scapularies, agnus Deis, and religious medals and ornaments. The short but
handsome and often recurring bridges, the bent double old women muffled
in cloaks, who want but the coloured handkerchief twisted round the head to
be completely French. . . . The noble public edifices, with bookstalls nestling
under the lee of their porticos, and blind men basking in the sun on their
steps. All these, with the sun and sky and genial atmosphere, are so many
points of affinity between the quays of Eblana and Lutetia.

We set out on our ramble down the length of the Quays at the Royal
Barracks, close to Arbour Hill, where is the great military hospital, and adjoining the Phoenix Park. We stand before a huge pile of stone buildings,
calculated, so my information goes, to accommodate two regiments of cavalry
and one of infantry. There is not much to repay curiosity in a barrack, wherever it may be – whether on Dublin Quay or the Quai d'Orsay, or the Birdcage
Walk, or in Berlin, Vienna, or St. Petersburg. When we say that a barrack is
a barrack all is pretty nearly told. The same listless men, in apparently
unimproveable slovenliness, lolling out of open windows; the same men on
guard in as apparently an unimproveable state of neatness and disciplined
dandyism; the monotonous lines of walls and chimneys pierced by windows
and doors; the busy sergeants plodding past with parchment covered books;
the same sergeant-major with the same stick; the same weary parties at drill,
looking very much as if they did not like it at all, which is very probable; the
same slatternly women and children, with the unmistakeable baggage-wag-
gon stamp about them. . . .

Down the length of the Quays beyond the barrack, past busy shops and
through busy throngs, we find ourselves beside the oldest of the bridges. It is
a grim grey structure of heavy frowning arches upon solid piers. This is called
by the startling name of Bloody Bridge. Why, you shall hear. The first bridge
was built of wood in sixteen hundred and seventy; but in the following year a
great riot took place among a body of apprentices who assembled here for the
purpose of pulling the bridge down. The soldiers were called out, and took
some scores of the rioters into custody; but, in an attempted rescue, several
were killed and thrown from the bridge, and their blood mingling with the
water went purpling down the Liffey. The bridge was reconstructed, afterwards, of stone; but its evil name adhered to it, and it has been known ever
since as Bloody Bridge. . . .

Two more bridges – the Queen's and Whitworth; but just ere we come to the latter we pause before the Roman Catholic chapel of St. Paul, upon Arran Quay. Hither come on Sundays the Roman Catholic soldiers to attend mass. It is a sight to see them with their bright scarlet and brighter accoutrements. Pass Whitworth Bridge, and on the left banks of the Quays is a public building you have, I warrant, heard and read of many a time. On the site of a Dominican monastery, called St. Saviour, was built, in seventeen hundred and seventy-six, a pile of buildings devoted to the judicature of the Chancery, King's Bench, Exchequer, and Common Pleas, and known commonly as the Four Courts.

I have not the art of guide-book writing, or I would mention the exact dimensions of this noble structure, with full information in addition as to its friezes, entablatures, Corinthian columns, statues, &c. As it is, I am content to enter the great circular hall, with twelve windows, crowned by a dome. This during term time is open to all – serving, indeed, the purpose of Westminster Hall in London or the Salle des Pas Perdus in Paris; and here for a contemplative man is food for thought sufficient to last him for a month.

Suitors, witnesses, and idlers mingle with vendors of watch-guards, dog-collars, combs, oranges, hundred-bladed knives, memorandum-books, almanacks, and sponges; together with barristers, barristers' clerks, attorneys hard-faced and sleek-faced, all are mixed up in heterogeneous confusion.

How many lord chancellors that were to be have paced this hall briefless and in rusty gowns? How many chancellors that are to be pace it now in similar case? Here, in the good old times, how many an amicable arrangement has been made for a deadly duel next morning in the 'fifteen acres?' How many ghosts must haunt this hall of barristers shot by barristers, plaintiffs shot by defendants? What blood as well as dust in the Four Courts. But that pace is ended, and hair-trigger footsteps are lost no more.

We pass Richmond and Essex bridges – the last named after an Ear of Essex who was lord-lieutenant here in sixteen hundred and seventy-six – and which is said to have been erected on the exact model of Westminster bridge. It is of course smaller, but considerably handsomer, than that infirm old structure which has been patched and cobbled so often, that, like Elwes the miser's worsted hose, scarcely any of the original fabric remains.

Yet more quays, and more bridges. There is the metal bridge, constructed in eighteen hundred and sixteen, and is one hundred and forty feet long, I am told, consisting of one bold elliptical arch. Another quay – still lined on one side by busy, bustling shops – and we approach the termination of our ramble. We stand upon Carlisle Bridge, the most crowded thoroughfare in Dublin, leading from Westmoreland Street, the Bank, the College, &c., to Sackville Street, the Post Office, and Nelson Column.

Here, traveller, pause and gaze on the stately Custom-House, the ships –

too few, alas! – and the great port of Dublin. All lie eastward; and eastward, too, stretch more quays, lined chiefly with shipping and bonding warehouses, and shops for the sale of ships' stores. Southward runs the stream of life and motion: – jaunting cars and carriages; inside and outside cars; officers on horseback; parties of excursionists coming from the Exhibition; laughing children and comely peasants. Westward are the quays and bridges we have passed, and in the far-off distance rise, with purpling shadows against the summer sky, the crumbling towers of St. Audeon's and the cathedral of Christ Church. The setting sun has bathed tower and spire, mast and cupola, water and quay, in one flood of golden light; and the river dances, and the diamond-flashing windows seem to laugh, and from the crowds on the quays and streets comes up a cheerful murmur.

From my window at home, in the twilight, I can still see the length of the quays, the houses, the bridges, and the people. Presently the twinkling lamps are lighted; and these, with the gas-lit shops, and the deep red glow from the chemists, mirror themselves in the water, which grows darker and deeper every minute. . . ."

* * *

A DUBLIN MAY MORNING[5]

In 'A Dublin May Morning' the author visits Dublin to view the Great Dublin Exhibition of 1865:

"From a land that surely seems about as remote as – say – Spain, have been floating to us the strange cries of Tenant Right, Evictions, Distress, Established Church, Fenianism, and all the other 'isms' which belong to an Orange and to a Ribbon. But, a day's easy jaunting – eleven hours by train and 'new and splendid packets' – will set us down in the very country with all these popular cries echoing about us. . . .

And now, of all seasons in the world – when I look down on this gay May morning from a window into Great Sackville-street, where there is a huge column to Admiral Nelson, and a golden shop-front board dedicated to O'Connell, on the site for his statue, and which is by-and-by to be made into a French boulevard and planted with trees – I say, on this May morning it is easy to see that one of the many Great Days for Ireland has come round once more. For, the crowds in the great thoroughfares, and the 'Boys' sitting on the bridges, and the flags and streamers, and the rolling carriages, and the gen-

---

5. *All the Year Round*, 27 May 1865, pp. 421-424.

eral air of busy idleness, tell me that a great festival is toward; and placards in fiercely carbuncled letters proclaim in an angry fit of St. Antony's fire, that H.R.H. the Prince of Wales is to 'OPEN' something: which something a still greater scorbutic operation of type tells us is THE DUBLIN EXHIBITION OF 1865.

I think, as I look out on this May morning, that it is curious that a people popularly supposed to want 'self-reliance' and 'independence,' and who are utterly ignorant of the 'self-help' principle, should, after all, have done some few self-reliant things in this very matter of exhibitions. Some one tells me that many decades of years before glass palaces were thought of, and when the universal peace and brotherhood glass palaces were mysteriously supposed to bring with them were not quite believed in, this 'un-self-reliant' people had their regular triennial exhibition of manufactures, on the French model. Further, that close on the footsteps of the Hyde Park Exhibition came the great one of Cork, and closer again on the footsteps of Cork the really great Dublin Exhibition of 1853, the building of which cost nearly eighty thousand pounds, and which was remarkable for the first international collection of pictures, and for the first performance of Handel on a colossal scale. Not content with this, I am told that this people, who were not self-reliant, went further, had two more successful exhibitions on a smaller scale, and have now finally girded themselves up for this yet more complete effort of 1865. Not so bad, this, for our poor woebegone sister with the harp. . . .

It is known then, on this gay Dublin May morning, that the young prince, who in this island has always been looked to with an affectionate interest, has been in the city since overnight, and out at the pretty lodge, which lies out in the 'Phaynix.' Hence the flags and the streamers. Hence, too, in front of the palace, the balconies fringed with scarlet, and the softened and melodious buzz of distant military music, with the staff officers flying north and south, and the regiments tramping by. But the flags grow thicker, and the balconies gayer, and the music more distinct, as I find myself at the corner of the great place, or square, dedicated to St. Stephen, which is a good mile's walking all round, and near which I see the great building, with the heavy porches and pillars, round which, and over which, run delicately, the light entrance of a Moorish-looking glass temple – a silver howdah on the back of a grey elephant. Such is the rather novel design for this last comer in the long series of exhibitions.

There has been the usual crush and pressure, the tremendous toiling against time, to get all done; the straining of every nerve, the sitting up all night, the hammering and sawing, the stitching of a hundred workmen and workwomen, changing the utter disorder and the naked deal boards and the rude planks of five o'clock last evening to perfect order – to the regularity of a drawing-room and acres of scarlet cloth. And in a crowd of light May morning dresses we drift into the huge Concert Hall, which is to hold thousands, and to echo to brass throats, and where there are the great organ, and the orchestra which holds the musical army a thousand strong: on the floor of which has grown up beds upon beds of human lilies that flutter and flutter again, whose flowers are white parasols and gossamer shawls. This hall, as a feature, is not so remarkable, for there are many great halls; but at its far end it is open, and crossed half way by a gallery; and through this opening we see far on into a Winter Garden and Crystal Palace, where are the light airy galleries, with the old familiar crimson labels, and the French trophies, and the bright objects, and the great apse like a glass cathedral, and Mr. Doyle's pale colouring, the faint lines of delicate green, chosen with rare good taste, which in itself is a novelty.

Looking out through the open end of the Concert Hall, and facing the organ, I see a grand marone velvet Eastern canopy and dais, under which the Pasha of Egypt is to sit a few months hereafter and receive his tribes; and on this dais are the nobles and gentlemen gathering, in the fine rich theatrical suits which give a colour to a festival, and of which we have not half enough. Judges in scarlet and ermine, privy councillors with coats that seem 'clotted' with gold, the never-failing lords-lieutenant and deputy-lieutenants, knights of St. Patrick, deans, doctors in scarlet, soldiers in scarlet, a lord chancellor all black and gold, Eastern dervishes (it may be, from the pillow-case look of their caps), a lord mayor of York, a lord provost of Edinburgh; in short, all shapes of parti-coloured finery. Turning round for a second, I see that the black musical army has debouched and taken ground, and that the great orchestra has spread like a large dark fan from floor to ceiling.

Now, I hear the hum of distant martial music, and the yet fainter but more inspiriting sound of distant cheering. Then the scarlet and ermine, the privy council clotted gold, the May morning bonnets, glitter and rustle with excitement. The hum and chatter of voices full of expectation travels on softly down the glass aisles and into the great hall. There has been a grand plunging of military troopers outside, a violent arrest of fiery horses pulled up suddenly, and the prince and a royal duke and the vice-king and all their attendants have descended. From the outside, the shouting creeps in gradually, until at last, it comes to its fullest pitch, when the crimson and gold crowd parts a little, we see this prince standing modestly under the Egyptian pasha's canopy, with thirty thousand eyes upon him. At this moment a speck half way up the dark orchestra, but which is a very skilful and most musical speck, gives a signal with what seems a white pin, and the musical army advances with the line Old Hundredth. The grand Old Hundredth travels out in rising waves through the open end of the hall into the glass cathedral, then loses itself up and down in the aisles. For two verses the voices do the battle by themselves; but, at the third, the trumpets and the grand brass and the rolling of monster drums burst out, and every syllable is emphasised with a stirring crash. It is like the deluge after a drought.

Then the sun gets up, and the gold and coloured figures cross, and crowd, and fit past, as some business is being transacted under that Egyptian pasha's canopy; for there are addresses to be read and spoken, and there is much advancing and backing to be done. Now, the party under the pasha's canopy breaks up for a time, and the stiff gold and scarlet and privy council strait-waistcoats, and the corporate dressing-gowns, having formed themselves into a procession, take the prince round to look at the place.

And there is a great deal to see. There are many charming pictures, and among the choicest those of which the Queen of Spain has stripped her palaces, and sent here. Is there not a hint of many a Velasquez most exquisite, and of Mr. Stirling, which are worth a journey to the Escurial to worship! Here is many a rare Reynolds which Mr. Tom Taylor might find worth making a note of, and here are walls covered with noble cartoons of the severe Munich school. These, with the photographs and water-colours, and mediaeval objects, are common to many an exhibition held before; but there is one feature unique – a noble sculpture gallery, artistic, charmingly lighted, sufficient to delight Mr. Gibson, and drive the Royal Academy to despair. A sculpture-hall, in which you can look up to an arching glass roof, and, half way down again, to the balustrade just mentioned, which is dotted with small statues. A sculpture-hall, where I can walk round and think myself in a Roman palace, to which these fine objects belong, and not in a temporary shed where some scattered objects that have been lent are shown. For here I see that the Roman studios have been emptied of their treasures; that Miss Hosmer has sent her Faun, in toned yellow marble: a marvellous – if the speech be not impolite – work for a woman. With Story's wonderful Judith, and a Baby Girl by Mogni – a pendant for the now famous Reading Girl. But it is easy to prophesy that this Baby Girl will be photographed, and stereoscoped, and binocularised in a hundred ways, and watched over by policemen specially, and visited by a steady crowd. This hall and its contents – the like of which it is no boast to say has not been yet seen in these kingdoms – is the feature of this exhibition.

Then, having seen all that is most curious and beautiful – in the fashion in which such things must be seen where there is only a quarter of an hour to see them – the stiff gold and crimson strands, which we call the procession, came back to the pasha's dais. And then, with a crash and a smash, and a thundering of monster drums, and the rattle and rolling of little drums, and the sharp brassy bark of trumpets, the true English national Old Hundredth, in which musical and unmusical – people with ears and people without, even people with voices, and people without – can join, then God save the Queen is sung. Sung! Rather fired off! Discharged! Salvoed!

And then the glittering mass begins to dissolve and fade away. The stage, which has been laid out under the pasha's canopy, gradually clears. At the door there is a struggle, and the scatter of new gravel, with the frantic leaping up behind carriages of many footmen, and the closing in of mounted soldiers. And then the pageant melts away, and the work of the day is done.

* * *

AN IRISH STEW[6]

In 'The Length of the Quays', the author stated that he had come to Dublin expecting to see the shabby side of the city but had only found grandeur. But on this occasion he found the Coombe.

"I have found them! The rags, the bones, the sawdust and the dirt, which I was at first unable, as I endeavoured to explain in a former paper, to discover in Dublin. But I have found them now. Not in Sackville Street, or Westmoreland Street, or Dame Street, or Grafton Street; not in aristocratic Merrion Square or College, or Stephen's Green; not in the Phoenix Park – but in the Coombe.

I have taken my fill of the monuments and public buildings, and of the Industrial Exhibition. But I have been keeping a wary look-out meanwhile in the rag and bone interest; hence I found myself in the Coombe. I did not know then that the Coombe was the Coombe; so I straggled out of it again, bewildered, dazed, in a labyrinth of dirty streets, rubbing the eyes of my mind, as one of the Seven Sleepers might have rubbed his corporeal eyes on his first ramble after his nap. The Lord Lieutenant (whose carriage I stopped to see sweep out of the Vice-regal yard into Dame Street) was the primary cause of my wandering Coombe-wise; but a personage somewhat removed from him in worldly station and appearance was the secondary loadstone which pointed to this pole. This was no other than a Dublin fishwoman, very much disguised or rather undisguised in rage and alcohol, who was scattering the flowers of her eloquence broadcast on a female with a barrow at the door of a whisky shop – the casus belli being a disputed question as to the right of property in a flat-iron – here called a 'smooth.' – 'Isn't it the smooth that's mine?' and, 'Sure is's not a skirrick of it that's yours,' were bandied about for some time, till the dealer in mulluscae, after the manner of persons quarrelling, diverged from the main point at issue to some retrospective griefs and torts by her suffered at the hands of her opponent. 'Isn't it yerself,' demanded this female Demosthenes in a concluding Philippic, 'that daren't go to chapel, forbye Father M'Anasser forbad ye ivery brick of it? Isn't it herself that kem

6.   *Household Words*, Vol. 7, 1853, pp. 617–620.

down only Wednesday was a fortnight to the corner of the Coombe, foreninst
the whole world and called me a murthering ould excommunicated
gaseometer?' With which latter trope she folded her arms and looked oyster-
knives at her enemy. . . .

I found the Coombe – which is indeed a very long, straggling estuary
between houses (I cannot call it a street) running from the bottom of Francis
Street to Ardee Street and Pimlico, and possessing vomitoria seemingly innumerable, in the shape of lanes, back streets, courts and blind alleys – to be a
thoroughfare of the same description as its neighbour, with a strong additional dash of Petticoat Lane, Broker's Row in Birmingham and Newgate
Market; but with an almost indescribable aspect of dirt and confusion, semi-
continental picturesqueness, shabbiness – less the shabbiness of dirt than
that of untidiness – over-population, and frowsiness generally, perfectly original and peculiarly its own. I wandered up and down and about the Coombe
for hours, till I was hungry, thirsty, and tired, and I would strongly advise all
travellers in Ireland, all painters of still life and genre subjects, and lovers of
the picturesque catholicity, by no means to omit a walk in the Coombe when
they visit Dublin, the silence of the guide books and the ciceroni notwithstanding. Let me see if I can, in my small way, recall a few of the oddities I
saw.

First the old clothes. A man who has seen the Temple in Paris, and Rag-
fair in London, is apt to imagine that very little can astonish him in the cast-off
garment line. Let him come to the Coombe. This, its subsidiaries, succursals,
and tributaries, don't teem but swarm, don't swarm but burst, with old clothes.
Here is a shop out of a hundred which is a mass of old clothes, so thickly
sown, so deeply heaped, that the proprietor and proprietors, squatting among
them smoking their pipes, look like bundles of old clothes (they are little else)
themselves. Every imaginable article of male and female attire seems clus-
tered together in this shop. The broken windows have old clothes stuffed into
their shattered panes; the sleeping department of the establishment is walled
off by a screen of old gowns and petticoats; the wind is excluded by old
stockings thrust into chinks, and sleeveless coats laid at the bottoms of doors.
There is a tattered shawl for a carpet, and a fragment of some under-garment
for a table-cloth; old clothes for counterpanes, old clothes for window cur-
tains; the pockets of old clothes (I shouldn't wonder) for corner cupboards.
All the mortals that sleep in the valley of dry bones seem to have left their
garments here.

Yes, here they all are, and you may see yourself retrospectively in a
mirror of rags. Here is the black frock and black sash and broad-flapped hat
with the black plume you wore for your father's death. You wear these rags,
ay! You wonder now whether you could ever have worn them, as much as
when at five years old you marvelled why they were substituted for the glow-

ing plaid merino and showy Leghorn purchased for you only three weeks before. Here are your first school-clothes, the marks of the wiped pen yet on cuff and collar, the whitened elbows attesting how doggedly you leant with them on the desk, over verbum personale – the wrinkled arms, and frayed cuffs, and cracked seams, bearing witness how much too big you grew for that last jacket before you were provided with a new one. Here is the tail coat you courted your first wife in; here in dank sable tatters is the black suit you wore at her funeral; and here is the blue body coat and fawn-coloured kerseymeres you made the second Mrs. Reader a happy woman in. Here is your school-master's grey duffel dressing-gown, the very sight of which throws a shudder through you, even now; your grandmother's well remembered black satin (worn only on high days and holidays, and reposing during the rest of the year in a dilapidated piebald hair trunk like a quadrangular cow); your sister's cashmere shawl you brought her after your first voyage, and in the centre of which Gyp the puppy bit a neat polygonal hole. Here are all the boots and shoes you ever wore – that have paced the deck, or plodded Cheapside, or tripped along chalked floors to merry tunes, or crawled through mud and mire up to high places, or shuffled about prison-yards, or faltered in docks, or stumbled in drawing-rooms, or kept the 'pot a boiling,' or stood on the damp ground over the dampest clay beside the dampest grave, while you peered down to see the last of kindred or of love. . . .

Seriously, (if among bizarre and fantastic speculations a man can claim credit for seriousness) there is really and truly a cause for this extraordinary accumulation of old clothes not only in the Coombe, but in every back street of Dublin. The Irish, from the peasantry even to the numerous class of petty shopkeepers and mechanics are, it is patent, almost universal wearers of old clothes. At what season of national depression, what climax of suffering and destitution they were first reduced to this degrading strait is yet to be discovered; but to this day, and in this day thousands of persons (whose equals in England would disdain it) are content to wear second-hand garments – not only outer but inner and under. Again, the extraordinary exodus, which every year takes tens of thousands of Irishmen from their native shores (principally to America) creates an enormous demand for second-hand wearing apparel; for in the United States clothes are among the very dearest articles of supply, and a newly arrived emigrant without money or without some wardrobe, however tattered, would soon have to go as Adam did. And again, many many hundreds of poor creatures (I have seen it and know it) are only enabled to cross from Dublin to Liverpool (even on the deck with the pigs and geese) at the sacrifice of a waistcoat, a shawl, or a coat sold for anything they will fetch. In like manner, in Liverpool, is the passage-money to New York often completed, or the miserable stock of provisions eked out by the sale of such old clothes as can be spared. Thus a great system of clothes barter and exchange, sale, purchase, and re-sale, goes on in Ireland. . . .

Diverging, temporarily, a little from the Coombe I enter Patrick Street, which leads to Patrick's Close, and to the great Protestant Cathedral of St. Patrick. Patrick Street is of the Coombe, Coombish. One side is occupied by an imposing manifestation of the old clothes interest, the other by a continuous line of stalls for the sale of butcher's meat and provisions in general – the stalls being overshadowed by projecting bulkheads prodigiously productive of chiaro oscuro, picturesqueness, rottenness, and dinginess. This and the neighbourhood is the most ancient, raggedest, dirtiest, wretchedest part of Dublin's proud city. I become sensible of the presence of incalculable swarms of tattered children nearly all without shoes or stockings, and the average number of whose articles of dress varies from one and a half to two and three-eighths; likewise of a multiplicity of grown-up females, also barefooted – the elder ones astoundingly hideous, the younger ones not unfrequently exceedingly well-favoured, and for all their bare feet, modest and demure. The men seem to carry the allowance of shoes for both sexes, exhibiting their lower extremities cased in huge shoes, which in heavy weather on heavy roads must make walking anything but a labour of love. I opine the men of all ages and the women of mature years are nearly all smoking the national short-pipe, its top protected by a small leaden cupola, perforated, like a miniature dish-cover with a hole in it. . . .

You will say that a visit to any London or Anglo-provincial district, colonised by Irish, will show you what I have been describing; but there are sights here, in addition, that you will not see out of Patrick Street and the Coombe. Groups of men and children carrying neatly-cut sods of 'turfs,' peat sods for fuel, about for sale; little dusky shops, full of big white jugs and huge iron-hooped buckets and churns full of buttermilk; more pork and bacon and eggs within a few square yards than you would see in some town-miles; open shops like coal-sheds, but where, instead of coals, there are piles on piles and sacks on sacks of potatoes . . . numerous stalls for the sale of salt fish – cod and ling – for this is Friday, and the Coombe, though hard by the cathedral close, is Catholic. . . .

At the first cursory view, Dublin seems very deficient in houses of public entertainment. No swinging doors invite the passer by – no glistening bars dazzle the toper's eyes. He sees plenty of hotels and plenty of grocers, but few what may be called public-houses. When, however, he has been a very few days in Dublin, he discovers that in almost every 'hotel' (the Sackville Street and aristocratic ones I exclude, of course) he may be provided with refreshment as moderate as a 'dandy' of punch, or modicum of whisky and hot water, which costeth twopence; or that in almost every shop where tea and coffee and sugar are sold, there also is sold the enlivening beverage extolled by poets but denounced by Father Mathew, the 'rale potheen,' from a pennyworth up to a gallon, which costeth eight shillings. There are, I believe, some excise and municipal regulations, limiting the drinking of whisky on the premises, which prompt some grocers of tender consciences to provide back yards, with back outlets, into which customers accidentally stray to drink their whisky, and find, as accidentally, such waifs and strays as 'materials,' i.e., hot water, sugar, and lemons, under a water-butt, or what not; but, in general, there seems no disguise about the matter; and, in the dram-drinking line, the grocery as plainly means whisky, as, in England, the Alton ale-house means beer.

I turn into Bull Alley, a very narrow and filthy little bulk-headed avenue of butchers' stalls – the very counterpart of a street in Stamboul. I have but time to notice that the butchers' wives and daughters are very rosy and comely looking – as all butchers' wives and daughters in all climes and countries seem to be – and make my escape as soon as ever I can; for Bull Alley has anything but an agreeable perfume, and there are puddles of blood between the uneven paving-stones, and should an animal of the species from which Bull Alley derives its name be disposed to manifest himself therein (which I do not consider unlikely), stung to frenzy by a 'sense of injured merit,' I would rather (Bull Alley being but contracted) be anywhere else, so I wend my way into Patrick's Close,

Where, looming large in the very midst of the old clothes, dirt, bare feet, slaughterhouses, and whisky-shops, is the metropolitan church of Dublin – the Cathedral of St. Patrick. It is a venerable majestic building – a chaste and elegant example of that most glorious period of pointed Gothic architecture, the close of the twelfth century. Originally built, so it is said, by St. Patrick, the present church dates from the year one thousand one hundred and ninety, when John Comyn, Archbishop of Dublin, demolished the elder structure.

It is magnificent in conception and detail, built in one uniform style, with a glorious nave and transept, a chapter-house and a Lady chapel. The banners of the Knights of St. Patrick hang over the arches of the nave. There is a fine choir, and monumental tombs, and cathedral service daily; but within and without the whole fabric is in a lamentable state of decay, and the feelings that come over one in gazing on it are inexpressibly melancholy. With its gray tower and noble proportions it dominates the city; but it stands here an anomaly, a discrepancy, an almost unused fane, unreverenced, unsympathised with, unhonoured, disavowed, disliked."

* * *

NEW MOVE IN THE LIFFY THEATRE[7]

"Seeing that there is a temple to love, and brotherhood and peace in, full work in Ireland, and doing a good peace and brotherhood business, it is gratifying to me to find the ROYAL LIFFEY THEATRE sharing in the general prosperity of the hour. It is, so to speak, in full swing; that is, if there ever was swing in lavish pink and yellow posters, and plenty of flaring fiery-looking gas, and an eager crowd about the yellow door at the end of the lane, and a bouquet of its own, not yet 'extracted' by Messrs. Piesse and Lubin. There is such a theatrically thriving air about the whole, that I cannot resist, and, wishing to contribute my little mite to peace and brotherhood, enter by the yellow door.

And yet, when I think that not so long ago the Royal Liffey Theatre was a sort of howling wilderness, where bats, and things more unpleasant than bats, might have their carnival; that it was given over to slow decay and desolation; that no happier personification of mildew and dry rot could be conceived – the present transformation seemed almost bewildering. The oldest theatre certainly in the kingdom – for here, in the year 1741, Handel tinkled the Messiah at his harpsichord, and Signora Avoglio sang 'I know that my Redeemer liveth,' and Mr. Dubourg, the state composer, led off the fiddles. It must have tumbled into sure ruin, gradually mouldered into a nuisance, and have been taken down and cut out of the street, like a gangrene, to prevent its corrupting the houses about it, unless – unless my friend MR. MALACHY had stepped forward, secured a lease on easy terms, and opened to peace and brotherhood at 'one shilling private boxes, with access to the stage,' and prices judiciously graduated to a penny.

Mr. Malachy had taken deep thought, and, like an inspiration, it had entered into his brain to produce the piece I was now looking at; that drama – like Pope's Kitty, 'ever fair and young,' the Vicar of Wakefield of the stage – THE COLLEEN BAWN! – on a grand new principle.

Seated in my private box – which is so far from being private, that there are three other persons occupying it – I find that we are well on in the fortunes of the ill-fated Eily. I look round the house, and find it crammed to the ceiling. I make out the old rococo shape, the remains of fossilised pilasters, and mouldering bits of florid stucco, which is so far good, for it helps me back to the old magnificence of a hundred and twenty years ago, when 'Mr. Handel' was sitting down below me, there where the four fiddlers are, 'thrumming' away at his harpsichord, of which I have now actually a fragment before me; and when the 'lord-lieutenant' and his court were all crowded together where

---

7.   *All the Year Round*, 7 October 1865.

the ragamuffins are; and when Mr. Dubourg was leading off his fiddlers to the
Hallelujah chorus, then heard for the first time. . . . And surely this is some
ghost of that ancient Messiah of a hundred and forty years ago! No. It is only
Myles singing the Cruiskeen Lawn, which he is not allowed to sing long, for
here is the whole house coming in in obstreperous and frantic chorus, shrieking their satisfaction in their 'li-li-li-tle Cruiskeen Law-n!'

When encored unreasonably over and over again in that 'Cruiskeen Lawn'
(from motives of pure selfishness in the audience, who only want to encore
themselves), with singular tact he substitutes for the last verse, 'And when
grim death appears,' &c., which even I was growing a little weary of, some
lines to this effect:

> And when your hearts are sore,
> Ye need but look before,
> And come here when ye can-an-an;
> Here MALACHY you'll find,
> And FARRELL's not behind,
> (Pointing to his own waistcoat)
> With the heart of a thrue Ire-ish man, man, man!
> The heart of a thrue Ire-ish MAN!

But for little eccentricities I know well that Malachy is not responsible. He has
his mind on greater things. He is unconsciously preaching Ruskin and Mr.
Carlyle, and we are now drawing on to the water cave, where these principles
will be revealed.

It came on me like a surprise. I was not prepared for such Realism. As
the scene drew aside, to my astonishment and delight I found the stage three-
quarters covered with a dark gloomy-looking pool. The necessities of the stage
had indeed compelled him to a slight concession to some of the popular
conventionalities: for the margin of the pool had to be masked by a canvas
bank, and similarly the approaches at each side, where the hill leads down to
the edge of the water, had to be lined with profile declivities. This fiction was
unavoidable. But there below us was the real water, cold, still, deep, impen-
etrable, and looking perfectly black, Stygian, and uncomfortable.

I joined cordially in the praise given in the bill to the author of this arrangement, where it is stated that 'the tank was under the arrangement of Mr.
Malone'. . . .

Hush! they come now at last. More Realism. A real punt, with Danny
Mann and the Colleen – ah, in her old red cloak! – on board. Yet more
Realism: for it will be recollected that the Danny, in order to stifle the sense
of the crime he is about to commit, has almost stupefied himself with liquor;
and it seems to me, from a certain unsteadiness in the management of the

punt, that the conscientious actor has been 'priming' himself. This would be quite in keeping with what I know of Malachy's character. Onward they move over the dark water, amid the cheers of the audience; but the punt is ill trimmed and ill managed, and rocks fearfully, and just as they touch the centre rock, the Danny is overboard, and the Colleen is prematurely submerged up to her middle. With infinite presence of mind the Danny rights the punt, has clambered on board, has landed the Colleen Bawn on the rock, and has proceeded to execute his purpose according to the programme. I am ashamed to say that indecent laughter greets this casualty.

Now, comes the well-known murder of the girl; and, having a commanding position, I see that a sort of dry wooden cell, or caisson, has been contrived next the rock, into which the poor struggling thing is plunged. Another concession to old prejudices, or rather to the Colleen's own private feelings, who, for no consideration of salary, could be induced to consent to realistic immersion! And I can make all allowance, seeing a wasted-looking neck over the red cloak, and a very spare figure, and something like a consumptive chest, and I can very well excuse Miss Lydia Rooney.

Now comes the retribution. Myles is at hand on the canvas bank, swings himself over by the rope – but mark how different the effect of swinging across real water instead of across 'some ribbons of blue muslin,' as Malachy puts it, for here is the sense of danger – sees that otter we all know of, and fires his – pistol in this case. It misses, but Danny, wishing to save the situation, plunges backward into the water, is seen struggling there for a time, and is got off at the wing somehow.

Then comes the 'Header' – mark you, a true header. Nothing finer could be conceived. A splash of water that goes up to the ceiling. Even the very noise is satisfactory, for we always missed that in the other performance. Myles is an accomplished swimmer. . . . At last he gets near to the dry caisson, out of which he draws the hapless Eily, raising her to the surface, and he gasping and leaning on the rock for support in the traditional way. Poor Eily! She has her wet probation in the cause of duty also, and not the least unpleasant portion must be that damp embrace.

Talking the matter over with Malachy afterwards, and I need hardly say congratulating him on his exertions, he tells me the difficulties he had to encounter were most dispiriting. The construction of 'the tank,' even with the aid of Malone, was almost disheartening. The water would come through; and for a long time there was a steady ooze, which defied discovery, until it was found that the pit was rapidly becoming an unreclaimed bog. This element, however, was baffled – perhaps by the ingenuity of Malone. He bore generous testimony to the 'willingness' of Myles, who was ready on any night, no matter what the weather. Even last March, when every one was enjoying his skating, this devoted gentleman went through his duty as usual; but the performances had to be suspended, owing to Myles, not unnaturally, contracting a rheumatic fever.

Taking it all in all, it is a move in the right direction, and the least I can wish Malachy is a 'collar of gold."

CHAPTER ELEVEN

Dickens visits Ireland: 1867

C harles Dickens's second visit to Ireland was in March 1867 when he first stayed in the Shelbourne Hotel on St Stephen's Green, Dublin. It was part of his readings tour of England, Scotland and Ireland, travelling to Belfast from Dublin while in Ireland. For a number of years the Fenian movement was astir in Ireland and a series of articles about the Fenians had appeared in *All the Year Round*. The Fenian rebellion took place on 5 March but had been put down by government troops, the government having prior knowledge of the uprising.

Setting out for Ireland from London on 13 March, Dickens and his party encountered very bad weather en route to Holyhead, as he described in a letter to his sister-in-law Georgina Hogarth.

> We made our journey through an incessant snowstorm on Wednesday night; at last got snowed up among the Welsh mountains in a tremendous storm of wind, came to a stop, and had to dig the engine out. We went to bed at Holyhead at six in the morning of Thursday, and got aboard the packet at two yesterday afternoon. It blew hard, but as the wind was right astern, we only rolled and did not pitch much. As I walked about on the bridge all the four hours, and had cold salt beef and biscuit there and brandy-and-water, you will infer that my Channel training has not worn out.

It was still snowing and bitterly cold in mid-March when Dickens and his party crossed over to Ireland where there was a state of alert against a feared general Fenian rising on St. Patrick's Day (17 March). It was to be a ten-day visit crossing the Irish Sea on 14 March. On arriving at Kingstown [Dun Laoghaire] they were met by police who began searching their luggage and "who could not imagine that the box containing the gas-piping could be anything but firearms for the use of the Fenians, and insisted, in spite of our protests, on having it searched before they allowed the box to be put in the train. When nothing but the innocent gas-piping was discovered, the breathless bystanders seemed quite disappointed."

Writing to Georgina Hogarth on arrival at the Shelbourne Hotel, he said:

The Chimes (*Christmas Stories*)

There is no doubt that great alarm prevails here. This hotel is constantly filling and emptying as families leave the country, and set in a
current to the steamers. There is apprehension of some disturbance
between to-morrow night and Monday night (both inclusive), and I learn
this morning that all the drinking shops are to be closed from to-night

until Tuesday. It is rumoured here that the Liverpool people are very uneasy about some apprehended disturbance there at the same time. Very likely you will know more about this than I do, and very likely it may be nothing. There is no doubt whatever that alarm prevails, and the manager of his hotel, an intelligent German, is very gloomy on the subject. On the other hand, there is feasting going on, and I have been asked to dinner-parties by divers civil and military authorities.

Don't you be uneasy, I say once again. You may be absolutely certain that there is no cause for it. We are splendidly housed here, and in great comfort. . . .

George Dolby, the tour manager, further recalled:

When we got to Dublin, we could see that there were good grounds for alarm; the whole city being alive with constabulary and soldiery, and a visit to our local ticket agent on the following morning convinced me that for our first Reading certainly our house would not be very good; but as St. Patrick's Day would intervene between the first and second Reading, it was fair to suppose that unless some serious disturbance took place on that day, matters would speedily right themselves, and that Mr. Dickens's reception would be as cordial as it always was in Dublin.

On the eve of St. Patrick's Day, a dinner party was given in Mr. Dickens's honour by an old and intimate friend, to which were invited all the luminaries of the city, and amongst them many of the official dignitaries and several of the highest military authorities, amongst whom was a distinguished colonel of Guards, who up to that time had made the Fenian organization his special study, being reputed to know more about it than any one in the service. During the dinner orderlies were continually arriving at our host's house with despatches, giving such details as could be collected of the probably "rising" that night, and it was clear that had any such movement taken place, the authorities would have proved fully equal to the occasion.

As a precautionary measure, the public-houses were ordered to be closed from Saturday evening, March 16th (St. Patrick's Eve), till the following Tuesday morning. The public buildings had strong forces within their walls, and the troops were all confined to barracks. Notwithstanding all this, the city life went on as if no danger were anticipated, and hospitality played – as it always does in Dublin – a leading part in the affairs of life.

At dinner, Mr. Dickens expressed a wish to make an inspection of the city, and as some of the guests at our friend's house had to do the same thing officially, his desire was very easily gratified. Returning to our hotel for a change of costume, we sallied forth in the dead of the night on outside cars, and under police care, to make a tour of the city; and so effectual were the precautions taken by the Government, that in a drive from midnight until about two o'clock in the morning, we did not see more than about half a dozen persons in the Streets, with the exception of the ordinary policemen on their beats. Several arrests of suspected persons had been made in the night, and some of these became our fellow-travellers in the Irish mail on our return to England.

Contrary to our fears, the political disturbances had done no harm to Mr. Dickens's reputation in his capacity as a reader, for our audiences were quite up to the average of our visits to Ireland in quiet times; and what at the outset looked most embarrassing, turned out a really enjoyable time, which was rendered not the less pleasant by a demonstrative reception in Belfast, where no trace of Fenianism could be discovered.

The first reading, on Friday 15 March, was of Doctor Marigold and "Trial from Pickwick".

Contrary to all expectations, the first reading in Dublin proved an unqualified success. Two days previously scarcely 50 stalls had been let, while for the single Belfast reading over 300 had been booked a long time in advance. As the evening drew on, however, a great change set in; crowds began to wend their way to the Rotunda, and long before eight o'clock the room was packed to excess. Among many well-known persons present on this occasion were the Protestant Archbishop Trench, Professor Dowden, Rev. Dr. Tisdall, Mr. R. Keating Clay, Master Lytton, the Dean of Emly, Mr. Percy Fitzgerald, Sir Charles Cameron and others. Professor Dowden says that as a reader Dickens was not to be compared with Mrs. Kemble, whose reading of The Tempest still lingers in his ears. Dickens's eye, he says, in speaking of the reading, kept roving throughout his audience from this face to that, as if seeking for some expression of the effect he was creating.

Dickens was delighted with his first night and wrote from his hotel to his daughter Mary Angela (Mamie) the next day:

My dearest Mamie, – I daresay you know already that I held many councils in London about coming to Ireland at all, and was much against it. Everything looked as bad here as need be, but we did very well last night after all.

There is considerable alarm here beyond all question, and great depression in all kinds of trade and commerce. To-morrow being St. Patrick's Day, there are apprehensions of some disturbance, and croakers predict that it will come off between to-night and Monday night. Of course there are preparations on all sides, and large musters of soldiers and police, though they are kept carefully out of sight. One would not suppose, walking about the streets, that any disturbance was impending; and yet there is no doubt that the materials of one lie smouldering up and down the city and all over the country. (I have a letter from Mrs. Bernal Osborne this morning, describing the fortified way in which she is living in her own house in the County Tipperary.)

You may be quite sure that your venerable parent will take good care of himself. If any riot were to break out, I should immediately stop the readings here. At Belfast, we shall have an enormous house. This is all my news, except that I am in perfect force. . . .

Next day, Sunday, St. Patrick's Day, writing again from the Shelbourne Hotel to Georgina Hogarth, he said:

Everything remains in appearance perfectly quiet here. The streets are gay all day, now that the weather is improved, and singularly quiet and deserted at night. But the whole place is secretly girt in with a military force. To-morrow night is supposed to be a critical time; but in view of the enormous preparations, I should say that the chances are at least one hundred to one against any disturbance.

The most curious, and for facilities of mere destruction, such as firing houses in different quarters, the most dangerous piece of intelligence imparted to me on authority is, that the Dublin domestic men-servants as a class are all Fenians.

I am perfectly convinced that the worst part of the Fenian business is to come yet. . . .

Another letter to a Mrs Fergusson, the same day, indicates how would-be writers pursued him, seeking his approval in submitting their articles to his journal *All the Year Round*. But Dickens could be quite blunt in his editorial role:

Your letter has been forwarded to me here. There is but one honest answer that I can give to it, and that answer is that I cannot make you a writer if you cannot make yourself one. I have many correspondents very near home whom I should be glad to turn into successful authors and authoresses if I could, but transformation is beyond my power.

Pray consider that my mere selfish editorial interest must be to discover suitable literary merit if I can. . . .

On Monday 18th, the day of his next reading in Dublin, he wrote to Frank Finlay of Belfast (where he was due to read on Wednesday 20th) expressing regret that his friend was indisposed with a back complaint:

> You know by this time, I may assume, the importance of always using an open-work cane chair? I can testify that there is nothing like it. Even in this episodical hotel-life, I invariably have my cane chair brought from a bedroom, and give the gorgeous stuffed abominations to the winds.
>
> A horrible fellow-creature (female as I judge) is practising the scales on a bad piano in the next room, where the sound is worse than it would be here. It irritates me to that degree, that I feel I shall magnetically irritate you, if I and the scales go on together.
>
> Do let me know when you are satisfied that you are really better, and believe me ever. – Faithfully your friend.
>
> Dolby sends kind regards and best thanks. The readings making a great noise in Dublin.

On that evening Dickens again drew an enormous audience to the Rotunda to hear him read *David Copperfield* and "Bob Sawyer's Party."

The next day he went to Belfast. On the previous visit he wrote from the northern city as follows: – "This is a fine place, surrounded by lofty hills. The streets are very wide and the place is very prosperous. The whole ride from Dublin here is through a very picturesque and varied country, and the amazing thing is that it is all particularly neat and orderly, and that the houses (outside, at all events,) are all brightly whitewashed and remarkably clean."

The reading took place in the Ulster Hall on the evening of 20 March, the programme comprising Doctor Marigold and "Trial from Pickwick." The following is an extract from the *Northern Whig* of 21 March 1867:

> The large hall was crowded in every part last night to hear Mr. Dickens reading Doctor Marigold and the "Trial from Pickwick." All yesterday, indeed, disconsolate persons were going about vainly seeking for tickets of admission. The audience was brilliant, and the appearance of Mr. Dickens was, of course, the signal for an enthusiastic greeting. Mr. Dickens is one of the very few great authors who are also great actors. Had not Mr. Dickens been the unrivalled delineator of modern English life, he might still have been one of the most vigorous and versatile of actors. If we take the most popular and well-known passages of his

works, with Mr. Dickens himself as the interpreter, we shall find that, as he speaks, many latent beauties rise vividly before us, and our old friends are endowed with a life which the pen, even at best, cannot fully depict. Mr. Dickens carefully avoids making the dramatic faculty too prominent in his reading. He calls the imagination of his audience into play; they are to fill up what he leaves incomplete. This is just what the very best reading, that is reading and not acting, ought to be.

Doctor Marigold, the first of Mr. Dickens's readings last night, is one of his latest productions. The Cheap Jack coming into the world by the assistance of a doctor who would accept no fee but a tea-tray, was immediately accepted as one of Mr. Dickens's most successful characters. Doctor Marigold had all the author's humour and pathos, and blended both these qualities in a graphic picture which posterity will not willingly let die. We should say that this creation is one of Mr. Dickens's own favourites, for we observed that he spoke the words, and never referred to the printed page of All the Year Round. What a lesson is taught by the affection of the rude and boisterous Cheap Jack for his little Sophy who dies in his arms, and by the adoption of that other child who could not be "deafer nor dumber," and whose torpid faculties are gradually called into action! The philanthropist can heartily sympathise with it; the clergyman may advantageously study it, and acknowledge that he can learn something of that religion of which the basis is love. The applause of the audience was not loud throughout the reading of Doctor Marigold; but Mr. Dickens fully commanded their sympathies, and tears were in many eyes.

In Belfast Dickens stayed at the Imperial Hotel. Writing to his daughter Mamie from Belfast on Thursday, 21 March he was still very worried about a general Fenian uprising:

In spite of public affairs and dismal weather, we are doing wonders in Ireland.

That the conspiracy is a far larger and more important one than would seem from what it has done yet, there is no doubt. I have had a good deal of talk with a certain colonel, whose duty it has been to investigate it, day and night, since last September. That it will give a world of trouble, and cost a world of money, I take to be (after what I have thus learned) beyond all question. One regiment has been found to contain five hundred Fenian soldiers, every man of whom was sworn in the barrack-yard. How information is swiftly and secretly conveyed all over the country, the Government with all its means and money cannot discover; but every hour it is found that instructions, warnings, and other messages are circulated from end to end of Ireland. It is a very serious business indeed. . . .

He returned to Dublin for the final reading of the series on 22 March. Writing to Georgina Hogarth on his return he said:

> We got back here to dinner last evening, after an extremely cold journey. It then began to snow furiously, and snowed all night. But the wind at length changed this morning to S.W. and very little of the snow remains in the streets. . . .
>
> Orderlies were riding all over the streets yesterday, bearing invitations for a grand dinner at the Castle in my honor tomorrow. Of course on finding the card awaiting me, I begged through the aide de camp in waiting, to express my high sense of the courteous consideration of the Lord Lieutenant and the Marchioness of Abercorn, and my great regret that I could not have the honour of dining with Their Excellencies, as I must return to London by Saturday morning's mail.

Writing to John Forster from the Shelbourne Hotel he said:

> You will be surprised to be told that we have done WONDERS! Enthusiastic crowds have filled the halls to the roof each night, and hundreds have been turned away. At Belfast the night before last we had £246 5s. In Dublin to-night everything is sold out, and people are besieging Dolby to put chairs anywhere, in doorways, on my platform, in any sort of hole or corner. In short the Readings are a perfect rage at a time when everything else is beaten down. . . .

He read *A Christmas Carol* and the "Trial from Pickwick", and the *Irish Times* hailed his performance and looked forward to Dickens's next visit to Dublin. On the following day Dickens left Ireland, which he visited for the last time early in 1869. But his leaving Ireland on this occasion was somewhat similar to his arrival, as his manager George Dolby recounts:

> As the mail boat leaves Kingstown for England at an inconveniently early hour in the morning, we decided on sleeping on board the steamer, on the night after the last Dublin Reading, and, accordingly, we drove down to Kingstown for this purpose.
>
> The intention was good, but the execution was a failure, for at about two-o'clock in the morning we were awakened by the tramping of soldiers on the deck overhead, and as the sound was a disconcerting one in such a place and at such a time, we went up to see what was the

matter. there we found a strong escort of marines in charge of some of the arrested Fenians of the previous week, on their way to England for safer custody.

These persons having been carefully stowed away in the lower part of the vessel, the marines and the police were free to roam about the ship at their will, and they created such a disturbance as to prevent anything like sleeping in comfort; so Mr. Dickens and myself spent the three or four hours before daybreak in the saloon, playing cribbage, after which we started off for a walk round the harbour until the time for the sailing of the mail boat.

Arrived at Holyhead, all the passengers were detained on the steamer until the Fenians were disposed of in the train, and at every stopping-place on the road from Holyhead to London there were strong escorts of police.

At Euston Square we were all locked in our carriages until the cavalcade of mounted police with the vans containing the prisoners had left the station, and then we were allowed to go our several ways, and glad we were to do so after ten days full of adventure, and many fears and anxieties as to the result of our visit to Ireland in troublesome times.

CHAPTER TWELVE

Stories of Irish Rebellions

Throughout Dickens's journals, both *Household Words* and *All the Year Round*, there are a number of stories of Irish rebellions – the rebellion of 1798, Robert Emmet's rebellion of 1803 and the Fenian rebellion of 1867 – of which the following are examples.

THE LAST HOWLEY OF KILLOWEN[1]

The American and French revolutions spurred on Irish nationalists to break free of English rule. The rise of the United Irishmen in the 1790s and the abortive French landing in Bantry Bay in 1796 led to a serious general rising in 1798. In Wexford a rebel camp was formed at Vinegar Hill and both sides displayed great bravery and gross cruelty until the camp was captured by

The Emigrants (*David Copperfield*)

---

1.   *Household Words*, July 15, 1854, pp. 513–519.

Crown forces in June 1798. The rising was a key event in the development of Irish nationalism.

The first story, "The Last Howley of Killowen" is set in Wexford of 1798.

"At the beginning of the year seventeen hundred and ninety-eight, a respectable family, named Howley, resided in the neighbourhood of Wexford, in Ireland. They consisted of the father; two sons, Mark and Robert; and a daughter, named Ellen. That was the year of the Great Rebellion, when the patriot volunteers having taken successively the titles of United Irishmen and Defenders, openly declared themselves in revolt, against the government of the sister country. The civil war raged fiercely in the southern provinces; and the Howleys speedily became involved in it. The father, who assumed the title of colonel, and placed himself at the head of an armed band, chiefly composed of peasants on his own estate, fell, fighting, at the battle at Vinegar Hill. Both the sons were taken prisoners with arms in their hands by the king's troops, during the terrible fight in the streets of Ross: and Mark, who was the elder, was shot, without trial, on the spot where he was captured; Robert, being a slim youth of fifteen – and of an appearance even younger than his years – was spared, and sent to Dublin for trial. His sister Ellen, who was then a girl of seventeen, and of very remarkable beauty, set out without consulting any one . . . contrived to traverse a country, still swarming with troops and insurgents, and arrived safely in Dublin.

There, with no friend or acquaintance in the city, she remained from the month of June until the February of the following year. During that time she was not allowed to see or communicate with her brother; but the misfortunes of her family, and the loneliness of her situation, transformed the young girl into a self-reliant woman. Every day was methodically spent in some endeavour, direct or indirect, to save her brother's life. She sought for friends, and succeeded in interesting those who had been mere strangers. Day after day she haunted the courts, listening to the speeches of the various counsel, in order herself to form a judgment of their skill. When she had fixed upon one to undertake her brother's defence, she instructed him herself, paying his fees out of a little treasure she had brought with her, and which had been kept by her father against a time of need.

The barrister whom she had chosen was a young man named Roche, then but little known in his profession. He felt for her sorrows, and began to take an interest in his client's case. Every day, after visiting the prisoner, he brought her some intelligence from him, and succeeded in whispering to him, in return, a word of consolation from his devoted sister. He also entered into her schemes for interesting influential persons in her favour; but he was a young man, and, having risen by his own efforts above the humble position of his own family, he had but little personal interest. . . .

Meanwhile, Roche directed all his energies to preparing for the defence. The morning appointed for the trial came. It was a showery day. Gloom and sunshine changed and counterchanged a dozen times, as the young maiden trod the quiet streets near the prison-walls, awaiting the hour when the court should open. It was an anxious moment when she stood in the presence of the judge, and heard her brother's name called, and watched the door through which she knew that he would come. . . . . Roche calmly arranged his papers without looking towards her, and the faint shriek that she uttered when her brother appeared, after all that long, dark winter, seemed to have caught all ears save his. But the young barrister, though seeming to be wrapt in thought, lost nothing of what passed – not even the impression that her beauty made upon some persons present. Though the evidence against the youth was too clear to be doubted, Roche dwelt strongly upon his youth, and the misfortunes his family had already suffered, and told, in simple and affecting language, the story of the sister's struggles. The effect of the appeal upon an Irish jury, was the acquittal of the prisoner; who, after a solemn warning from the judge of the danger of being ever again accused, left the court with his sister, and the friend to whom he owed his life.

The impression of that trial, and of his interesting client was not easily to be effaced from the mind of Roche. . . . He corresponded with Ellen Howley at intervals; and delighted by the womanly sense and tenderness of her letters, he soon became aware of his attachment for her. A journey to Wexford – though only sixty miles distant from the capital – was not a slight matter then, and a year and a half elapsed before he was enabled to quit his duties and pay a visit to the Howleys.

Killowen, where the Howleys resided, was at a distance of three miles from the town. The way lay down a cross country road in the neighbourhood of the sea-coast; a lane, partly through an enclosed plantation overgrown with rank shrubs, conducted to the house. . . . The residence of the Howleys was a large red-brick mansion, by no means old or dilapidated; but the railing that surrounded the shrubbery had been torn out for pikes, leaving square holes, in which the rain had accumulated, along the top of the parapet wall. . . . . There was a kind of porter's lodge beside the rusty iron gate; but its shutters were closed, and its door was nailed up. . . .

In this desolate and solitary spot, Roche remained two months with the Howleys. The rebellion had left Ellen no relative except her brother. The serving-man, who had lived in the lodge, had also lost his life in the insurrection, and his place had never been filled up. The brother and sister, and an old woman servant, now formed the whole household. Owing to the political troubles of the country, the land belonging to them was then in great part uncultivated; but the brother collected such rents as could be recovered, and the Howleys, though impoverished, were still in easy circumstances. Roche accompanied the brother in fishing or shooting excursions on the banks of the Slaney, during which he frequently spoke of political matters, and hinted that the rebellion might again break out before long; but Roche, who had no sympathy with the insurrectionists, always turned aside the conversation, or spoke to him of what his family had already suffered, and warned him of his imprudence in approaching such matters. Robert was of a gay, reckless disposition; but the sister was the same subdued and thoughtful creature. The sad and solitary spirit of the place seemed to centre in her. Roche remarked, at first with surprise, that no visitors ever came there; but, he soon grew accustomed to their lonely life, and began to feel a pleasure in it. . . .

Roche's visit to Killowen naturally increased his affection for the young lady. When the day of his departure drew nearer, he frankly told her his circumstances, and solicited her hand. She set before him, like a noble girl, the injury that might result to him in his profession from alliance with a family considered as rebels by the government; she reminded him that her brother was rash and hotheaded, and that their troubles might possibly be not yet over; she prevailed upon him at last, to postpone the marriage for a twelvemonth. On this arrangement, made with the approval of her brother, and on the understanding that he was to return in the same season of the following year, Roche bade her farewell, and returned to Dublin to follow his profession.

The appointed twelvemonths had nearly passed away, when one of those minor outbreaks which, for many years, followed at intervals the suppression of the Great Rebellion, again involved the Howley family in trouble. On the twelfth of July (the anniversary of the Battle of the Boyne), a party of the Society of Orangemen, which had grown bolder than ever since the triumph of the loyalists, assembled in the town of Wexford, and marched across the bridge, and through the principal streets, in procession, carrying banners inscribed with mottoes offensive to the Catholics, and preceded by musicians playing 'Croppies, lie down', and other tunes known to be irritating to them. The Ribbonmen remained in-doors; but it was whispered about that it was intended to light bonfires in the streets at night, and to burn in effigy some of the favourite leaders of the united Irishmen, who had suffered for their treason; and it soon became known that a riot would take place. The Orangemen, who have since been found to be so mischievous a body, were, in those days of party warfare, openly encouraged by the authorities, and looked upon as a useful barrier against the revolutionary spirit of the common people. No pains therefore, were taken to stop their proceedings, and several frays ensued, in which some lives were lost. One of these occurred in the market-place, where a large fire had been made. The attacking party were at first beaten off, and the Orangemen's bonfire had sunk into a great heap of embers, glowing and rustling in the wind, when a man named Michael Foster, who was in the act of raking the fire with a pole, was shot by an unseen hand, and immediately fell forward on his face. A few persons who were standing near him (most of the Orangemen had already dispersed), fled at the report of the gun; before any of his own party returned there, the head, and a portion of the body, of the murdered man, were almost consumed by the fire. There was then a dead wall on one side of the market-place, from an angle of which some persons pretended to have remarked that the shot was fired; however, in the hurry and bustle of that night the murderer escaped.

Outrages had been committed on both sides; but so strong was the prejudice of the authorities in favour of the party who gave the first provocation, that no Orangeman was apprehended, while a great number of Ribbonmen were taken, and lodged in prison; on the following day, a diligent search was made for others, who were known to have been connected with the affray. The murder of Michael Foster in the market-place, made remarkable by the mystery attending it, and the horrible circumstance of the burning away of the head, was the subject of much investigation.

Suspicion, casting about for some person known to have a plausible motive for the crime, was not long in finding a victim. It was remembered that the murdered man had been a witness against young Howley on his trial; he was, moreover, said by some, to have openly boasted of having with his own hand cut down the father, at the fight at Vinegar Hill. This clue was at once seized, and, on the night following the Orange riot, young Howley was arrested, and conveyed to the gaol at Wexford.

Evidence, true or false, was quickly procured against him. One of the Orange party now came forward, and (for the first time) stated, that as he stood near the angle of the dead wall, on the night of the murder, he heard a voice, which he recognised immediately as that of Howley, exclaiming, "By the Holy Ghost, I'll make a hole through that villain!" Immediately after which, he heard the report of a gun, and fearing that there were many armed men of the Ribbon party at hand, fled with others. Young Howley admitted that he was at Wexford that night, and that he carried his gun with him, but solemnly denied that he was the murderer of Foster; declaring that he had never heard of his boast of having slain his father until that moment, and that he did not believe it. Nor could any witness now be found who had ever heard of such a boast. But the magistrates committed him; a special commission was appointed; and, for the second time, young Howley was to be tried for his life.

On the day of her brother's apprehension Ellen Howley had written to her lover the intelligence of her new trouble, and again imploring that assistance which had already served to rescue him from a violent death. But the difficulty was now greater than before. The trial was to take place at Wexford, instead of at Dublin; and the inhabitants of that town were strongly against the rioters. Roche knew that it would be extremely dangerous to the prisoner if he were to plead his cause a second time. He therefore secretly instructed a barrister who was a warm friend of his, besides being a Protestant and a strong government man, to proceed to Wexford, and conduct the defence. The day of trial arrived, and Howley's counsel would probably have succeeded in neutralizing the feeble testimony against his client, but for a circumstance which, though probably intended to save him, was undoubtedly the cause of his destruction. On his way to the court-house to give evidence on the trial, the principal witness against Howley was fired at from a plantation beside the roadway, and wounded in the arm. The ball passed through the flesh, without breaking the bones, and the man, after having the wound dressed, persisted in presenting him self at court to give his evidence. The appearance of this fanatic, who, whether speaking truth or falsehood, had wrought himself to a belief in his own statement, created a deep impression on the audience. His pallid countenance, his arm in a sling, his narrative of the attack upon him by a secret assassin, presumed to be a friend of the accused, and his statement – not to be shaken – of the words used by Howley, decided the minds of the jury. The eloquent appeal of his counsel was often interrupted by murmurs in the court; and the young man was found guilty and sentenced to death.

The execution of Howley, with five others, found guilty of taking a part in the riot, was fixed for the afternoon of the second day after the trial. The magistrate, apprehensive of disturbances, had despatched a messenger to Waterford for a small reinforcement of soldiers; but some hours had passed since noon, and the men had not yet arrived. It was not until sunset that it was determined to proceed to execution without them. A large crowd had assembled; but the yeomanry were in great force and well armed, and the populace confined their marks of disapprobation to yells and groans, until the prisoners appeared upon the scaffold. At that moment, some symptoms of a disposition to renew the riot were remarked; and the executioner was ordered to hasten with his task. Young Howley was executed, repeating his declaration of innocence. The six men suffered their sentence, the mob dispersed, and no traces of what had passed were left, all within one hour.

Since the day of her brother's second apprehension Ellen Howley had never rested from her endeavours to save him. But all hearts were steeled against her. . . . On one only, of all those to whom she applied, did the sight of her beauty and misery make any impression. This man was the sheriff of the county; but he had no power to help her, and he did not even dare to delay the execution. There was but one favour he could procure for her. . . . It was that – contrary to custom – the body of her brother should be given up to his family, to be decently interred in their own burial place. Accordingly, about dusk on the evening of the execution, the corpse was privately removed, in an undertaker's car to the house at Killowen. . . .

It was not until the day after the funeral that Roche arrived in Wexford. Trusting to the skill of his brother counsel, he had proceeded to London to endeavour to interest some powerful persons in favour of the accused. Only on his return to Dublin did he learn that the execution must have already taken place. He hastened, therefore, to Killowen, in the hope – though too late for aught else – of consoling his unhappy friend.

It was evening when he arrived there. Though in full summer, the place struck him as far more desolate and lonely than it had seemed in the dull autumnal day when he had first visited it. The heavy clank of the bell that hung somewhere between him and the house, startled him as he pulled the handle. No one answered his summons; and seeing no light at any of the windows, he began to fear that its inmates had left the place. Gently pushing open the gate, he made his way through the shrubberies around the house. The place was quite still; but, listening awhile, he fancied that he heard a noise within, like a faint moaning and sobbing, yet he doubted whether it came from a human being. . . . Tormented by vague surmises, he made his way back to the front of the house, and mounting a flight of stone steps, knocked loudly at the door. Some minutes elapsed before a voice answered him, and inquired his business. It was the old woman servant. She admitted him, and refastened the door with a chain.

'Where is your mistress?' inquired Roche.

The woman, with a strange bewildered look, motioned to him to follow her. She led him into a little room lined with books, and faintly lighted by a lamp hung from the ceiling; there, seated in a chair by the table, pale and motionless as death, he recognised the form of his betrothed. Roche would have sprung forward to clasp her in his arms; but the thought of her recent sorrow, and the coldness and silence of her manner, awed him.

'I am glad you have come to-night,' she said, as soon as they were alone. 'This very hour I have formed a resolution, which would give me no rest until I had told you of it.'

'No, no,' said Roche, anticipating her meaning. 'This terrible affliction must not separate, but link us closer to each other!'

'Roche,' she replied, in the same chilled unimpassioned voice, 'I declare to you solemnly and before Heaven, that the promise I gave to you last year can never be fulfilled!'

'I came to-night in the hope of consoling you in your sorrow,' replied Roche. 'Do not think that I would press you, now, on any thing relating to my own happiness. Let me do something to cheer your solitary life. . . .'

'A reason that I cannot name to you,' she replied, 'compels me to appear ungrateful. I entreat you to leave me. This interview is more than I can bear. Believe me, the pain our parting gives me is equal to yours. I ask of you the greatest proof you can give me now of your affection. It is that you believe my resolve to be forced upon me inevitably; but that it is firmly and for ever taken; and that you take my hand, and promise never to seek me, to see me, any more.'

Roche took her cold hand, and turned away. 'I cannot promise this,' he exclaimed passionately. 'I will leave you to-night, since my presence gives you pain. But I declare to you, I cannot cease to hope that you may, one day, repent of this cruel determination.'

In compliance with her entreaties, he promised to leave the neighbourhood; but, only on condition that she would meet him that day six months, and assure him, from her own lips, that her resolution was still the same.

Roche returned to the capital, where, in the increasing labours of his profession, he endeavoured to bury his thoughts, until the six months should have passed. The appointed day – the very hour he had named – found him again at Killowen. Ellen Howley received him as before. . . . She repeated to him her determination, and Roche, according to his promise, departed from her again. Thus, for several years, at long intervals, the barrister returned to Killowen, and always with the same result. In the course of time, her obstinacy irritated him, and the repeated disappointments he experienced gradually wore away much of his love for her. He pitied her lonely and cheerless life, and would gladly have restored her to the world; but, by degrees, he came to know that his affection for her was not the ardent passion that it had been. One day, upon the occasion of one of these visits, Ellen Howley spoke to him of the injustice he did himself, in continuing to wait for a change which could never, in this world, come. Not without a sorrowful heart, when he knew that the moment for separation had at last arrived, Roche entreated her to remember him whenever she had need of aid or counsel; and finally bade her farewell.

Many years passed, and Ellen Howley continued to live, shut up in the great house at Killowen. No visitor ever entered there, and she rarely went abroad. When she was seen, it was noted that her looks grew more and more careworn. . . . The house in which she lived, looked every year more dreary and neglected . . . strange stories circulated, of curious noises heard at night; and the country people, who knew the history of the family, would not pass there after dark. . . . One day, a woman servant who had been occasionally employed there since the old nurse's death, declared she had seen the ghost of Robert Howley. She said that she was going up the stairs at the back of the house, at night, and that as she came to an upper landing, she distinctly saw, by the light of the candle in her hand, the young man, whom she remembered well. His face, she said, was ghastly pale; he did not speak; but stood rolling his eyes, and making strange grimaces at her, until she dropped the candle, and swooned. . . .

Thus Ellen Howley lived, for seventeen years. Meanwhile, Roche had become a thriving man in his profession. Years after the impression his first passion had left had begun to wear away, he had won the hand of the daughter of a wealthy merchant in Dublin, and had settled down in life, a quiet, unromantic lawyer. The name of Ellen Howley had long been absent from his thoughts, when he received a letter from her, begging him to come to her. She told him that she was very ill, and that she desired to make a settlement of her property before she died. He left Dublin immediately, and travelled in all haste to Wexford. . . .

It was getting dark when Roche arrived at the well-known house of Killowen.

. . . He rapped at the door; the noise gave a hollow echo, as if the house were empty. Having repeated his summons several times, without receiving any answer, he went round, as he had done long ago, to the back of the house. He had brought with him a dark lanthorn; by this, he guided himself, until he discovered steps ascending from a lawn; mounting them, he found that he could open the door by means of the latch. To his astonishment, at that moment, he caught again the very same noise that had startled him before. It was a long plaintive tone, interrupted now and then by a noise, like the sobbing of a child; at length the whole died away, and the place was silent.

The barrister was a man of nerve; but he hesitated a moment. . . . Drawing out his travelling pistol, however, he entered. With the light from the lanthorn in his left hand cast before him, he walked up the hall and down a passage, calling aloud, 'Miss Howley!' until, finding the doors on each side of the hall, locked, he began to mount the wide staircase. More and more surprised by the silence of the place, he was relieved by seeing a faint light through a door which stood ajar upon the landing above. This door opened wide; and a man stood on the threshold. Roche felt a chill pass through his body, for he recognised, in his wild look, and distorted features, the face of Robert Howley.

'Howley!' cried Roche, grasping his pistol firmly. 'Speak, in the name of God, if this be you?' . . .

The figure moved towards him, and said, in a whisper, 'You may come in. Come in, if you will. Keep the crowd away. They must not see her.'

Too much astonished for reflection, Roche followed him into a large chamber. . . . There, beside an ancient bedstead, stretched upon the ground, was the figure of a woman, dressed. Roche knelt beside her, and raising her, felt that she was cold. Her hair was grey, and her features sharp and wasted, like her body. Ellen Howley.

'She is dead!' exclaimed Roche; 'she is dead!'

His companion regarded him with an idiotic stare; and then burst into the same loud whine and sobbing noise, which he had heard twice before.

A suspicion passed into his mind, that she had suffered violence at the hands of the idiot; but he found no marks of injury on her, and he had known that she was ill. It was evident to him that she had perished without medical aid, or any one near her, save her crazed companion.

He had no alternative but to leave her there, while he rode back for assistance. That night he learned the truth. In a letter, addressed to him, and only intended to reach him after her death, she related the terrible history of seventeen years. In the confusion and hurry of the execution, and under the fear of an attack from the mob, her brother had been taken down from the hanging-place within a few minutes; and, some time after the removal of his body to Killowen, he gave signs of life. Aided by the old nurse, she succeeded in slowly restoring him; but wholly deprived of reason. Then it was that she resolved to keep her dreadful secret, and devote her life wholly to him. In later years she had wished to dispose of her property, and leave her native country with him; but he could not be prevailed on to go out into the daylight, or to meet the face of a stranger. Since the nurse's death, and the day when the woman servant accidentally met him, she had lived alone in the house with him. Satisfied in her own mind that she had done right in setting her lover free from his engagements, and bidding him farewell, she had resolved never to see him again; until her long continued illness, and her anxiety for her brother's fate, compelled her to write to him.

Robert Howley lived only a few months after the death of the sister who had sacrificed her love and her life for him. He was buried beside her, in the parish church near Killowen; the last of his unfortunate family."

* * *

THE FENIANS[2]

Many Irishmen migrated to America and fought in the American Civil War. They hoped that the hostility between the United States and Great Britain, which was so strong about 1865, would result in war and organised the Fenians ("Celtic Warriors") in order to take full advantage of any opportunities to set up an independent republic in Ireland. The central authority of the society was in New York where the Irish-American element was strongest.

An abortive Fenian invasion of Canada (not supported by the American government) in 1866, a planned attack on Chester Castle in England in 1867 were followed by a Fenian rising in Ireland on 5 March 1867, which was quickly put down. Though further outrages were unsuccessful they had an important political result. They compelled England to realise "the vast impor-

---

2.   *All the Year Round*, 27 October 1865.

tance of the Irish controversy" (Gladstone) and brought the Irish question into the realm of practical British politics.

An article about the Fenians published again in *All the Year Round* initially looked back to the early Fenians:

"We have to go very far back to discover anything about the true Fenians, who were a very different class of heroes from those who have been recently trying to revolutionise Ireland, and whose head-office must surely be in some Dublin Tooley-street. Some fourteen or fifteen hundred years ago, Ireland was distracted by the battles of two enormous clans, who represented both halves of it pretty fairly – the Clan Boisgne, which included the Leinster and Munster warriors, and the Clan Morna, those of the north. . . . In these disturbances, figured Con of the Hundred Battles, Art the Melancholy, Cumhail (pronounced cool), and other poetically-named chiefs. The struggle was carried on by an enrolled standing army massed over the country in regular battalions, and called the Fionians. Finnians would be, therefore, a more correct representative of the Irish word than Fenians. 'Cool,' the father of 'Fin,' was killed in battle by a general called Goll, but who had a more showy name in 'The Son of Morna,' who was succeeded by young Fion, who became the famous Finn Mac-Cool.

Such a leader would have been invaluable at the present crisis. The origin is easily explained. He watched seven years at the Boyne for the Salmon of Knowledge, and when he had caught that invaluable fish (now-a-days the Fenian salmon are in deserved repute), his patience was rewarded by being appointed leader of the Fenians. . . .

The strange body of men over which this youth was called to rule, were surprisingly disciplined. They are the men who wore those elegant and exquisite golden ornaments that are dug up now and again. Their proceedings were as chivalrous as King Arthur's court. . . . The postulant was obliged to have certain physical qualifications, and 'pass' satisfactorily in the following branches: He had to parry nine javelins thrown at once, with only a hazel stick. He had to run at full speed through a wood, and tie his hair up so as it should not come down. He was to run under a stick as low as his knee, and jump over a stick as high as his chin, while pursued at full speed by the examiners. He had to tread on a rotten stick without breaking it, and to pull a thorn out of his foot when running. He had to be musical, to write verses, and to recite poetry. He had to take an oath to relieve the poor, and never to offer an insult to a woman. Nothing more chivalrous than the Fenian behaviour to the 'fair sex' can be conceived. Anything a lady ordered her lover to do, must be done – such as leaping across a fatal chasm. Finn was once required, by a lady he admired, to jump over a pillar as high as his own chin, with another pillar of the same height in the palm of his hand. He succeeded; but, in a private conversation with his father-in-law, he afterwards owned that it was the most ticklish thing he had ever attempted.

A Fenian had great privileges, as indeed such an accomplished fellow deserved to have. He was at free quarters wherever he went. Salmon, deer, and game of all sorts, were kept strictly for hunting and shooting. If a common fellow killed a stag, he had to replace it by an ox, and was well off if he did not fare worse. The Fenian knights had all sorts of accomplishments, were fond of playing chess, kept paid bards to sing to them, and could do feats (or some of them could) that rivalled professors at Franconi's. We all have seen the gentleman with the symmetrical legs and fleshings, and with the silver fillet about his head, who keeps his footing on a large globe as it rolls down an inclined plane... But Diarmid was before him by at least fifteen hundred centuries, and went up a hill and down again, on a large tun of wine, to the amazement of a sort of open-air circus. . . .

They seem to have been sumptuously appointed, and to have lived magnificently – feasting, drinking, and fighting. 'Tell me,' said Conan, an Irish gentleman, at whose house Fion was on a visit, 'what are the sweetest strains you every enjoyed?' Fion answered him in a song that breathes the spirit of poetry:

> 'When the seven battalions of Fenians assemble on our plain, and raise their standards over their heads; when the howling whistling blast of the dry cold wind rushes through them and over, that is very sweet to me. When the drinking hall is set out in Almin, and the cup-bearers hand the bright cups of chaste workmanship to the chiefs of the Fenians, the ring of the cups on the tables, when drained to the last drop, that is very sweet to me. Sweet to me is the scream of the seagull and of the heron, the roar of the waves on Tralee, the song of the three sons of Meardha, the whistle of Macluagh, and the voice of the cuckoo in the first months of summer.'

A couple of centuries later, we find the Fenians in possession of a code of laws more minute than, and quite as philosophical as, those of Justinian, illustrated by commentaries, glossary, and interpretations, divided into elaborate systems of the law of distraint, and debtor and creditor, of 'fosterage' . . . One of the remedies of a creditor against his debtor was 'fasting' at his gate until he paid.

Of a very, very different pattern are the modern gentry who take to themselves the name of those Ossianic heroes. . . ."

*   *   *

THE FIFTH OF MARCH IN DUBLIN[3]

In "The Fifth of March in Dublin", published in *All the Year Round* on 6 April 1967, the author recalls his experience of the Fenian rebellion on that date, less than two weeks before Charles Dickens came to Ireland on his second visit.

"I had been absent from Dublin on leave during the whole month of February. When I left the city, on 27 January, the Fenian conspiracy would have seemed to an ordinary observer utterly collapsed. Arrests were occasionally made, but were chiefly confined to Americanised Celts. If these men had been born in Ireland, the soil and climate of America had a strange effect upon their constitution. They were tall, pale-faced, bearded – in every respect presenting the appearance of the genuine article. My duty brought me into contact with many of the prisoners, and I found that for one who came from New York, three came from Massachusetts. They seemed to me to court arrest, for the were singularly rude and insolent, swaggering through the streets, jostling the passers-by, and walking at a rapid pace three or four abreast when the footpath was crowded during the fashionable hours for promenading or shopping. I remarked that several wore large stars of silver on their left breasts, ugly ornaments enough; for they were, in all respects, like pieces of block tin. All had hats, a compound between the 'pot hat' and the 'Jerry'. All, too, had loose overcoats of different shades of grey.

When many were seen together, it became plain that their dress was a kind of uniform. Nothing was found upon these men when searched. Documents they would not carry, revolvers and ammunition were thrown into the river before the police could seize them at the quays.

In my retreat I heard of the fiasco at Cahirciveen, and the curious movement on Chester; but my newspaper was always three days late, and was read, I verily believe, by every person in the village before it was allowed to come to me. There were Fenians, as I afterwards found, in my neighbourhood, and accident taught me that the maid-servant in my lodgings was enlisted in the plot. A secluded glen some distance from my home was a favourite haunt of mine, but I found that whenever I walked out in that direction, she placed a candle in an upper room, the window of which could be see from the glen. I noticed the light, but did not discover that it was a signal until informed by the constabulary on the night before I left.

I was sitting at breakfast on the morning of 5 March, wondering whether all my friends had forgotten me, seeing that I received no letters, when a

---

3. *All the Year Round*, 6 April 1867.

jaunting-car was driven up before my window, and a boy handed me a telegram. It was very brief, containing an order for my instant return to Dublin and my (?). I felt that 'something was up,' and asking the carman to wait, made my hurried preparations. While I was wrapping a rug about my legs, the servant-girl, looking piercingly at me, inquired: 'Have they kept their word?' As I hesitated, not knowing what answer to give, she inquired again: 'Are the boys up in Dublin? They said they would rise today.' 'Indeed?' said I. 'You know much more than I do.' As I dashed down the road leading to the station, I noticed that a loose pile of straw at the head of the glen had been fired, and now sent up into the clear air on the rolling column of white smoke. In ten minutes similar smoke signals were seen on seven hillocks stretching round and past the glen, and then I believed that there really was 'something up.'

I travelled to town by the Great Southern and Western Railway in a third-class carriage. I wished to hear the talk of the country people. I counted nine young athletic fellows in the carriage; they were all singularly silent. We took in few additional passengers until the train reached successively Straffan, Celbridge, Lucan, and Clondalkin. At the last two places passengers became so numerous that accommodation could not be provided for them. There was evidently an understanding between many of the young peasants and two American Celts who got in at Celbridge. The moment these men entered, every pipe was put out. They had with them a stout deal box about twenty inches long and sixteen deep, braced at the corners with iron, and evidently of great weight.

There was no confusion or crowding at the terminus. I noticed that three men stepped out from among the carriages and cabs, and addressed a very brief sentence to the two Americans who had travelled with us. The young men regularly 'fell in' and marched rather than walked down the quays. Suddenly they broke up into twos and threes, and disappeared rapidly up the lanes leading to Thomas and James-street. Three hours afterwards, I recognised five of them at Tallaght.

Coming down the north side of the quays, here and there scarcely seen – for the gas was peculiarly dim – I saw policemen wearing swords standing in sixes together with their backs against shop shutters. They looked like a black wall. Further on, a group of boys, youths, and men would be formed around one person in the centre, and, after receiving brief directions from him, also broke up into twos and threes and passed rapidly down the quay...

I counted thirty-one of these groups from the railway terminus to Sackville-street. But here there was a continuous stream of men and boys passing rapidly over Carlisle Bridge... Not a word was spoken, and though very large numbers poured out of Dublin together, there was not the slightest disturbance or confusion. I followed the moving stream up Westmoreland-Street, past the college in whose vast front not a light was to be seen, through Grafton-Street, up Stephen's green, and Harcourt-street. There I left them, and hurried home. I expected to find explicit orders awaiting me. . . .

In my own street every house was lighted up, and a large ball was being given in Harcourt-street. No chain was placed across my own hall door, and my servant, in answer to my inquiries, replied, as coolly as if it were a matter of no importance, that 'the Fenians had riz.' . . . A long envelope was handed to me, and in five minutes I left my home alone, to move with the Fenians up to a certain point. They had risen, and it was believed that they intended, when collected in numbers sufficiently great, to pour down upon the wealthiest portion of the city, and plunder there.

I found that the greater portion of the mass began to move slowly in the neighbourhood of Rathmines: a suburb consisting mainly of a single street of fine houses inhabited by the higher orders of the middle class. . . . At the extremity furthest from the city, it opens out into a spacious triangular place, at the two opposite angles of which two roads branch out: one leading to Rathgar, Roundtown, and Rathfarnham: the other, through an irregular line of buildings, to Palmerston-fields, which are skirted by the river Dodder, here exceedingly picturesque. There are some very fine old trees in the neighbourhood; and in a magnificent field surrounded by wood the multitude gathered. I think, however, that from the first many of the Fenians passed on rapidly, crossed a bridge over the Dodder, and made for the rendezvous at Tallaght, a village fully four miles to the right.

By this time the alarm had spread. Cavalry from Portobello, and infantry from other barracks, were on the rear of those stepping out for Tallaght. The cavalry did not proceed very rapidly; for, I believe, it was designed by the authorities to allow the mass to meet at Tallaght. The metropolitan police, whom I have spoken of as standing in sixes by the shop shutters, had now united into a very formidable body of tall strong men, and they moved after the insurgents as rapidly as the cavalry. They marched silent as death, each man fully able to deal with a dozen Fenians. Tired and worn out by my long travel, I stepped into a friend's house to obtain some momentary refreshment, but after a little rest I mounted my friends car, and arrived at Tallaght before the great event of the night occurred.

The lower order of Irish use the phrase 'Tallaght-hill talk,' to express boasts and menaces without power to enforce them. From the hill you can look down upon Dublin, 'the city of the black pool;' and on a summer's day or moonlight night the panorama is magnificent. A scout placed on Tallaght -hill could ascertain, without difficulty, every military movement in Dublin. I do not know the plans of the Fenians, but I think they expected large reinforcements to meet them at Tallaght from the counties of Meath, Wicklow, Wexford, and Kildare, and, when all were combined, to pour down upon that part of

Dublin which, from their eyrie, they saw to be least protected. Lord Strathnairn, however, was too quick for them, and while he and his strong force of infantry and cavalry were marching to cut off the approaches to the city, he had directed a portion of the 48th Regiment to move from the Curragh by the Southern and Western Railway, to leave the train at Celbridge station, and cut off the rear of the insurgents.

But, before the military had reached the Fenians, the latter were cowed and beaten. The tactics of the leaders were to attack police barracks, with their little garrison of from six to eight men. The constabulary barracks are nothing more than ordinary houses, usually one of a number, and in no way distinguished from the rest. The police barrack at Tallaght is a small building, incapable of resisting determined assailants. On the night of 5 March there were fourteen constabulary in the barracks, when an excited messenger gave information that the Fenians had risen and were marching on the Tallaght road. Almost at the same moment the sound of a very large number of advancing men was heard. The inspector who commanded the constabulary ordered his men to move out and face the enemy. These could be heard and seen advancing like an irregular moving wall. . . . Some order was issued to the insurgents, and then a volley came from the rebel ranks, irregular and scattered, but the light of the rifles pointed the insurgents to the constabulary. These had knelt down, and the insurgents' fire passed over them without wounding a man. Then the constabulary delivered their fire, all together, like one shot. There was silence for an instant, then terrific yells rent the air, and screams of men in agony. The insurgents recoiled and broke at once. . . . You could hear the pike-staves and revolvers falling on the ground, as they were thrown away in the panic.

The dark mass melted away, but on the ground lay two dying men: one clutching at the gravel, and screaming out, 'O men! O men!' The other was desperately wounded, and insensible. Two others were found next morning. They had been thrown into a ditch to die. The bullets of the constabulary did their work well; no one can tell how many were 'hurt badly' by that one volley. I know there have been several clandestine burials and unhonoured graves; and I believe that there are still many sorely mangled lying in outhouses, a terror to their friends. . . .

When light dawned, there were not more than three hundred men and boys together, the most timid of the lot, who had feared even to attempt escape. The military captured with ease one hundred and eighty-six of these miserable wretches, half dead with fear, and utterly worn out with hunger and fatigue. They were marched into Dublin, and 'paraded' in the Castle yard. Some begged for water, others for a morsel of bread; many threw themselves down on the flags to get a moment's rest. A more dismal and disgusting spectacle was never seen. There my duty ended. . . ."

CHAPTER THIRTEEN

Dickens in Ireland: 1869

Ireland was visited by Dickens for the third and last time in January, 1869. The readings were advertised as "the last that will ever be given by Mr Dickens in this country," and this announcement drew together unprecedented audiences. There were three readings in Dublin and two in Belfast. Those in Dublin took place on Monday, 11 January 1869, Christmas Carol and "Trial"; Tuesday, 12 January, Copperfield and "Bob Sawyer's Party," and Wednesday, 13 January, "Boots at the Holly Tree Inn," "Sikes and Nancy," and "Mrs Gamp." All the reserved seats for Dublin had been sold in advance, and Mr Dolby and his local agent were put to their utmost resources to meet the enormous demand on the space at their disposal. On this occasion also Dickens [and his party] stayed at the Shelbourne Hotel in St Stephen's Green.

For the first reading the Rotunda was filled to overflowing. An extract from the *Freeman's Journal* of 12 January 1869, describes it thus:

Mr Fagin and his pupil recovering Nancy (*Oliver Twist*)

Last evening the Round Room of the Rotunda was completely filled by an audience such as has seldom assembled within its walls. The rank, the executive intellect, and the appreciative intelligence of the Dublin people were amply represented. . . . At eight o'clock, when Mr. Dickens came on the platform, the popular goodwill and personal esteem were vented with native enthusiasm. The cheering lasted for some time. . . . Mr. Dickens is a little older than he was two years ago (!), his voice is a shade weaker, and his action more subdued than ever. His reading, however, is none the worse . . . he has always been a natural, plain, one might almost say a friendly reader; he reads as he writes, in the language of nature and simplicity. His reading of the introductory portion of the Carol was exceedingly graceful – quiet, natural, unaffected. . . . At every available point or casual pause the applause was instant and decisive; and when everything was coming right at last . . . the cheering was most unequivocal. When Mr. Dickens retired the people stood up and cheered him lustily. It is not that the world knows Mr. Dickens to be merely a great man; but we all know him to be a good man. And, therefore, his reading is not looked upon as a performance, but as a friendly meeting longed for by people to whom he has been kind. . . .

For the second reading the Rotunda was again besieged. The pressure at the entrance gates was so great that a strong force of mounted and foot police was requisitioned to regulate the traffic in the neighbourhood, while at the doors were stationed plain clothes officers. The taking of money at the pay-boxes was an utter impossibility, and it was decided to admit only those who had provided themselves with tickets beforehand. Even then the room was filled to its utmost capacity.

The third and last reading of all, in Dublin, was the most extraordinary scene of its kind ever witnessed in the city. Hours before the doors opened the vicinity of the Rotunda was densely thronged with persons awaiting admission. Mr. Dolby, anticipating what would happen, consulted with his "chief," and it was decided to fill every available spot with extra chairs wherever this might be done with safety. Nearly two hundred additional seats were thus provided, every one of which was disposed of at the agent's shop within two hours. Dickens was always most particular about commencing his readings precisely at the advertised hour, but on this last evening in Dublin he found it impossible to do so. An extra large staff had been employed for the occasion, but so taxed were their resources that Dickens was compelled to stand at his desk for a quarter of an hour. His presence, however, had a wonderful effect on the public, and in spite of the inevitable "scrowding" (as Mrs. Gamp would say) for seats, the utmost good-humour prevailed. At length Mr. Dolby and his colleagues succeeded in getting the people settled. Just as Dickens was about to commence his reading another interruption occurred owing to a gentleman – himself a noted author – making his appearance in the now silent room and endeavouring to reach his seat. He was hailed from the platform with an imperative "Sit down, Mr.——!" and the audience, with their characteristic perception of a joke, and knowing the gentleman to be an intimate friend of Dickens's, roared with laughter; while Dickens himself was so tickled by the whole scene that another delay was occasioned before he could compose himself to proceed.

Towards the close of the second of the three readings that night an incident occurred which might easily have ended in a catastrophe but for the ready resourcefulness of Dickens and his manager. A sudden downpour of smoke into the hall gave rise to an alarm of fire. The Rotunda is a large building containing several apartments in addition to the Round Room. It appears that a fire had been lighted for some purpose in one of the upper rooms in a grate which had been disused for a long time. A sudden draught carried the smoke downstairs. Fortunately the caretaker was ready on the spot with this explanation, and as the people were hurriedly leaving their seats Mr. Dolby stepped upon the platform and told Dickens, who immediately explained the matter to his audience in a most humorous speech, and succeeded in reassuring them at once. They all settled down in their seats again, and a great danger was averted. At the time of this occurrence Dickens was giving his famous "Sikes and Nancy" recital, to which the local papers the next day referred in eulogistic terms. With the following interesting extract we may close the account of the great novelist's associations with the city of Dublin:

"Sikes and Nancy" was a masterpiece of reading, quite unparalleled in its way; and it is with no small pride one feels it can honestly be said that Mr. Dickens is the greatest reader of the greatest writer of the age. It is quite useless to attempt to describe the emotions of the vast crowd which filled the room last night. It was but feebly represented by the enthusiasm which sustained the ringing cheers that burst out when Mr. Dickens had retired. Shortly before ten o'clock Mr. Dickens concluded, and looked his last good-bye. The cheering was sustained for several minutes in the hope that he might just come out a moment – but he didn't. Never have we seen on any occasion such assemblies as those that have met during Mr. Dickens's stay amongst us. There is hardly a man of note in the city that has not been present at one or all of the readings. Every part of the room has been filled every night by people who were there from – not a sentiment, but a principle; people who could not imagine Mr. Dickens in the city, giving readings from the books they loved, and not go to hear him.

The *Irish Times* on 13 January in its notice of Dickens' last Dublin reading that night said "On this night we shall bid a long farewell to one whose name is so familiar in our homes, the occasion is one of which none will fail to avail themselves." The next day the same paper in concluding its review of that last night said: "He has taught us in his recitations that the characters he portrayed partake less of fiction than of reality, and his efforts in the past will invest all his works with far greater interest in the hearts and minds of the many thousands of his admirers".

They had to leave for Belfast the following day, and so a supper-party of intimate friends was quickly arranged at the Shelbourne Hotel. At this Dickens was in one of his merriest moods, all traces of ill-health having for the time left him. George Dolby added:

> On occasions such as this he would entertain his guests with stories of the most interesting kind, and as they generally took a theatrical turn, it is painful now to remember the energy with which he illustrated the scene he was depicting, whether of a serious or ludicrous kind. In either case he was thoroughly in earnest, and it was difficult to believe that he had gone through so much on the platform, and that his never-flagging spirit came to his rescue when he felt bound to amuse his friends in the social circle.

Dickensians in Belfast were proud that theirs was "the honour of obtaining Dickens's last words," and the farewell readings in the northern city attracted great attention. The successes of his previous visits to Belfast were repeated, and the old enthusiasm was fully maintained. He read the Carol in the Ulster Hall on the Friday evening before going to Dublin (8 January), and returned to Belfast on 15 January for his last reading in Ireland. The *Northern Whig* of 9 January 1869, reported:

> Charming is the only fitting phrase to describe the entertainment in the Ulster Hall last night. Mr. Dickens has come back to us in improved health and spirits, and never read more delightfully than he did last night. All learned criticism on Mr. Dickens as a public reader – all erudite analysis of his dramatic faculty – all exhaustive display and elaborate investigation as to the relative powers of his combined functions of author and reader are now behind the times. We have done all that... Once more we had the humour and the pathos; once more the tender phrasing of soft words that stirred the heart and made the eyes grow moist; once more the quick turn and lively banter that sent a

ripple of sweet laughter through the hall. Once more bright eyes grew brighter and soft eyes grew softer, beneath the influence of the author-reader's voice.

After the final reading on the 15th the *Northern Whig* again reported:

We have had the honour of obtaining his last words, and we are certain that all who saw the great English novelist make his final bow last night will remember all their lives with pleasure, and will have equal pleasure in telling to the next generation, that they were present when "Boz" took his leave of Ireland.

It was proposed to give a large public dinner to Dickens and his friends by the Mayor (Frederick Harry Lewis) and Corporation, but owing to prior arrangements connected with his tour Dickens was reluctantly obliged to decline this invitation which was made through his friend Mr Frank D. Finlay, the then proprietor of the *Northern Whig*. The next morning (16 January) Mr. Finlay saw Dickens off at the Great Northern Railway.

On leaving Belfast Dickens had a second unpleasant experience in a railway accident, described as follows:

The party left Belfast on Saturday by the midday limited-mail in order to catch the evening boat at Kingstown. The train consisted of two passenger cars with the usual postal and luggage vans. In order to secure rest and quiet on the journey a coupé had been engaged. The coup, held four persons, and was composed almost entirely of plate-glass. It was situated right in front next to the engine, and it was owing to this fact that it proved so dangerous. About forty miles from Belfast, on the Belfast and Newry line, when running along at a high speed, a sudden jolt was felt by the occupants of the coup,. Looking out, they saw an enormous mass of iron hurtling past the window. Next came a terrific crash on the roof of the compartment, and the brakes were suddenly applied. Dickens, probably in recollection of the dreadful accident at Staplehurst, instantly threw himself to the floor of the carriage and his friends all did the same. The train was speedily brought up, and, dismounting, they learned the cause of the accident. The tyre of the great driving-wheel of the engine had broken, and huge masses of the iron had been driven through the air with terrific force. One of these had fallen on the roof of the coup. Had it struck the glass side instead, the consequences might have been very serious. As it was, the promptitude of the driver in bringing the train to a standstill prevented it leaving the metals, and no one was injured in the slightest, though everyone was considerably alarmed by the occurrence. After an hour's wait, in that bleak spot, while another engine was despatched from Belfast, the party proceeded on their journey to Kingstown, and that evening Charles Dickens said has last farewell to the Emerald Isle.

His general farewell readings tour was abandoned at Bolton in April 1869 when he nearly collapsed and was ordered by his doctor to rest. He had never recovered from the punishing American tour of 1867–68. He now began to write another novel, *The Mystery of Edwin Drood*, and gave a short farewell season of twelve readings in St James's Hotel, London, ending on 15 March 1870, with the famous speech:

> Ladies and Gentleman, – It would be worse than idle, for it would be hypocritical and unfeeling, if I were to disguise that I close this episode of my life with feelings of very considerable pain. For some fifteen years in this hall, and in many kindred places, I have had the honour of presenting my own cherished ideas before you for your recognition, and in closely observing your reception of them, I have enjoyed an amount of artistic delight and instruction which perhaps it is given to few men to know.
>
> In this task, and in every other I have ever undertaken as a faithful servant of the public, always imbued with the sense of duty to them, and always striving to do his best, I have been uniformly cheered by the readiest response, the most generous sympathy, and the most stimulating support.
>
> Nevertheless, I have thought it well in the full flood tide of your favour to retire upon those older associations between us which date much farther back than these, and thenceforth to devote myself exclusively to the art that first brought us together.
>
> Ladies and Gentlemen, – In two short weeks from this time I hope that you may enter in your own homes on a new series of readings at which my assistance will be indispensable; but from these garish lights I vanish now for evermore, with a heartfelt, grateful, respectful, and affectionate farewell.

Those immortal words – "From these garish lights I vanish now for evermore. . . ." – were repeated, less than three months later, on his funeral card. He died suddenly on 9 June 1870 and was buried in Westminster Abbey. People all over the world lost "a friend" as well as a great entertainer and creative artist, and one of the acknowledged influences upon the spirit of the age.

The Dickens Fellowship in Ireland

The Dickens Fellowship, of which there are now branches in the United Kingdom, Argentina, Australia, Canada, France, India, Japan, The Netherlands, New Zealand and the United States of America, is a world-wide fellowship of lovers and scholars of Dickens. Although there is no branch in Dublin at present there remain lovers and scholars of Dickens here. This appendix records the activities of the Dublin and Belfast branches of the Fellowship in the early part of this century.

Dublin 1907–1919 and Belfast 1908–1912

The Dickens Fellowship was founded in London in 1902. It is open to all lovers of Dickens and is more than a literary society. Its four principal aims are:

1. To knit together in a common bond of friendship, lovers of that great master of humour and pathos, Charles Dickens.

2. To spread the love of humanity, which is the keynote of all his work.

3. To take such measures as may be expedient to remedy those existing social evils, the amelioration of which would have appealed so strongly to the heart of Charles Dickens, and to help in every possible direction in the cause of the poor and oppressed.

4. To assist in the preservation and purchase of buildings and objects associated with his name or mentioned in his works.

The Dickensian, a thrice yearly publication, was begun in 1905.

The Dickens Fellowship in Ireland was in existence from 1907 until the troubled year of 1919 when the political situation in Ireland made it not feasible to continue. Likewise in Belfast, this branch, initiated in 1908, went out of existence in 1912, the year of the Ulster Covenant, when again the political situation was unsettled.

The inaugural meeting of the Dublin branch took place on 25 July 1907 at the Sackville Café in Sackville Street (now O'Connell Street). The chair was taken by Sir Charles Cameron, C.B., who was elected president, with

W.H. Huish as vice-president, and Jack Shaw as recording secretary and treasurer. The organising secretary was Mr G.A. Prescott; the committee was comprised of William Reid, John T. Robson, D. Collins, Kathleen Slyne, Mrs Culwick and Anna M. Gibbons. Many persons present handed in applications for membership and the large enthusiastic crowd gave assurance of success.

By 10 October ninety-three members were enrolled. A programme of music and recitals was planned. Pianoforte and violin solos were performed by the Misses Alton. Mr W.H. Huish gave an impersonation of Sergeant Buzfuz's famous speech and performed other humorous sketches throughout the evening. "The Murder of Nancy" by Sikes was read, as was "The Dancing Academy". Professor Dowden, Trinity College Dublin, was elected a vice-president and new members were added to the committee. By the end of the meeting the membership had grown to 150.

On 30 October the fellowship visited the residence of Mr and Mrs Martin Harvey. Martin Harvey, an actor, said that actors owed a great deal to the novelist. He personally owed a debt which could never possibly be paid. He said that the character of Sydney Carton exemplified perhaps the very prototype of Christianity. It had made him many friends, and brought him into close touch with humanity at large.

In subsequent meetings Mr McHardy-Flint, the elocutionist, with his wife and daughter presented many Dickens sketches from the novels and from *Sketches by Boz*.

In December, Arthur Humphreys from Manchester, presented "An Evening with Dickens" and a scheme was announced to provide a free dinner to some 150 newsboys of Dublin on Christmas Day. There was a generous response to this appeal and the Sackville Café was to be the venue. In the event 170 boys and one little girl (who succeeded in obtaining admission unnoticed, and received a good dinner as the reward for her ingenuity) were given soup, roast beef and vegetables, and plum pudding. In addition, each juvenile guest was presented with a surprise-packet containing a mince pie and fruit before leaving.

So successful was this charitable venture that the Fellowship almost immediately provided a New Year's treat for the adult poor of the city, two hundred of whom, including fifty girls, were entertained to a meat tea and concert in the Molesworth Hall on New Year's night (1908).

To celebrate the birthday of Dickens a conversazione was held in the Sackville Café, on 7 February, comprising sketches, readings and musical items.

On 19 March Mr Jack Shaw's paper "Are Dickens's Female Characters True to Life?" was read and discussed. Various other topics from Dickens's writings were debated at subsequent meetings, the August meeting being held "al fresco" on Howth Summit.

On Christmas Day 1909, 350 juveniles were again treated to a Christmas dinner, 250 boys and 100 girls. And on New Year's night a further 250 adult poor were again treated as the previous year. In addition, a cabful of toys was dispatched to each of the two Dublin Children's Hospitals, and the surplus from the Dinner Fund, almost £4, was sent to the Shelter for men.

Again Dickens's birthday was celebrated with a special meeting on 11 February. In March a "Jenny Wren" Guild was formed in connection with the Dublin branch. On 8 April the subject for discussion was "Was Dickens a Socialist?" Both sides of the argument were put and debated. When the vote was taken a large majority indicated an affirmative view.

On 22 April Miss Mary Angela Dickens, the novelist's eldest granddaughter, was present. She was introduced by the president, Sir Charles Cameron, to rapturous applause. Miss Dickens gave her own early recollections of her grandfather and congratulated the branch on its proceedings to date. Miss Dickens was elected an honorary member of the branch and an evening of recitals and music followed.

Again at Christmas the newsboys and adult poor were treated to a Dickensian meal and entertainment as heretofore. At a meeting on 12 January 1910 the Misses Ramsey were thanked for their kindness in organising a recent concert on behalf of the annual Christmas charities. On the Evening of 12 April a "Cinderella" dance took place in the D.B.C. (Dublin Bread Company), Lower Sackville Street, and was attended by 100 members and friends of the Fellowship, who thoroughly enjoyed themselves, dancing being kept up with enthusiasm until after midnight. In July a day's excursion to Lucan Demesne was held and at the evening supper a telegram was dispatched to the president, Sir Charles Cameron, wishing him a speedy recovery after his recent sad accident. [Sir Charles recalled in his "Reminiscences" that he escaped from death on this occasion, 10 June 1910, due to his wearing a tall hat. He had been investigating a case of diphtheria at the Viceregal Lodge and was returning to the city on an outside car when the horse fell in Parliament Street and threw Sir Charles into the road, breaking his collar bone and three ribs and causing other less serious injuries. If he had not been wearing his tall stiff hat his skull would have been fractured. He was laid up for several months.]

On 17 October the branch hosted a lecture by Mr Alfred Tennyson Dickens, a son of the novelist, in conjunction with the Presbyterian Association and afterwards the president and committee entertained Mr Dickens to supper in the Gresham Hotel. The 2 November meeting heard a paper on "Dickens's Child Characters". Membership stood at 113, rising to 140 by January 1911. Meetings had now transferred to the XL Café in Compton Street. At the Dickens birthday celebration meeting in February Mr and Mrs

Edward H. Lucas, who were appearing during the week at the Empire Theatre, delighted the audience with selections from their repertoire of "Scenes from Dickens". At the fourth annual general meeting on 11 October 1911 it was stated that seventeen meetings had been held in the previous year. At the November meeting the paper read was entitled "Dickensian Courtships".

The year 1912 was the centenary year of the birth of Charles Dickens and was celebrated with many literary and musical evenings and the odd whist drive. At the centenary meeting on 8 February, Sir Charles Cameron mentioned that he had met Dickens on a few occasions and treasured the memory very dearly.

The Belfast Branch, 1908–1912

Before continuing with the account of the Dublin branch it is timely to note the existence of the Belfast branch from 1908 to 1912. The inaugural meeting of this branch took place in the Visitors' Room, Assembly Buildings, on 2 October 1908. Mr John Mcarthur's inaugural address on Dickens was reported in the Belfast Northern Whig. At the second meeting on 10 November Mr Joseph R. Fisher B.L. was elected president, Messrs John Macarthur, J.E. Archibald and E.J. Elliott vice-presidents and Mr John S.B. Shaw hon. secretary and treasurer. A strong committee was also elected.

The first social gathering of the branch took place in Ye Olde Castle restaurant when over 80 members sat down to tea. Mr Fisher said that one of their main aims was to help the poor and oppressed. Recitals and musical items entertained the audience and the meeting was deemed a great success. The meeting of 6 January 1909 heard a paper by Mr John W. Renshaw, B.A., on "Dickens as a Social Reformer" which was well received. At the March meeting each member wore a badge or design representing a Dickens character or book-title, some of these being ingenious and original. After tea the task of guessing was gone through and afforded much pleasure. Regular meetings were held each month. The meeting of 6 January 1910 welcomed Mr John Shaw from Dublin who gave an illustrated talk on the early life of Dickens and of his family. He said he hoped the Dublin branch would soon have the pleasure of a visit from some of the Belfast members.

A commemorative service of the birth of Charles Dickens was held with the approval and permission of the Dean of Belfast in the Cathedral on 24 March 1912, the proceeds from the collection going to the Ulster Hospital for Women and Children, Templemore Avenue. The sermon was preached by Rev. W.S. Kerr, B.D., of St Paul's who emphasised Dickens's Christianity. This was the last recorded meeting of the Belfast branch.

The Dublin Branch 1913–1919

On 1 January 1913 in the Molesworth Hall, the Dublin branch entertained 300 to 400 poor men and women, similar to the newsboys' treat on Christmas Day. The meeting on 26 February heard a paper by Mrs E.A. Montgomery entitled "Music and Dickens". It was shown conclusively that Dickens loved music, that many of his characters sang or played, all kinds of songs were sung and all kinds of instruments were used. Dickens wrote the words of "The Ivy Green" and the "Christmas Carol" in Pickwick Papers. The 5 December meeting took place in the College Restaurant and a wide programme of musical items was enjoyed.

During 1914 successful meetings were held throughout the year, with a whist drive being held on 18 November in aid of the Belgian Relief Fund. In 1915 a Dickens Character Tea was held on the Birthday Anniversary meeting on 10 February. This event had now become a regular feature of the year and again much ingenuity was displayed in the various costumes and badges worn. On 24 February a whist drive was held and on 3 March an invitation concert was given in aid of the Red Cross. As usual the president, Sir Charles Cameron, C.B., occupied the chair. They hoped to continue their work for the Belgian Relief Fund and the Red Cross. Sir Charles Cameron was elected a vice-president of the Dickens Fellowship at headquarters.

On 17 November a whist drive was held in aid of providing comforts for the Dublin Fusiliers at the front. On 1 December a paper entitled "Dickensian Domestics" was read by Miss Hogg who dealt with female domestics only. Mrs E.A. Montgomery contributed a short paper on some of the male domestics and an interesting discussion followed. Another concert in aid of the fund for the Dublin Fusiliers was held on 15 December.

At the meeting on 12 January 1916 Mrs Montgomery read a very clever and humorous paper in which the story of David Copperfield was related by Mrs Gamp, who said she was tired of the people in Martin Chuzzlewit and just went into another book to see what they were like.

On 15 March 1917 a concert was given in aid of the New Dublin Central Club for Soldiers. Its object was to provide a place for soldiers passing through Dublin where they could rest and refresh themselves and, if they wished, to deposit their money and kit if they wished to go sight-seeing in the town. The Club did a great deal in guarding the men from the dangers that might befall them in a strange city.

Though the membership had fallen slightly this year, doubtless owing to many people being occupied by various forms of war-work, the financial state of the branch was healthy.

In December a whist drive was organised by Miss Wheeler and Miss Woodhouse in aid of the Soldiers' and Sailors' Help Society (Disabled Sol-

diers' Employment Bureau) and in the same month a concert was organised
by Miss L. Ramsey in aid of St Dunstan's Hostel for blind soldiers in January
1918. This year all further funds raised were devoted to the Red Cross
Society.

The meeting of 8 January 1919 heard papers on "Objectionable Characters in Dickens", contributed by Miss W.J. Lawrenson and Miss McCurdy.
The former laid emphasis on the preponderance of objectionable characters,
especially of hypocrites, in Dickens's works, and said that without these characters the author could not have accomplished a tithe of the good done by his
books. Miss McCurdy said the title of the paper was rather a misnomer; that
these characters were not objectionable to the reader at all and that she
would object rather to some of the good characters much more than to the
bad ones.

The last recorded meeting of the Dublin branch was on 19 February, the
subject for discussion being "Some Little-Known Dickens People" with Mrs
E.A. Montgomery conducting the delivery of papers and readings from the
Reprinted Pieces, Christmas Stories, Sketches by Boz, and Pictures from
Italy. A veil then falls on further reports in the Dickensian. Sir Charles Cameron
had been president throughout the period 1907–1919. It can only be sur-
mised that the political state in Ireland during the War of Independence
made it dangerous to travel out at night. And so ended the music, the recitals, the papers, the discussions, the sketches and the fun of the Dublin branch
of the Dickens Fellowship.